Praise for Sister Cities

"I am very happy to recommend readers to the important new book _Sister Cities_, which recounts the story of our Richmond-Ségou adventure. As the Bamako Representative of Virginia Friends of Mali, I have been involved in every step along the path of friendship between our two cities, our countries, our two civilizations. There is no 'clash' of civilizations: that is a piece of propaganda meant to divide people. _Sister Cities_ proves my point, for this is a story about uniting people, about building peace and security through 'citizen diplomacy,' just as President Eisenhower imagined his sister city program would work. The book is an excellent introduction to citizen diplomacy, decentralized international development, civil society empowerment, women's empowerment, and the way in which the world can really work well if men and women of every background pull together. Every teacher and every student should study Ana's and Robin's book, _Sister Cities_. This is a model story of cooperation and peace building, and will be valuable for travelers and for students and researchers. Read it!"

-Mr. Kalifa Touré, economics and finance professor at the University of Bamako

"Americans need to learn about Africa, and _Sister Cities_ will teach them. Written by a black American and a white West African, both educators and civil society leaders, _Sister Cities_ tells the story of the Mali Empire in West Africa (founded in 1235 by the Lion King) illustrated by health projects and contemporary cultural exchanges between the people of Richmond, Virginia and Ségou, second city of Mali. West Africans helped build the USA. Many of the earliest African slaves, who came to America in the most horrendous circumstances, were from Mali. Most American music was originally Malian music. Southern cooking was Malian food. Southern houses have porches because West African houses have verandas. We learn these facts in this readable book filled with colorful people. Malians discover the music, museums, and universities of Richmond, while Virginians dance at Ségou's famous Festival of the Niger River. In both cities, the mayors place urban poverty at the top of their agenda: their school and health problems are different, but equally urgent. Sister city partnerships build 'citizen diplomacy,' a pathway to international friendship and cooperation. Every diplomat, every aid worker should read this sister cities story. I congratulate the authors on their exciting book, filled with real stories about Ségou and Richmond—long may their partnership continue!"

-Mme. Safiatou Ba, author and international civil servant living in Washington DC

"As Mayor of Ségou, I congratulate the authors on their excellent book. *Sister Cities* does a wonderful job of presenting great stories, as well as the fascinating personalities involved in the Richmond-Ségou twinning experiences over the past ten or twelve years, including the many projects that our two cities have completed together. As examples of joint success stories, I must mention: medical and scientific research projects partnering experts from Ségou and Richmond who have worked particularly on AIDS; the improvement of medical facilities in Ségou, with hospital equipment and the construction of a maternity ward and a laboratory for medical analyses; building latrines to improve our city's hygiene; educational campaigns that teach the people of Richmond about the many things that Malians have imported to America since the 1600s, including the discovery of our craft products, cooking, arts, music; English and French language internet teaching for Ségoviens and for Richmonders; our cultural exchanges through our two great annual Folk Festivals for music and craft; our personal visits and the development of strong and sincere friendships between Segoviens and many citizens of Richmond. The work has begun so well; let the partnership continue!

—*Mr. Nouhoum Diarra, mayor of Ségou*

"The sister cities partnership between Richmond and Ségou began with MUSIC! We founded Ségou's Festival of the Niger River at around the same time that the National Council for Traditional Arts in Washington DC founded what became the Richmond Folk Festival, which I have attended several times beside the James River. The Ségou Festival gave birth to the Centre Culturel Kôrè to promote the arts, while the Richmond Festival gave birth to Virginia Friends of Mali (VFoM) and the sister cities.

"By writing *Sister Cities*, Ana and Robin have borne witness to the story of our collaborative work. Our festivals have huge budgets, but they exist only thanks to the efforts of volunteers. The work of hundreds of people in Ségou and in Richmond is celebrated in this new book, which I endorse with pleasure and recommend without reservation. *Sister Cities* is a tribute to international peace building through culture, generosity, and voluntarism. *Sister Cities* tells a story of development and friendship-building, and adds an important insight to the literature of peace and culture and citizen diplomacy. This is a must-read book for every student of international affairs. I hope that we will be able to encourage the production of a version in French. Thank you, Ana and Robin, for your work and for your witness!"

-*Mamou Daffe, founder of the Ségou Festival, director of the Centre Culturel Kôrè*

"I have been working with Sister Cities International for more than 40 years, and I was delighted to find a book in the pipeline about the Richmond-Ségou relationship when I returned to become the 2018-2019 Chair of the Richmond Sister Cities Commission. Our relationship with Ségou has been rich, both because of the personalities involved (at both ends) with their dedication to international peace and friendship, and also because there are genuine links of history and culture between our two cities.

"Virginia's food and music have West African roots. Their origin was the terrible slave trade of course, but the result is a commonality of culture and experience that Malians and Virginians can exploit to build deep friendships and new, shared re-interpretations of history. I have never seen these issues better described that in the new book SISTER CITIES, where Ana Edwards and Robin Poulton illustrate our 400 years of our shared history with stories, conundrums and solutions in both the Ségou and the Richmond environments.

"I recommend that every sister city commissioner in the world should read this book – as well as teachers and students of Africa and of the African American experience. Readers will find out how joint sister city projects work (or sometimes do not work) and how our rich shared history has created the opportunities for Citizen Diplomacy that President Eisenhower envisaged more than half a century ago. This is an interesting book, an exciting book, a satisfying story of peace building. It is a truly great read!"

—Thomas Lisk, 2018-2019 Chair of the Richmond Sister City Commission, former Board Member and Chairman Emeritus of Sister Cities International, Attorney.

"The publication of a new book always creates a moment of reflection and pleasure. Some books are easy reading for bedtime; some are academic studies for serious learning. What Ms. Edwards and Dr. Poulton have produced is easy reading for serious learning! The book is well-paced, filled with interesting discoveries, and a pleasant read. We meet interesting Virginians (some of whom I have met personally) and plenty of interesting Malians, women as well as men. I was born in Ségou, and therefore it is a particular pleasure for me to see that the Richmond-Ségou friendship story has not only flourished, but it has become a book.

"There is plenty of history in *Sister Cities*, just as there is plenty of history between Mali and Virginia, dating back to the slave trade of the 1600s. The authors bring this history right up to date, not fearing to discuss the Charlottesville killing of a woman by an angry white supremacist, nor the issue of how we should treat the statues of war heroes and the racism they represent both in Ségou (French repression) and in Richmond (the Civil War). But the history of Virginia is much more closely linked to our Malian culture through food and music and family structures, all of which comes through in the writing of this useful book. I myself have visited Richmond; my daughter's business studies at VCU are one small part of the inter-city partnership, and I have received Richmond students and faculty members here at my university. The friendships we have created are genuine and lasting; the story is good, and the lessons are good. Every professor and student of Africa—and of international relations—needs to have *Sister Cities* in their course reading matter or on their bookshelf. I recommend it very strongly.

"Congratulations to Ana and Robin for this wonderful initiative. I'd like to thank you for your continued efforts to develop a fruitful cooperation that is of mutual interest between my hometown and Richmond. You can understand how greatly honored I am to write a recommendation to support your book."

—*Dr Macki Samaké, professor of English Language and Literature and rector of the ULSHB at the University of Bamako*

"I strongly recommend this wonderful book that tells the first ten years of our sister cities story! As the former mayor of Ségou, it was my honor to sign in 2009, along with Mayor Dwight Jones, the official Sister City documents between our two cities. We have been able to develop rich personal and professional relationships with Richmond City Council and with the Sister City Commission. I have fond memories of many valuable meetings with city urban planning officials, with organizers of the Richmond Folk Festival, with faculty, researchers, and students of Virginia Commonwealth University, Maggie Walker Governor's School, Virginia Fine Arts Museum, Virginia Union University Art Museum, and with many Richmond citizens who generously offered hospitality in their homes each year to the Ségou delegation members. I must not forget the French-speaking students and professors (Dr. Patricia Cummins, Dr. Kathryn Judy-Murphy, Dr. Macky Tall, Dr. Oumou Koné, Dr. Fanta Diabaté, Dr. Macki Samaké and his Malian daughter Kadidia, who studied at VCU, as well as our dear friend from Ivory Coast, Professor Brahima Koné), all of whom ensure that we Francophones from Mali are able to remain in constant and fluid communication with our Anglophone friends in Richmond.

"I also joined Richmond's campaign to save the Malian cemetery, where our ancestors are buried after they were torn from the African motherland and taken to build Virginia as we know it today. The richness of the Richmond-Ségou sister cities derives partly from our cruel shared history of slavery, our ongoing struggle for justice, and the elimination of poverty. This important and eloquent book reminds us of the ancient relationship of domination, as well as our modern partnership in trying to build a better future.

"It is not the citizens of Richmond and Ségou alone who deserve our thanks.

I need also to salute the participation of the organizations that have supported our sister city work financially. The regional hospital in Ségou is engaged with VCU in AIDS research, both on the medical side (Dr. Susan Kornsten and Dr. Daniel Nixon) and in anthropology (Dr. Christopher Brooks and his Ségou partner and doctoral candidate Salim Coumaré); the hospital and the community health centers (CSCOMs) have received new equipment from Physicians for Peace in Norfolk, Virginia, Cheikh Mansour Haïdara Foundation (Ségou), Supplies Over Seas (Kentucky), Project C.U.R.E. (Colorado), Orange Foundation (Bamako), Rotary International, and the Bill & Melinda Gates Foundation. VCU and our sister cities have also received support from the US government. We thank them all. Not one of them would have participated without the active leadership of Virginia Friends of Mali, based in Richmond. Many actions succeeded only through the efforts of project managers Allan Levenberg in Richmond, and Madani Sissoko, who piloted the sister city projects in Ségou.

"I cannot recommend too strongly this wonderful book, *Sister Cities*, in which Ana Edwards and Robin Poulton tell the story of all these projects and partnerships that have enriched our city and built up the awareness of our young people. The future of Ségou is filled with opportunities because they have been created by the past ten years of work. *Sister Cities* is valuable because it bears witness to the successes of our immediate past and pushes us to seize future opportunities for Africa."

—*Mr. Ousmane Simaga, former mayor of Ségou, businessman in transport and hospitality*

"I strongly commend Ana Edwards and Robin Poulton for writing the story of the Ségou-Richmond sister cities relationship, which brings into the classroom and into our emotional experiences so many wonderful and different lessons about intercultural friendships and successes. The authors—who know Mali well and have implemented several projects in and with Ségou—provide humor and insight regarding connections between Mali and Virginia. This partnership is key, particularly with the strong focus on elementary education. Virginia's elementary students, as part of their mandated history Standards of Learning, delve into the medieval Empire of Mali-Sonrai. They learn about the medieval Islamic University of Timbuktu, the actual conquering Lion King, and the trans-Saharan trade routes exchanging gold (from the forest) and salt (from the desert). All this brings into the classroom an exciting set of discoveries about commerce, language, religion, and different lifestyles . . . yet it sometimes seems too exotic and distant in time. I wonder how many elementary students realize that they are actually studying parts of their own history when they are studying Timbuktu and the Lion King? That is what our African heritage is all about. The Mali Empire, for example, is where much of our American pop, jazz, reggae, soul, blues, and rap music emerged.

"*Sister Cities* is a story about shared Virginian and African heritage, today and for the past four hundred years. Ana and Robin retell the story of Sunjata Keita, the Lion King, in their new *Sister Cities*, but here it is updated because Mali, Ségou, and Timbuktu become real places with live people, some of whom visit Richmond. In *Sister Cities*, we meet plenty of colorful Malians from Ségou who discuss commerce with Virginia businesses. And while they are not selling salt from the Sahara desert, they are playing and dancing at the Richmond Folk Festival. The Malian visitors also meet students in school classrooms, bringing Mali into their modern reality. This new book allows teachers and students to relate a real-life story to our common heritage: our American music was originally Malian music; our southern food is largely Malian food; our houses have porches because Malian houses have porches; many of our Virginia citizens share some of the same DNA. This is why *Sister Cities* is an important educational book that deserves to enter the classroom in elementary, middle, and high schools, as well as colleges and universities throughout the Commonwealth of Virginia."

-Laura Lay, teacher working with VCU's School of Education and Richmond Public Schools, board member of the Virginia Council of Social Studies (VCSS), board member of the Virginia Conference of Social Studies Educators (VCSSE)

"I was born in Ségou, and my mother still lives in that city; meanwhile, I was living and working in Virginia. I was naturally thrilled when my Malian home city, Ségou, became linked with Richmond, near where I was living in America. I soon became involved in selling Malian textiles and crafts at the Richmond Folk Festival, where I met Ana and Robin and became a member of Virginia Friends of Mali (VFoM). For the next ten years I watched—and encouraged—the progress of cultural exchanges (music, art, education, and language teaching) and development projects that included building a maternity clinic and analysis laboratory in Ségou, supporting local community health clinics, and equipping the regional hospital. I especially like encouraging women's entrepreneurship in Ségou.

"The new book *Sister Cities* provides a wonderful telling of this story of international friendship. Authors Ana Edwards and Robin Poulton have visited Ségou several times, and my hometown has made them both honorary citizens—a title they wear proudly! Many of the projects they have supported in Ségou (and I have not forgotten VFoM's work with the schools, their support for girls' education, the university exchange programs, the building of latrines to improve hygiene) could not have happened without the members of VFoM in Richmond, the Ségou Sister City president Madani Sissoko, and Mayor Ousmane Sissoko. Readers will meet all of these people in the book, as well as some marvelous Malian women entrepreneurs and women politicians in Ségou. *Sister Cities* confirms this. Readers will meet farmers and artisans, teachers and health workers, on both sides of the Atlantic Ocean, as well as politicians. Readers will discover that Malian and American historical relations go back to the early 1600s, when the slave trade first brought Malians to Virginia.

"I agree, as the authors suggest *Sister Cities*, that the biggest benefit of this international friendship story will accrue to Richmond. The African-Americans of Richmond need to learn their ancestral history, and learn about the deep Malian roots of their black and southern culture. The music, food, crafts, and family structures of the southern states are not inherited from slaves: these qualities are inherited from a magnificent series of medieval African kingdoms since at least the fourth century, and from the glorious Mali-Sonrai Empire founded by Sunjata Keita, the Lion King, and that lasted from 1235 until 1591. Black Americans can claim descent from the Lion King, and that is really something to be proud of!

"I recommend this excellent book, *Sister Cities*, completely and without reservation. It should become a part of the African studies curriculum at every college, as well as informing teachers in America's elementary, middle, and high schools to understand the culture of their African American students, and help the students to transmit the good news to the rest of American society. *Sister Cities* will help develop friendships well beyond Virginia and Mali, for its message covers the whole of America and the whole of Africa."

-Mme. Haoua Cheick Seip, program sustainable business social entrepreneur, active member of VFoM, importer of Malian textiles and crafts

"I am very happy to be able to give my support to *Sister Cities*, which I welcome enthusiastically. Imagined and written by two great friends of Ségou and of Mali, the book makes a significant contribution to Mali's development and to the expansion and understanding of civil society. Ana Edwards and Robin Poulton (known in Mali as "Macky Tall") are among the founders of Virginia Friends of Mali and the Ségou-Richmond sister city relationship. The ten years of sister cities friendship described in this wonderful book are rich with great stories. I have been working for the past twenty-eight years between the two cultures of Mali and America. The new book *Sister Cities* reveals the complexities on cross-cultural partnerships, and explains how to overcome the obstacles. This exceptional book will become required reading for every student, every development agent, and every African diplomat. Good reading!"

-Mr. Yacouba Deme, West African regional director and Mali director of the Near East Foundation

"I would like to congratulate Ana Edwards and Robin Poulton on writing *Sister Cities*, that begins with a Forward by the Vice-President of Sister Cities International. The authors describe ten years of spectacular sister cities friendship-building between the river-cities Richmond, Virginia and Ségou in Mali. Richmond has half a dozen sister cities, but none has brought the common histories of our two cities to life in a more dramatic manner than Ségou, nor produced so much action and inter-action, so much education and excitement. This very readable book tells a wonderful story filled with great anecdotes and even greater people. It is valuable for every teacher of African culture and international relations. Anyone who reads this fascinating book will want to create their own sister cities adventure."

-Mr. Marcus Squires, past president of Richmond Sister City Commission

"It is a pleasure and an honor for me to recommend *Sister Cities*, conceived and written by two great friends—friends of mine and of my hometown, Ségou, which has made them both honorary citizens. It is largely thanks to the efforts of Ana Edwards—a dear sister who has lived in my house and become the bosom friend of my spouse—and Robin Poulton (*dit* "Macky Tall"), who is my host in Richmond, that the sister cities program linking Richmond and Ségou has become a model. For our umbrella association Sister Cities International (SCI) in Washington DC, we were indeed a model—a noisy and demanding model—during the African Urban Poverty Alleviation Program (AUPAP), funded by the Gates Foundation to improve hygiene in selected African cities. Our actions were a triumph, as *Sister Cities* explains.

"For seven of the ten years covered by *Sister Cities*, I had the honor of leading the Ségou Sister City Commission. This made me the direct partner of Ana, Macky, and their colleagues Allan, Lydie, and Dana in the Executive Committee of Virginia Friends of Mali (VFoM), which is a 501.c.3 association based in Richmond. I was present at the meetings that led to the twin signing ceremonies: October 2009 in Richmond and February 2010 in Ségou. We created this twinning adventure together.

"All the projects described in the book were implemented under the influence of the authors, the VFoM Executive Committee, the Mayor of Ségou, and myself. With Allan Levenberg, VFoM Treasurer, I acted as project manager for the various projects we put in place. *Sister Cities* evokes many memories of pride for my city and for my own contribution. You can actually visit the clinic and the latrine blocks that we built with the support of SCI and the Bill & Melinda Gates Foundation. You can admire the medical equipment in the community health centers (CSCOMs) and in Ségou's Niankoro Fomba regional hospital, supplied with VFoM's assistance by a number of different partners including Physicians for Peace in Norfolk, Virginia, Cheikh Mansour Haïdara Foundation (Ségou), Supplies Over Seas (Kentucky), Project C.U.R.E. (Colorado), Orange Foundation (Bamako), and Rotary International (including the Rotary Club of Bamako).

"Other actions are less visible, yet may have an even greater influence on the future of Ségou. I am thinking of sports activities and education actions, including visits to Ségou schools by visiting Richmonders—and of course, there have also been regular visits to Virginian schools and college classes by Malian delegation members. I think also about the weekly internet exchanges taking place between groups of Malian students learning English, and American students studying French; about initiatives undertaken to support girls' education in Ségou, as well as early childhood education initiatives. Nor should we forget the exchanges between musicians, artisans, and craftspeople, and Ségou's entrepreneurs and researchers exchanging with their American counterparts, who sometimes offer new ideas, or who open doors for Malians. These invisible contributions have the capacity to transform the lives of Ségoviens. They may also transform the lives of Americans, as we see from the large number who play Malian music on Malian instruments: a way for them to rediscover the deepest roots of American music.

"For those who have had the opportunity—as I have—to visit our sister city, Richmond, the experience opens our minds to a wide range of opportunities. We are astounded by the quality of Virginia's health clinics, by the size of the education buildings in which students are taught, by the cleanliness of Richmond's streets, and by the wealth of their museums (and these are just a few of the things we admire). These are models we might try to emulate in Ségou.

"Other discoveries are less pleasant, and we are duty-bound to mention them as friends of Richmond: the urban poverty and the discovery that many Americans cannot access those impressive health clinics; the obesity in Richmond, which we are told is a sign of poverty and bad eating habits; the isolation of old people, destabilized by the disintegration of the American family; the separation of the races that continues despite the campaigns of Martin Luther King Jr.; the violence in a society where armed policemen (mainly white) killed unarmed citizens (often black); the Path of Shame leading from the port of Manchester-Richmond, along which slaves had to walk to reach the auction houses of Shockoe Bottom in the center of Richmond; and not far from there, the desecration of the African cemetery in which our Malian ancestors are buried. When we first visited, the cemetery was an asphalt parking lot. But we have also seen some progress: the African cemetery is now covered with grass; the movement called "Black Lives Matter" is sending warning signals to a society dominated by the money of white men; and the debate in Richmond around the future of Shockoe Bottom and the creation of a slavery museum has had repercussions in Ségou, where we have our own sacred burial ground in front of City Hall. Heads of forty families in Ségou were massacred in April 1890 and buried in a common grave on the orders of the French Army conqueror Archinard. This brings us to a similar confrontation as in Richmond, around the statues of men who ordered massacres with strong racial overtones: Ségou has Archinard, and Richmond has Robert E. Lee.

"The authors of this remarkable book do not shy away from raising these subjects, which gives their volume a precious historical dimension. Our two cities have been linked for a decade as sister cities. We have been linked for four hundred years by the slave trade. *Sister Cities* offers rich material to inform teachers, historians, diplomats, and development agencies. We hope that the authors will have the courage to produce a French version of their book, so that young Africans will be able to take advantage of its lessons and share the partnership that we, their fathers and mothers, have enjoyed. While we wait for the French version, I am proud to recommend this remarkable book, *Sister Cities*, as easy to read and rich in information about Mali and about Virginia."

-Mr. Madani Sissoko, former president of the Ségou Sister City Commission;
businessman in carpentry, metalwork, poultry raising, and restaurants;
and owner of a sports gymnasium and dojo

"I am very happy to recommend the exciting new book *Sister Cities*, which tells the story of an innovative development partnership between Richmond in Virginia and Ségou in the modern Republic of Mali. The book is well-written by two educators who know Mali very well. Ana Edwards and Robin Poulton have been leaders in the sister city process, and leaders for many years in civil society development and justice programs on both sides of the Atlantic. The story they tell so well, describes intercultural exchange and discovery. They introduce us to many interesting Malian and Virginian people, explore the ways that Americans and Africans work together, and they show how development projects can succeed as well as how they can fail.

"As a professor of World Studies, I will use this valuable book to teach intercultural relations. It will offer my students new and challenging interpretations of American history—and of the Richmond-Ségou friendship—focused on the arrival in 1619 in Virginia of the first Africans (who came from Angola), followed by the installation of slavery and the forced and brutal import of tens of thousands of Malians to work the tobacco and cotton plantations that made Virginia rich. Malians built the many beautiful houses with elaborate wrought-iron railings that made Richmond beautiful. Richmond's African Burial Ground at Broad Street and 15th Street is filled with Malian Ancestors: not Americans, because the USA was not created until 1789.

"As a French teacher, I have been very excited to be able to work with Mali. France is the home of the French language, but France is only one of many countries that use French as the language of business and commerce. Commercial French is one of my specialties, and I have been delighted to serve as an intermediary between Malian entrepreneurs, women's cooperatives, as well as Francophone women novelists and their American partners. Later, I became Chair of the Richmond Sister Cities Commission, which gave me the opportunity to visit Ségou as well as other cities in West Africa. On some of my West African visits, I have traveled with Ana and Robin (and other academic colleagues), and they are very entertaining companions. Everyone who reads this fascinating book with discover the same: the authors are entertaining, knowledgeable, insightful, and wise. Every teacher, every traveler, and every diplomat should read this book and learn the lessons of *Sister Cities*."

-Dr. Patricia Cummins, professor of French and world studies at VCU, former Richmond Sister City chair, co-chair of Women, War & Peace and Doing Business in Africa conferences

"I am happy to be able to offer my enthusiastic support to *Sister Cities*, written by two great friends of Mali and of my hometown, Ségou. It is thanks to the titanic work of Ana Edwards and Robin Poulton (whom we know in Mali by the name "Macky Tall") that I personally had the opportunity to visit Richmond and to study with my distinguished friend Dr. Christopher A. Brooks, Professor of Anthropology at Virginia Commonwealth University (VCU), focusing on the sociology of AIDS among the women of the Ségou region. Our book—the result of two years of research—appeared in 2017 under the title 'The Most Vulnerable: Women with AIDS and Islam in Mali' (Linus Books, 2017).

"As the title indicates, women are the most vulnerable to AIDS infections. In the majority of cases, it is the husband who brings AIDS into the family and infects his spouse with the virus. It is not Islamic beliefs that obstruct governmental and NGO campaigns to fight AIDS infection and transmission: it is the ancestral taboos and social prejudices of Malian society that prove obstructive. We were able to bring out this information thanks to the sister city program and a research grant, awarded under the US government's Title VI program to Professor Patricia Cummins of VCU who was also—at that time—the president of the Richmond Sister City Commission. Without the Richmond-Ségou sister cities relationship, our sociological research would not have taken place, nor would the parallel scientific AIDS analyses undertaken by our medical colleagues in Ségou and Richmond (at VCU's Medical College of Virginia).

"The marvelous sister cities story of our ten years' partnership has allowed Edwards and Poulton to produce a book rich with tales of success, proving the value of president Dwight Eisenhower's innovative sister city initiative. Sister cities has opened doors for the citizens of both our home cities. VCU faculty and students would never have visited Mali without the sister city relationship. Neither would Ségou's entrepreneurial men and agribusiness women have been able to visit Richmond; nor our teachers and elected councilors, many of whom have traveled to seek American partnerships and economic opportunities. These spectacular results are revealed in *Sister Cities*, which describes wonderful successes in the medical field and the difficulties faced by certain projects. Usually the problems boil down to the complexity of regulations, although sometimes the fault lies with officials and their lack of energy. We should also note the precious financial support our various sister cities actions have received from foundations including Bill & Melinda Gates; Orange; Conrad Hilton; Rotary International; Project C.U.R.E; Supplies Overseas; Physicians for Peace, and many generous private donors. Let me thank them here!

"Complexity is a part of international cooperation, including linguistic barriers that the sister city relationship is helping to defeat through our French-English language-teaching programs. *Sister Cities* tells us what is takes to win, despite everything! In spite of difficulties and vast distances, the voluntary commitment of some and the creativity of others has turned the Richmond-Ségou partnership into an undeniable success. The work and devotion have created a strong platform for long-term future partnerships between Mali and America, and the excellent *Sister Cities* book tells us how it happened. This easy-to-read book is a MUST-READ for every student of America or West Africa, and for every African diplomat."

-Mr. Salim Coumaré, philosophy teacher, socio-anthropologist, former member of Ségou's Sister City Commission, doctoral candidate in sociology at Gaston Berger University

"As President of Virginia Friends of Mali (VFoM), it is both a pleasure and an honor for me to recommend most strongly the readable and amusing book *Sister Cities* and the amazing ten-year story it tells about friendship between Virginia and Africa. Since the first Africans came to Jamestown, Virginia in 1619, slavery has been a part of our landscape. The lands of the Empire of Mali are connected by forced migrations to Virginia. Richmond became a slave trading center. *Sister Cities* describes twenty-first century connections with Malians who visit Richmond for pleasure, talk to Virginian students, and dance at our Folk Festival. It also shows us their reactions to Richmond's slave history. Mutual visits of Richmond and Ségou citizens since 2006 have provoked debates on both sides of the Atlantic Ocean, not just about our common history of music and food, but also about colonialism and statues, cemeteries and massacres and remembrances, as well as about promoting economic, educational, and cultural exchanges.

"For sister cities is very much a two-way relationship. Indeed, Richmond may be the greater beneficiary of our sister cities friendship. While VFoM and the Richmond Sister City Commission have been able to facilitate physical exchanges for students and teachers, as well as funding to build a maternity clinic, equip health facilities and support AIDS research in Ségou, the greatest value for Richmonders will be understanding that our history is not one of slavery only, but of the rich cultural and social inheritance of West Africa: of Sunjata Keita, the Lion King, whose rich and famous Mali-Sonrai Empire lasted from 1235 until 1591 and covered parts of nine modern West African countries. Many—perhaps most—African Americans have DNA from the Mali Empire. What a wonderful heritage! *Sister Cities* tells the Sunjata story too. With Ana and Robin, we visit the shared music and art and food and families of Virginians and Malians, whose lifestyles are molded by a shared history. This book should be read by every African American and by every Virginian. *Sister Cities* should be compulsory for study in every Virginian high school, and this book should be incorporated into African studies courses across the Nation from Sea to Shining Sea."

-*Mrs. Lydie Alapini Sakponou, attorney, teacher in Chesterfield County Schools, president of the Virginia Friends of Mali*

"As president of the Association of Malians living in the Washington DC area, it is a great pleasure for me to congratulate the authors, and the 501.c.3. association Virginia Friends of Mali, on producing this exciting book, *Sister Cities,* about the developing relationships and increasing friendships between the cities of Richmond, Virginia and Ségou in Mali. The concept of town-twinning, or *jumelage* in the French language, developed after the terrible desecration of the second World War. It really was a 'world' war: there are plenty of Malian military cemeteries in France that attest to the numbers of my fellow countrymen who died fighting fascism. President Eisenhower, the top allied general, believed that 'citizen diplomacy' would help people to know one another and make them less inclined to kill each other. When he became the American president, he created Sister Cities International.

"The Richmond-Ségou partnership is a perfect example of sister cities and citizen diplomacy at work. At least forty Virginians have visited Ségou, and at least as many Malians have visited Richmond. We play music at each other's festivals; we visit each other's schools and clinics; we promote links between businesses; we teach and learn about the many cultural commonalities that join Virginia and Mali: the food and the faces, the music and shared our joint history of colonialism and slavery. Ana Edwards and Robin Poulton describe all of these shared African and American experiences in *Sister Cities*. They describe health and education projects in Ségou, and their exciting Teaching Timbuktu program in Richmond. The authors show us a positive picture of citizen diplomacy and friendship-building, filling their book with interesting stories and lessons learned, but without covering up the problems or hiding contradictions. This is an important book about America and about development issues in West Africa. *Sister Cities* contains many cultural lessons and introduces important historical debates. *Sister Cities* should become a major source book for African Studies courses, for African American Studies, and for Schools of Diplomacy. I recommend it most strongly."

-Mr. Issa Sangare, president of the Association of Malians (AMAW) in Washington DC

"As a Richmond councilman responsible for the Sister City Commission, I am delighted that two of our stalwart supporters—Ana Edwards and Robin Poulton—have written an exciting book about Ségou, our sister city in West Africa. Like Richmond, Ségou is home to a famous music festival, a center for agriculture and commerce, and a river port . . . situated beside the Niger River, Africa's third greatest river. Africa contains fifty-four nation states, and the medieval empire of Mali covered nine of them.

"Every third grader in Virginia learns that the Mali Empire was founded by Sunjata Keita, the real Lion King. Parents who read this wonderful book about Richmond and Ségou will know as much as their kids. They will discover the roots of Virginia's food and music and lifestyles. *Sister Cities* provides a window to the world, where all citizens can become involved. I strongly recommend that every Richmonder read this fascinating book."

-Councilman Andreas Addison, Richmond

"Thanks to the Richmond-Ségou sister city relationship, I made my first-ever visit to Africa in early 2019, seeking new suppliers of cotton yarn for my business. I bought yarn from the Ségou cotton factory Comatex, but the overall experience of visiting Mali turned out to be overwhelmingly more important for me. The vibrant colors of West Africa, the generous friendship of Malians, the sister city achievements in Ségou, the wonderful music and art of the Ségou Festival, and the lovely children swarming around Robin's compound—these are my dominant memories of the visit, and this book brings them all to life in a wonderful way. Everyone needs to read this book to discover West Africa as it really is!"

-Elisabeth Drumm, artisan and owner of Wolle's Yarn Creations
wollesyarncreations.etsy.com

SISTER CITIES

A Story of Friendship Between Virginia and Mali

SISTER CITIES

A Story of Friendship Between Virginia and Mali

Richmond in Virginia and Ségou in Mali, West Africa:
Twelve Years of Citizen Diplomacy and International Friendship

by Ana Edwards
and Robin Poulton

Brandylane
Publishers, Inc.
Publishing books since 1985

ISBN: 978-1-947860-58-2
LCCN: 2019905794

Designed by Michael Hardison
Production management by Christina Kann

The front cover shows Africa, represented in the paintings that author Ana Edwards presented at the Ségou Festival when she was artist in residence. She created these works of art using the famous, mystical red soil of Mali, ink from charred millet, and brown dust from the roadway to develop a theme of "Earth and pavement." Between the art pieces, a photo depicts African soil in a Sahelian savanna landscape from the Ségou region.

On the back cover, fishing pirogues (canoes) float on the Niger River in Ségou. The other back cover photos take us to Virginia and the Sister City story. We see Robin Poulton and Ana Edwards in a Richmond delegation with some leading Ségou women. We also find Ana—as President of Virginia Friends of Mali—receiving an award from the Malian Ambassador to Washington, His Excellency Al-Mamoun Keita, during the 2013 Women War & Peace conference, which was organized by VFoM in partnership with Virginia Commonwealth University, the Liberian Association of Virginia, the Richmond Peace Education Center, and the Richmond Sister City Commission.

Printed in the United States of America

Published by Brandylane Publishers, Inc.
5 S. 1st Street
Richmond, Virginia 23219
brandylanepublishers.com | belleislebooks.com

Brandylane
Publishers, Inc.
Publishing books since 1985

This book is for the young women of Ségou and Richmond, who will—we hope—be the greatest beneficiaries of the Richmond–Ségou sister city relationship over the coming years.

We also want to offer a special dedication to Kadidia Samaké, a civil society activist and Virginia Friends of Mali's student board member from 2013 to 2017. She graduated from Virginia Commonwealth University on May 13, 2017 and returned to Mali one month later with her diploma and her new baby, Macki Konaté, who was born in Richmond between Kadi's exam period and graduation. Kadi managed her studies, her marriage, and her first baby, all in four years. That is a high rate of productivity!

Fig. 1. Djita's World: Important locations in the life of Djita, a Malian girl born in Virginia. Illustrated by Ana Edwards, Virginia Friends of Mali (VFoM).

CONTENTS

Four Hundred Years of Historical Ties
Between Mali and Virginia

2006 - 2007
Teaching Timbuktu to Virginia

Teaching Timbuktu to Virginia

The First Sister City Projects in Richmond and Ségou

2008- 2009
New Ségou Visits Richmond

Acknowledgements

Our first thanks go to the people of Ségou, who have received and befriended us over the years. It has already been ten years since the official sister city agreement between Richmond and Ségou was signed in 2009; more than twelve years since we began the sister city adventure, back in 2006; and more than thirty years since Robin first visited Ségou. We must mention the amazing hospitality provided since 2005 by Ségoviens Mamou Daffé, Ousmane Simaga, Madani Sissoko, Abdoulaye Diop, Fabété Tall, Safiatou Kamaté, Abdoulaye Coulibaly, Mohamed Doumbia, Hamma Ag Mohamed, Yah Traoré, and Salim Coumaré. In particular, let us thank Maha, the late Mamadou Haïdara—teacher, author, and dear friend, who was president of the association of Ségoviens living in Bamako when we first sent a Virginia Friends of Mali delegation to Mali in January 2006.

Let us follow thanks with an apology, for we know that this book tells only half of the story of our sister city adventure. For the world to hear the other half, someone in Ségou must write it—or at the very least, we would need to spend enough time in Ségou to listen to everyone and their mother-in-law, to hear and understand and write their side of the story and to ensure we could reproduce it faithfully. Dr. Christopher Brooks and Salim Coumaré did exactly that for their fascinating book about AIDS, *The Most Vulnerable: Women with AIDS and Islam in Mali* (New York: Linus Books, 2017). They give voice to twenty citizens of Ségou, mainly women; and their work is a valuable product of the sister city relationship. In 2019, *Le Ségovien,* Ségou's newspaper, will publish a special review of the sister city relationship thus far, and this will offer a Ségovien view of the story. Meanwhile, Richmond's side of the story will tend to dominate the rest of this book, and we apologize to the people of Ségou if it seems one-sided.

As well as thanking the Ségoviens, we must add thanks to all the Richmonders who have participated in this sister city adventure, and recognize the active Virginia Friends of Mali whom the reader will meet. Let us start with Mr. Tom Lisk, a lawyer and former chair of the Richmond Sister Cities Commission (RSCC) who was on the national board of Sister Cities International in 1981 and again in 2009, and served as its national chairman from 2012 to 2014. Next, let us salute the sister city commission presidents who served during the period of this story: Madani Sissoko in Ségou; My Lan Tran, Susan Nolan, and Patricia Cummins in Richmond. This list highlights one cultural difference between the two cities: Malian leaders tend to remain in their positions and are often men, while Americans change their leadership much more often—and more readily embrace female leaders. Our three RSCC presidents since 2006 have all been women, although Marcus Squires took over from Patricia in September 2017.

Specific thanks go to people who have helped us write and correct the chapters in this book, starting with Tallie Hauser, a young lady with a good eye for facts and style; and Cole Cummins. Like Tallie, Cole is a smart student from Richmond's Maggie L. Walker Governor's School, where our Malian visitors have often given lectures about Africa and received generous hospitality. Other precious readers, friends, and advisors include Carol Warner, Patricia Cummins, Allan Levenberg, Dana Wiggins, Carol Hart, Zakiyatou Oualett Halatine, Ibrahim Ag Youssouf, Dara Bayer, the Sakponou family, the Samaké family, Christopher Brooks, Shawn Utsey, Kathryn Murphy-Judy, Marya Dull Washington, Laura Lay, Brahima Koné, Kapanga Kasongo, Robert Pringle, Adam Kaplan, Richard Woodward, and Omilade Janine Bell. Photographs have been provided most generously by Allan and Ana of Virginia Friends of Mali, by Africa Sam photography, by Ęlęgba, by John Moser, by the Wikipedia Foundation (to which some of us donate monthly), and by Michael Covitt and the Malian Manuscript Foundation. Thank you all for your time and friendship.

Finally, we want to thank the embassies of Mali and of the United States, and all the ambassadors and consular officers who have supported the Ségou-Richmond partnership over the years with hospitality, with diplomatic help, and with visas. In particular, the five-year visas they have granted have made our lives so much easier than the three-month or one-year visas that are awarded (often with reluctance) by some other countries. You cannot work if you are denied the tools with which to do so, and visas are a key part of our development toolbox. If we had to beg for a visa for every single visit, we sometimes would simply not bother. Such diplomatic support—in the spirit of President Eisenhower's concept of fostering "citizen diplomacy"—is very important in helping us and all our friends in Sister City International to promote peace and friendship between peoples.

Foreword
by the Vice President of Sister Cities International

It's more than a little strange to see a lasting social movement come out of a not-very-well-funded presidential initiative, but sister cities are the beneficiaries of a few key foundational beliefs that have served them well (and they've always been a bit quirky). When Eisenhower launched sister cities at the People to People conference on September 11, 1956 and spoke to a few dozen well-heeled civic and business leaders, I'm not sure even he imagined that it would grow to include hundreds of US cities with thousands of partnerships in almost every country in the world.

First and foremost is the mission: "to promote peace through mutual respect, understanding, and cooperation—one individual, one community at a time." This foundation, that the sister cities movement is first and foremost a peace-building movement, has been its greatest strength. It inspires people to donate their time and energy; it acknowledges that the smallest change, affecting "one individual" is worth the effort; and it gives us the framework to engage constructively with new people and cultures. Respect, understanding, and cooperation aren't just clichés. At a time when cross-cultural communication continues to expand exponentially, these principles become more and more relevant: respecting our shared humanity, seeking to understand why each of our communities is the way it is, and using this knowledge to cooperate for mutual benefit.

Another key to sister cities' persistence has been their flexibility. It doesn't matter if an exchange is about youth or business or the arts or humanitarian work or municipal governance. Does it involve people? Is it mutually beneficial? Are you respecting the other person and trying to understand them better? Then we're all set! It's this flexibility that excites people and draws them to sister cities. When you explain sister cities to a teacher, artist, baker, farmer, architect, or any other person, you can see their eyes start to light up as they imagine the projects they would do, and a smile might start to draw across their face, and they'll share what their "dream exchange" would be.

Last but not least is the focus on engaging a city, one of the most enduring social structures we have. You could say "sister cities is older than Mali," since the country only gained modern independence in 1960, but while that would be technically true, you'd be hard pressed to tell folks in Ségou, Bamako, or Timbuktu that their communities are young. Mali has been home to empires and kingdoms, with communities that have thrived with their own identities for hundreds of years. This is why it's here that a lasting peace can be built. As nations are created, divide, combine, and otherwise shift, it is our cities, rooted in their locations, that are constant, that carry the thread of our cultures and communities forward. In many—if not most—places, our identity is defined first by the city where we've grown up, and only afterward by nationality (and even then, sometimes only grudgingly).

But there are also more than a few city-centric initiatives around the world, promoting cooperation or knowledge sharing, so what makes sister cities special? I think it's because those in the sister cities movement treat the relationships between cities like the relationships between individuals. They have start dates, but they don't set end dates. They are open commitments, meant to grow and expand. They take precedence over any one activity or transaction, since there will always be a "next time." They are there in good times and especially in bad times, and help us grow to better ourselves. They often start small, in one part of our cities or lives, and then expand into so many other areas that we couldn't imagine who we'd be without them. They are best when they are relations of partnership and not patronage. And we cherish them because we realize life is so much richer with them than without them.

We were very lucky that President Eisenhower, from his perch at the height of individual and institutional power, saw that enduring peace had to be a grassroots effort. It starts with one individual, in one community. Or sometimes a few, as is the case with Richmond and Ségou. I have worked with hundreds of sister city programs, and when people ask me about successful relationships, I often think of this pair of cities.

I was fortunate to come across the small group that started the sister cities relationship early in my time at Sister Cities International in 2009, and to meet and work with so many of the incredible people in this book. It's an amazing thing to watch a relationship blossom and grow, and to see more people drawn in. This group has encompassed everything that has made sister cities special: a dedication to building peace, exchanges that engage people from all walks of life, and a commitment to keep and expand the relationship though thick and thin.

I think that too often people think of peace building only in terms of "settling disagreements." And there is certainly a time and place for that. But my experience with sister cities has taught me that peace building is not always a grim slog, and that the most successful peace building is *fun*. It's filled with music, and new friends, and delicious food, and opportunities, and adventures, and learning things that will change your life. It's true, and you'll see it in the pages of this book—and the most amazing thing about it is that it's a story that never has to end, and one that can be told in any community around the world.

Adam Kaplan
Vice President, Sister Cities International
915 15th Street, NW Fourth Floor
Washington, DC 20005
(202) 347-8630
www.sister-cities.org

Introduction

The Richmond-Ségou sister city adventure actually has its roots in 2003. That year, the Virginia Department of Education created a Mali Standard of Learning (SOL), a state-imposed regime mandating that third-grade students learn and answer questions about Mali for an examination given to every third-grader in Virginia. My wife Michelle and I had raised our children in West Africa, in the lands of the medieval Mali Empire. In 2003, we were living in Richmond, where I discovered that the triumphs of Martin Luther King had often been reversed, and where many African Americans attended schools that were *de facto* segregated still. I wanted to help Virginians emancipate themselves from the legacy of the slave trade; meanwhile, those who had created the new SOL had done so wanting to help Virginia's African American schoolchildren to discover that they were descended not just from enslaved persons, but from a rich and glorious medieval civilization founded by the famous Lion King. Our objectives seemed a perfect match.

I went to visit Thelma Williams-Tunstall, one of the originators of the new SOL, who was then overseeing history and social science teaching in Richmond Public Schools. Thelma honored me with an invitation to speak to her teachers at their annual conference. Suddenly, teaching third graders seemed more important than teaching undergraduates.

My lectures in schools and exhibitions of Malian artifacts in museums and libraries led Mali's prime minister and his ambassador in Washington to visit Richmond in November 2005. They talked to children who were learning about Mali; they met Governor Mark Warner and several university presidents, including VCU's Eugene Trani; and at the end of his speech to five hundred students and faculty at VCU, the PM produced an invitation to Richmond from Ségou (the city of Ambassador Diop, whose idea this was) to become sister cities.

Citizen Diplomacy and the Sister City Idea

The concept of sister cities was a creation of President Dwight Eisenhower, an initiative to promote peace following World War II. "Ike" reasoned that people who get to know each other, will be less likely to make war on each other. The website of Sister Cities International explains how President Eisenhower's "citizen diplomacy" works in practice:

"Sister city relationships offer the flexibility to form connections between communities that are mutually beneficial and which address issues that are most relevant for partners. A sister city organization is a volunteer group of ordinary citizens who, with the support of their local elected officials, form long-term relationships with people and organizations in a city abroad. Each sister city organization is independent and pursues the activities and thematic areas that are important to them and their community including municipal, business, trade, educational and cultural exchanges with their sister city. Sister city organizations promote peace through people-to-people relationships—with program offerings varying greatly from basic cultural exchange programs to shared research and development projects between cities with relationships."

On November 12, 2005, Virginia Friends of Mali (VFoM) was founded as the citizen organization that would manage Richmond's sister city relationship with Ségou. The meeting at which it was founded took place at Virginia Commonwealth University, in the very same room where the Malian prime minister had presented the sister city invitation the previous week.

This study of the Ségou-Richmond sister city relationship seeks to analyze and illustrate the meaning and practice of President Eisenhower's "citizen diplomacy." How has it helped form relationships and "build partnerships that would lessen the chance of new conflicts?" How have we Virginians and West Africans managed to "share research and development that advance peace and prosperity through cultural, educational, humanitarian, and economic development exchanges?" How do both our cities benefit, and how—a personal injection, this—have the women of both cities been able to expand their horizons and partake, equally with men, in these benefits?

Sister city success is based on growing friendships. People from Ségou come to Richmond every year. Frequent visits to Ségou from a varied number of Richmonders keep up the momentum of our activities. Though emails are a wonderful tool, and Skype and WhatsApp are useful for those of us who speak French—the official language of Mali—personal connection is vital. Ségou receives visits from one or more Richmonders every year. These visits keep both us and the Malians on our toes. The frequent visits in both directions enrich friendships and broaden the sister city experience beyond the organizers in each city. VFoM estimates that more than thirty Ségoviens had visited Richmond by the end of 2016, some of them multiple times. Four or five even spent several weeks living in Richmond, staying in the homes of Virginian Friends of Mali to study English. Kadidia Samaké was the first full-time undergraduate to choose Richmond for her studies because it is a Malian sister city. She studied social justice at VCU from 2013 to 2017.

In the other direction, since 2005, more than forty Richmonders have visited Ségou. Members of the VFoM executive committee have visited many times. Some have spent significant time in Mali: two volunteers, Lakshmi and James, worked there for several weeks. Two high school girls, Rachel and Virginia, spent their junior years in a Malian *lycée*. Dana (given the name Aisha Diallo) and Craig (Waraba Doumbia) were Peace Corps volunteers. Ana acted as artist-in-residence for several weeks, and exhibited her work at the Ségou festival in 2011. Several musician friends of ours—Heather Maxwell, Corey Harris, Seth Swingle Diabaté, Chuck Kerwath, Allan Levenberg, Joshua Stevens, Rusty Ekland, Omilade Janine Bell, Orimolade Ogunjimi, and Julie and Andrew Moore—spent years learning to play Malian instruments while searching in West Africa for Virginia's musical soul. And several Friends of Mali worked in Mali with the UN, USAID, Child-Fund, Africare, and other development agencies. We are not in touch with all of them all the time, but we shall meet some of these interesting people in this book.

Any group in civil society runs the risk of becoming closed to outsiders. VFoM has tried to spread the net so as to include an ever-wider number of people in the sister city experience. Each year we make new connections in Virginia, and search for new Friends of Mali who can help us teach, or who will offer their homes as accommodations for one or two Malian visitors, leading to blossoming friendships. Hundreds of elementary-age students learn about Mali every year in school, but very few of their parents are engaged with their sister city. We need to reach more of them.

We keep making new friends. When I visited Ségou in February 2014, for example, I became good friends with Salim Coumaré, a teacher whom I had not really known previously. He was my host on this visit, because the usual key players in the Ségou Sister City Commission were hosting other people: Madani Sissoko, the sister city president, had four people from the Ségou's French sister city, Angoulême, staying in his home, while Madame Diao Fabété Tall—another member of the commission and one of my Malian "sisters"—was acting as hostess to a new sister city delegation from Ngor, in Senegal.

Salim, my new host, gave me a new vision of Ségou. Salim is a teacher of philosophy in Ségou's Cabral High School, and I attended several of his classes. I spent time with his fellow teachers and friends, and met his students in the classroom. My visit forged new partnerships with English teachers at Cabral and—later—with a Ségou-wide English Teachers' Club that partners with teachers in Richmond and also with the cultural section of the US embassy in Bamako. Soon I was able to send a box of English-language books and maps to the English teachers. I also had the chance to meet the French and the Senegalese sister city delegations. New friendships can lead to new activities: with the French, we envisaged joint activities in teaching using three-city photo exhibits, and I promised to visit Senegal one day.

Three months later, Dr. Christopher Brooks, a professor of anthropology who teaches classes about Africa at VCU, arrived in Ségou to work on his anthropological AIDS research. Salim Coumaré became his research partner. At his own expense, Brooks generously invited Coumaré to visit Richmond to coauthor a book, and together, they presented their work at Virginia Commonwealth University. This rich experience inspired Salim to start a PhD program at Gaston Berger University in Saint-Louis, Senegal.

Thus, like the snowball collecting snow as it rolls, the sister city relationship grows in its influence as it attracts interested parties through regular visits in each direction. Without these visits, activities, and a strong effort on both sides, its dynamism would dissolve like snow melting in the sun, and soon nothing would remain but the memory of a former friendship. But through each shared story, each kind thought, and each attempt at understanding, we strengthen our bond, fortify our friendships, and ensure that this will never happen.

This book is the story of our sister city snowball, of friendships old and new, and of the continuously active cooperation between our two cities. Here is how I summarized "the story so far," in an op-ed piece I coauthored with Dana Wiggins for the *Richmond Times-Dispatch* in 2012:

The Lion King Lives in the Schools of Richmond, Virginia
By Robin Poulton and Dana Wiggins
Published September 19, 2012 in the Richmond Times-Dispatch

World-famous musician Cheick Hamala Diabate will sing the praises of the Lion King at Virginia Commonwealth University on Saturday. There is a link between Richmond and the lion king—not the Disney cartoon, but the true African story of Prince Sunjata Keita, who lost his throne as a child and returned in 1235 to create the Mali

Empire. Many Richmonders came from there. The ancestors buried in Richmond's African Cemetery (at the junction of Broad Street and 15th Street) were Malians and—in the mid-1700s—not yet Americans.

In 1865, fully 630 years after Sunjata wrote his constitution, freed black Americans came to camp under the protection of the Union army in Richmond and they called their camp "Gorée" after the West African slave island, the last piece of Malian soil their ancestors had trodden. Soon after that, they began to build Jackson Ward. This explains why all third- and sixth-grade students in Virginia study Mali as a Standard of Learning in history and civics. In support of this SOL, Virginia Friends of Mali founded its program "Teaching Timbuktu"—named for the famous Islamic university city that is the northern capital of modern Mali.

The Mali SOL was created in 2003 by the Virginia Department of Education to promote understanding of our African cultural heritage. In 2005 came an invitation from Mali for Richmond to become the sister city of Ségou, an old riverside capital city like Richmond. Ségou is situated on the banks of the Niger, Africa's third-greatest river. A formal agreement was signed in October 2009 by Mayor Dwight Jones of Richmond and Mayor Ousmane Simaga of Ségou. Since then the cities have worked together on education, health and economic exchanges, and numerous musicians have played in their music festivals: In the past four years Virginia musicians the Old Time Hill Folk, Seth Swingle, and Heather Maxwell's *Afrika Soul* have played at the Ségou Festival, while Cheick Hamala Diabate, Vieux Farka Touré, and Bassékou Kouyaté's Ngoni Ba have all played in Richmond.

In February 2012, Ségou opened a maternity clinic and three blocks of latrines, built with support from Sister Cities International. The work was jointly supervised by Ségou's mayor and by VFoM: former Christian Children's Fund Vice-President Michelle Poulton and former Peace Corps volunteer Dana Wiggins both visited the sites. Working in West Africa changes the life-vision of any American woman. Malians have great dignity and beauty, but they lack many things we take for granted. When you pull your water from a well, washing clothes and dishes takes on a new meaning: You don't waste water! We know many Malian women who have lost babies in childbirth or from sickness, emphasizing life's fragility. In Africa, death is truly a part of daily life.

Virginia has received so much from Africa: Most of our music (rock, jazz, soul, blues, rap) has African roots; our family values and Virginian front porches are African; so too are foods like hush puppies and doughnuts, fried chicken and peanut butter, okra and gumbo. We celebrate Mali's National Day every year in Richmond, on-or-around September 22nd—and we celebrate with Malian food and Malian music. Often we receive a visit from the Malian Ambassador in Washington, and always we include students and friends from Richmond, including members of Richmond's Sister City Commission.

Robin Poulton is professor of French West African Studies at the VCU School of World Studies (affiliate), and may be contacted at rpoulton@comcast.net. Dana Wiggins is a former Peace Corps volunteer in West Africa, and may be contacted at danawiggins@gmail.com. Both are members of Virginia Friends of Mali.

Ana's Impressions

First Impressions

1 February 2010: I had just been elected president of the Virginia Friends of Mali. Now, I was the last of the organization's members to arrive in Ségou, as part of a small delegation sent to inaugurate the sister city relationship between Richmond and Ségou. The first ceremony officializing the two cities' new relationship had taken place in Richmond in October the year before; now, we had traveled to Ségou to replicate the ceremony in Richmond's new sister city.

It was my first-ever trip to Africa, and the first time I actually used the French I'd learned in high school, thirty years before, in a French-speaking country. I was giddy as a teenager, and couldn't stop smiling. I was also nervous that I'd look like an idiot being so happy, but I decided common sense would catch up with me soon enough.

We were welcomed as guests of the city, and of the newly elected mayor of Ségou, Ousmane K. Simaga. As our official host, he had arranged lodgings for us in a lovely small villa near Comatex, a textile factory of which the region was particularly proud, because of both the quality of its goods and the fact that it was still Malian-owned.

Mayor Simaga was also responsible for our itinerary, and it was a full one: over the course of nine days, we attended thirty-three meetings! We met with public officials, including the governor of the region and all of the members of Ségou's city council. We attended a press conference with members of the local, regional, and national media, and engaged in dozens of informal discussions with people we encountered as we toured the city's markets, trade collectives, women's associations, NGOs, and historic sites. We even had dinner at the mayor's home, as guests of his wife and family.

On February 5, several of us were asked to make remarks at the opening of Ségou's annual music festival, *Festival sur le Niger,* which took place on grounds along the banks of the Niger River. Later that evening, at a local hotel, we held the second formal sister city signing ceremony, finalizing the agreement between our two cities.

Our nine-day trip was exhilarating, sobering, and exhausting. But when I look back on it, it is my arrival that remains my strongest memory: my first steps off the plane and onto the soil of Africa.

ᘒ

Two-thirds of my five-hour flight from Paris to Bamako was a night flight over the Sahara desert, without a city light in sight. The first lights that twinkled into view were those of the runway of Bamako-Sénou International Airport. When we landed and the doors opened, I at once smelled the earth of Mali—the red earth of the Sahara transitioning into the Sahel, the earth that, when dry, becomes the orange dust of Africa that I had read about, attended lectures on, heard about in the stories of other visitors. I had seen movies filmed on location in the orange dust of Africa . . . and there I was, forty-nine years old, standing on the black tarmac, breathing that dust into my lungs—a dust of joy heralding the unknown. I'll never forget that feeling.

The plane had arrived an hour and a half late. I had been traveling for three days without a working cell phone, and I was not sure if the other members of the group knew when I was supposed to arrive—so I was very happy to see familiar smiling faces at the end of the terminal walkway: Robin, Allan, and Kalifa.

Robin Poulton, a Scotsman, is a former longtime resident of Mali, and the founder of our organization. Allan Levenberg is a good friend from Richmond who had helped establish the community radio station, for which my husband and I hosted a show on the first slate of locally produced programs. It was Allan who had introduced me to

Robin, and who was responsible for my becoming involved with Virginia Friends of Mali. Finally, Kalifa Touré is of the Sonrai people, born in Gao in northern Mali, about two thousand miles from Bamako, Mali's capital city. He was the Bamako representative and host of the Virginia Friends of Mali, and this was my first time meeting him.

The three men bundled me into a small car, and soon I was breakfasting with Kalifa's wife Ami and their three children (four now, because they have a new baby) on the terrace amid the jasmine flowers and adobe walls of their small house. We drank sweet peppermint tea, and ate fresh-baked baguettes dipped in delicious local honey. "If you feel thirsty in this dry heat," I was warned, "and especially if your lips feel dry, then you have already started to become dehydrated." Here, on the edge of the Sahara desert, dehydration is the biggest health risk, followed by malaria. We typically drank a two-liter bottle of water two to three times a day to avoid dehydration and—in my case—prevent migraines.

Around 3:00 p.m. that afternoon, I met the red dust of the harmattan in the full light of day—the powerful, desiccating winds of December and early January that act as an essential seasonal cleanser, a precursor to the hot dry months that are followed by the downpours and runoff of late summer. The late summer rains herald the season of meningitis and malaria in Mali, but they also bring on the extraordinary greening of the Sahelian world, and usher in months filled with the promise of abundance as the growing season begins for farmers and herders alike.

The harmattan sometimes blows sand from the Sahara as far away as Europe. The minute I felt it hit my face, I understood instantly.

I grew up in Los Angeles, where we have the Santa Ana winds— winds that also usher in a season of desiccation and fire to strip the hillsides of dry brush and debris, followed by rain and mudslides and home destruction in southern California. But oh, I loved them! Somehow, the pressure and rush of the winds told me I was alive and part of nature. They swept the air and earth clean. They made us ready for soil-saturating showers that pulled flowers sparkling from the sands at the foothills of the San Bernardino mountains. The effects of the wind were no different in Mali: skin sandblasted dry and smooth; straw-like hair; bleeding, dust-laden nostrils; and a kind of clarity or cleanliness at the molecular level. It was unexpectedly familiar, and I was happy.

Second Impressions

4 January 2011: One of the most common flight routes to Mali runs through Paris, France, while another runs through Dakar, Senegal. On my 2010 trip, my route took me through Paris. For my 2011 voyage, I chose to travel through Senegal, with a twenty-four-hour layover in Dakar, Senegal's capital city. This allowed me to visit my father and his wife, who were reaching the end of their semiannual stay in their home away from the States.

My father, Melvin Edwards, is a sculptor with a long history of working in Africa, beginning in the early 1970s with a trip to Benin and Nigeria. His wife, Jayne Cortez, was a poet, and was on that first trip with him. Over the next three decades, they traveled throughout the continent together and independently. In 2001, they built a house in Dakar near the family of their close friend, artist Abdoulaye Ndoye. The house was adobe with a stucco finish, and had three floors, including an office for Jayne and a studio for Dad. The roof provided views of the surrounding neighborhood, a dense urban center. Except for the extra perk of seaside breezes, Dakar looks and feels very much like Bamako, steeped in the colors of a landscape not far from the Sahara desert, its streets busy with tailors, mechanics, blacksmiths, shopkeepers, fresh food vendors, and phone card sellers.

After an uneventful seven-and-a-half-hour flight across the Atlantic Ocean at thirty-seven thousand feet, I was met at the airport in the dark of morning by my father and his friend Bakry, who cares for the house when Dad and Jayne are away. Half an hour later, we had arrived at the house and were enjoying mint tea, baguettes with butter, and sliced papaya halves. My father's sister, Anne, was also there, on her first visit to Senegal as well.

This second visit to Africa contained so many firsts: my first time in Dakar, my first time seeing my father and Jayne in their Dakar home, and my first time being there with Anne. I'd grown up meeting her friends from Africa—Niger, South Africa, Uganda—friends from her days at the University of California at Los Angeles (UCLA). And here we were. In Africa, together.

My father determined that this quick visit should focus on two sites: the recently completed African Renaissance Monument and Gorée Island. So, after a long morning nap chased by a lunch of fish, vegetables, and fried *jola* rice (yum!), off we went to the embarcadero at Dakar's shipping port to catch the ferry to the island.

Once there, we walked straight to the *Maison des Esclaves* (House of Slaves), the combination auction house and jail, with its infamous *porte du non-retour* ("door of no return") through which Africans were shoved to board the wooden boats that would transport them across the Atlantic Ocean to exile and slavery. The house had once belonged to a mixed-race woman, Madame Anna Colas Pépin, who had been the mistress of French colonial governor Stanislas de Boufflers in the late 1780s. The building was pink and smaller than I had imagined, since I hadn't conceived of its origin as a residence, but when I imagined the tens to hundreds of thousands of people who had exited this door-of-no-return over the centuries, neither the size nor the origin of the building seemed to matter.

We passed the cells that had housed captives. Doorways long bereft of their iron bars displayed twentieth-century signage identifying the gender and age of the prisoners who had been housed within: *Hommes* (men), *Enfants* (children), *Petites Filles* (young girls), *Femmes* (women), and *Les Recalcitrants* (the incurably resistant). I didn't like to focus on why there would have been a special cell for young girls, but plainly there was no shame over the particular profits to be made from sex slavery.

Joseph Ndiaye founded this museum in 1962, and his children have kept up their father's mission since his death at the age of eighty-six, in 2009. The International Coalition of Sites of Conscience, and

University of Virginia architectural history professor Louis Nelson, are part of an international team working to restore the building. It is not the only one of its kind: several other auction houses like this one, both small and large, and all state sanctioned, stand scattered across the west coast of Africa. Some had apparently been owned by a particular category of slave traders: wealthy female merchants known as *signares*. These were the mixed-race daughters of European sea captains or traders; their mothers had been enslaved, but their fathers had acknowledged them by name or with financial support, so that they would not share the same fate.

Next, we visited the printmaking workshop of one of my father's friends, Mahmadou Kansy, who shared with us a folio of beautiful lithographs and etchings from a three-artist project he and my father were involved in back in 2005. Then we walked by the Gorée Institute, where Dad and Jayne had lived and worked in the late 1990s. Established in 1992 to further peace-building, development, and the promotion of arts and culture in Africa, the Gorée Institute was the result of a partnership between Senegal and South Africa, born of a historic July 1987 meeting between the exiled leadership of the African National Congress (ANC) and influential civil society representatives and researchers from South Africa, which opened the way to a negotiated settlement of the South African conflict. The spirit of the late Leopold Senghor, Senegal's inspiring poet and visionary leader in the struggle for independence, permeates the peace efforts of the Gorée Institute and its visiting scholars and artists.

Despite its painful history as a center for the slave trade, Gorée is a beautiful island. It is small, and there are no cars, as motorized vehicles are not permitted. People walk or use carts pulled by donkeys to travel between their homes and the market, passing by ancient merchant buildings and the occasional eighteenth-century cannon. We did not tour the fort, so I did not get a strong sense of its presence, except as a backdrop to the beach and docks. Gorée relies heavily on Western tourist dollars, and the most popular western iconography of 2011 was on display: teens and toddlers wore T-shirts sporting images of US president Barack Obama and his slogan "Yes We Can!" while barber and beauty shops promoted their services and their international savvy with hand-painted signs depicting the well-coiffed President and Mrs. Obama.

We retraced our steps, heading past the port and beach to visit the town hall, where a new art gallery was showing paintings and watercolor drawings by another of Dad's friends, Gorée native Souleymane Keita. On the way, Dad pointed out the deep red stucco house where Keita grew up. When it was time to leave, we bought water, regretfully declined to buy souvenirs, and waited for the ferry to take us back across the formerly shark-infested waters to smoggy Dakar.

It was now late afternoon, and as if escaping the fumes of cooking fires and old tires, we fled by car up to the Mamelles (French for "breasts"), a pair of round hills overlooking the city. Here we saw the new African Renaissance Monument: an enormous bronze statue, large as the Statue of Liberty, of a woman, man, and baby pointing upward and eastward, toward the continent. The tastes of the man who had commissioned the statue—the president of Senegal from 2000 to 2012, Abdoulaye Wade—suggested the aesthetic of 1930s heroic social realism. The hillside leading up to the monument was dotted with tall poles waving the flags of every African nation, to celebrate both African unity and the opening of the monument.

As the sun set, I photographed its light streaming brilliantly across the hilltop. Then we headed back down the hill, passing a beautifully situated new mosque tucked into a cove overlooking the ocean. Dakar is a lovely city, with ocean breezes that cleanse the smoggy air, as well as lots of hotels and restaurants not far from the sound of waves lapping on the shore. Along this waterfront, where the local soccer teams limber up, President Wade also erected the large statue of a man gesturing out to sea. His face resembles that of Wade when he was a younger man. I might not care for the egocentrism inherent in these statues, but they remind viewers that it remains important to look forward from and beyond the crushing legacies of colonialism.

The geography of the slave trade and the Age of Exploration, which one might also call the first age of global imperialism, links Senegal's history to Mali's history and the evolution of the American continents. Along with its neighbors Mauritania, Guinea, and The Gambia, Senegal was a part of the medieval Mali-Sonrai Empire created by Sunjata Keita, the Lion King—an empire that extended over an area as vast as Western Europe. Africa is a big, big continent, with fifty-four separate nations and a thousand different languages. It is amazing to think that the United States could fit comfortably inside Africa—at least three times! Mali alone is twice the size of Texas, and eleven times bigger than Virginia.

On the shore in Dakar, Senegal, I stood at a precipice overlooking the past and present and gazed west toward the sea, across the Atlantic to where people, along with their memories, were taken from their homelands and kin over nearly four hundred years. But that January, I was headed east, to Mali, where I would spend the next five weeks. There, from the edge of the Niger River in downtown Ségou, I watched the currents that once hid hippopotami and crocodiles and moved warriors and fishermen home to wives who wove cotton into cloth and cloth into clothing. Those currents have not washed up the technological progress one might expect from commerce and trade, hydro power, or floating hospitals and mass transit ferrying people efficiently between northern jobseekers and southern industry, eco-tourists and culture consumers. But I did see boats carrying travelers to the village of Kalabougou, where men still catch and sell fish and women make pots to be transported in large *pirogues*—wide, flat-bottomed canoes—to the Monday market in Mopti, nearly four hours up the Niger.

Artist and Citizen Diplomat in Residence

20 January 2011: I am living in the home of Madani Sissoko, president of Ségou's sister city commission. Down the street, a car mechanic has set up shop under a very large and shady mango tree. His customers sit in low chairs, drinking green tea while their cars are

repaired. In a couple of months, the small green fruit dangling from that tree will be ripe for plucking; customers will be sipping tea in the April heat, or dozing with their mouths open in anticipation of the fat, juicy mangoes. Across the street, under a neem tree, a barber is shaving the head of a customer to keep him cool—and "kool."

January 20 is a holiday celebrating the creation of Mali's national army, and the kids are off school for a four-day weekend. Madani's sisters all look like my cousin Stacy—especially his younger sister, Mah. His wife Fati reminds me of Marpessa Dawn, the actress who played Eurydice in the 1959 Brazilian film *Black Orpheus*. In the market, I saw a girl who looks just like a younger version of one of my local Richmond councilwomen, Cynthia Newbille. We *are* all descended from the peoples of the Mali Empire!

I wake up each morning to hear Madani calling me: "Aaanaaa! *On mange!*" Already dressed and fed, Madani waits for me at the little table in the courtyard so we can start the day. His wife, Fati Thiam, sets the table out early in the morning so that it is ready for whoever comes to eat, whenever they come, until 10:00 a.m. The courtyard is shaded by the house itself, and the air moves with a light river breeze. The table holds tins of Nescafé instant coffee, Nestlé's enriched powdered whole-fat milk, sugar, butter, jam, and a sack of French-style baguettes. On Sundays, protein is served: eggs scrambled with tomatoes and onions, pickled sardines drained and sautéed in oil, and canned beef that resembles Spam. This meal, like every meal, is followed by the traditional Malian green tea. This is the routine, whether the weather is a balmy one hundred degrees or a frigid eighty-five.

I take each of my meals like this, in the courtyard with Madani, while Fati and the kids eat in the kitchen. But as I become accustomed to the rhythm of this household, it gets harder to be waited upon with Madani as if I were an honorary man. I find myself slowly asserting small acts of solidarity with Fati. She speaks Bambara, Arabic, and a very little French, and I speak absolutely no Bambara, nor Arabic; but with her eldest daughter as translator, I can tease Madani in her presence about his chauvinism, or offer to help with the shopping. I can't clean anything, however, because it's not allowed. The family's two teenaged servant girls, Batoma and Naa, often manage to wash, dry, and fold my clothes before I realize they've even been in my room.

In the evening, we sit in chairs around the light of a fire fed by an eight-foot-long, four-inch-thick dry tree limb that Madani nonchalantly pushes into the flames. He and his male friends joke about how they might assimilate me into the world of Malian women; about the benefits of polygamy; about me adding a Malian man to my matrimonial harem. They tell me that there is a ratio of four women to every man in Mali, and give me instructions on how to make and serve the traditional Malian tea. I tell them that whether I was a Malian woman or an expatriate American, I would have to stay single!

These fireside jests complement the meetings I have with people working on social problems like domestic enslavement, child abuse, poverty, and malnutrition, which are sometimes caused and often exacerbated by the intersection of polygamy and the effects of Western interference during and since colonial times.

These meetings have also jarred me into recognition of another truth about my race and ethnicity: "It depends on where you're standing." On countless occasions over those five weeks in Ségou, I heard myself referred to as "the *toubabou* from America." *Toubab* (TOO-bahb)—probably derived from *toubib,* which is French slang for "medical doctor"—is the Bamanan term for all whites. Apparently, however, its meaning stretches further than that. As one young girl explained to me, *toubab* is a label applied to strangers, to foreigners. I had seen myself as an African American finally visiting the motherland, but to every other Malian outside of my small group of friends, I was just another "white" tourist from America. Isn't that something!

My retreat is the rooftop patio off my bedroom. I spend time each day drawing or watching the wind blow the branches of the *neem* trees to and fro. The temperature has been perfect. The sun, while high and bright, has been obscured by the seasonal dust stirred up by the harmattan. I have had no migraines, but the dust is so thick I fear I might develop asthma! To protect my skin from the dry, dry air, after bathing, I slather myself, and my hair too, in *karité* (shea butter) that has been blended with coconut and citrus oils into a dense pomade.

Like all the women, I usually wear a scarf, and a loose tunic over matching loose pants. When going about routine activities, women dress fairly casually, though my outfits still look pretty pitiful in comparison to their color-coordinated garments. But let there be a wedding, and you will never have seen such splendor in cloth! Spectacularly tie-dyed or printed cotton damasks of all colors, intricately patterned embroidery with gold thread; heads wrapped with a simple square of fabric that in two swift moves becomes a striking headpiece. Every woman will wear a different pattern and cut, and yet as a group, they will be flawlessly coordinated. Before the ceremony, they spend hours getting their hands and feet tattooed with henna in floral and geometric patterns, and their faces transformed by make-up artists whom Hollywood would envy. Each woman is more beautiful and more brilliantly done up than the last.

But as lovely as everyone is, and as much as I want to stay forever, I've been a guest, imposing on people's daily lives. And life here is hard for most people. Statistics reveal that the average Malian subsists on less than two US dollars per day. People often barter for basic goods and services, and sell whatever they must wherever they can: out of their homes; on the street in makeshift shacks; even on the road, approaching stopped cars. The women and girls usually work in the marketplace, while the boys and men hawk their wares on the streets. Young or old, everyone works to contribute something to the family income, no matter how small.

In the faces of young men and women, you can see how the hard work either makes them more beautiful or wears them out early in life. Women don't stop working until they are affluent enough to hire servants. If they never get them, they keep working. Domestic service is a prominent source of labor, and younger family members serve their elders, and their guests. The ease by which guests like me get to feeling that "life is good" is unnerving. I am provided more than is available for some families; and yet, every morning, Madani is visited by a neighbor or stranger who asks for money to buy food or school supplies for their children. Embarrassed at what I have spent on necklaces, I determine to leave a gift of money with the family before I return home.

3 February: I learned another new word—*vernissage*. Literally, it means "a varnishing"; practically, it is a first viewing or the opening reception of an exhibition.

I am one of a group of international artists who have been invited to participate in Ségou's 2011 music and cultural arts festival, *Festival sur le Niger*. The weeklong festival was held at Monsieur Amaghiré Dolo's Animy Sculpture Atelier in Sébougou, a suburb of Ségou along the river's edge just north of town. Its curator, Amadou Chab Touré, is a Ségou- and Paris-based photographer, art critic, and gallery owner. My fellow international artists were Anna Read (UK), Wren Miller (UK), and Leslie Lumeh (Liberia), while the Malian artists were Hama Goro and Amara Sylla (Bamako), Issa Koné, and Amaghiré Dolo himself (Ségou). Of the eight of us, four spoke English fluently, two of us spoke some French, and the rest spoke French and Bamanankan (Bambara). So we managed to talk about life and art pretty well.

We were provided with our own studios and basic supplies: canvas, gesso, and whatever else we had requested in advance. The theme of our show was to be *la terre,* the earth, and we were to provide creations inspired by Mother Earth and by the red soil of Mali. I had decided before arriving that I wanted to make pigments from local materials, especially from the red dust and from the charcoal of local wood.

Dolo's atelier is located beside the Niger River, and as we worked, we could watch men and boys casting fishing nets, poling canoes, or stretching sails to catch the breeze, while women and girls fetched water for the large riverside gardens or to use to wash clothes. On the first day of the workshop, we spent many hours observing the river as we waited for our studios and accommodations to be ready. Workmen continued to come and go, even as we began to move our supplies into the workshop. Issa Koné set up vats of leaf dye and river mud and prepared his precut wood tablets in the courtyard. I consulted him about using local materials, and together with Dolo, he taught me how to grind charcoal until it was fine enough to use as a pigment in paint.

We spent the morning stretching canvases, a process through which I earned my first ounces of respect as a stickler for rigorous stretching procedures. Everyone was busy at something until lunch was served at noon, after which the place became very quiet as all the men but Issa left to go into downtown Ségou.

It was at this point that two of us discovered we'd been robbed. During the chaos of the morning, Anna Read's passport, driver's license, money, cameras, memory cards, and cell phone, as well as my wallet, identification, cash, and cell phone were all stolen. It was a near-perfect crime of opportunity. Dolo and the festival organizers were appalled. The gendarmes were called and took testimonies, along with an inventory of the stolen items.

The festival's organizers almost immediately replaced our money and phones. Two days later, a local teacher found our wallets and documents in a trash dump on his way to school. Civic pride demanded that someone be held responsible, but as the actual thief could not be produced, the atelier's caretaker was arrested for negligence. Anna and I spent quite a bit of social and political capital (and all the French I could wrestle) trying to convince the gendarmes to let him go and the festival authorities not to fire him. That would not make for good art, nor good diplomatic relations in our very young sister city friendship. We—or someone—prevailed in the end.

☙

The workshop resumed, and the last of my five weeks in Mali whooshed by. Other crises related to our workshop, artistic differences, and curatorial frustrations arose, but were quickly resolved. We did not, however, develop much cohesion as a group. Dealing with the robbery had taken up a lot of time, so we had to focus intently on our work in the time remaining before the exhibition's installation. I made three abstract paintings using red dust (actually, it was closer to orange), brown soil, black charcoal, burnt millet ink, and white acrylic paint. The exhibition looked good. We had a wonderful vernissage and danced to spectacular music at the festival night after night, and our exhibit enjoyed lots of good press.

Four days later, I was on a plane on my way home, bringing to an abrupt end what had become a way of life. I knew immediately what I would miss:

I am going to miss the ritual call to prayer coming through the early morning dark, across the rooftops and along unlit city streets. I am going to miss the sight of trees unhindered by power lines and light poles in their growth to mature individuality. I am going to miss taking long walks in dark streets lit only by the flickering of fire pots, cigarette tips, black-and-white TV screens peering through windows, or the occasional neon of a part-time nightclub. I am going to miss Fati's extraordinary face; Mami's teenage reach for power; Lalu's joyful, girlish ferocity; Bouba's reserved, observant determination; Sidi's chocolate brown eyes and huge smiles at the least bit of attention. I am going to miss Batoma and Naa, servant girls who will receive no education, and who speak no French beyond « merci » and « bon jour » or « bon soir »—so I take every opportunity to be sure I greet them in Bambara. Madani has a huge heart. He is an advocate for the realities of people's needs and what motivates them; he greets everyone, knows almost everyone, and understands how to stay connected. My affection for the whole family is growing. They've given me a name — Awa Sissoko—making me a real « Tantie » in the family. I told Madani and Mayor Simaga I would like to come back and build a small house in Ségou, by the river. They both said, "No problem."

I was exhausted and numb when I got back home. I told my husband that a hole had opened in my chest, and when I thought of Mali, a portal filled that hole, and transported me back there—there where I could smell the dust, feel the wind, and hear the morning call to prayer and the birds that sang in the afternoon. When my father had our DNA tested, we had learned that our family originally came from the lands that make up what is now Benin, Nigeria, and Cameroon, and I plan to visit someday. But Mali turned out to be my way back to the motherland, and it will never leave me.

2003 - 2005

Teaching Timbuktu and Our First Visit

Starting Conversations Between Virginia and West Africa

The sister city idea fits perfectly into the framework offered by Oxford University historian and philosopher Theodore Zeldin, who in 1998 published a small but immensely important book entitled *Conversation: How Talk Can Change Your Life*. Originally a series of six BBC radio lectures delivered by the author in 1996, the *Conversation* is less than seventy pages long and able to fit into a breast pocket. Though small in size and volume, its message is huge. I quote, with the author's kind permission, from his sixth lecture:

> Bringing people of different nations together for sport and music is useful and fun, but only long conversations can reveal the full meaning of the deep resentment felt by many civilizations towards the West. What we consider to be our triumphs—our freedom, our empire or our technology—are viewed quite differently by them. Never has there been more need for conversations between civilizations, because never have they been able to inflict so much damage on each other. . . .
>
> Our sensibilities change when we visit the Islamic world, which at the beginning of the (previous) millennium was the most splendid of all civilizations at the time, and when we converse with Islamic women, to discover the enormous variety of conditions they experience, in different countries, in different classes, to realize how their position has changed many times in the course

of their history, and how it is changing now, when we appreciate that Islam has been interpreted in as many ways as Christianity or any other religion. God says in the Koran, "We have created you male and female and made you nations and tribes, *that you may know one another.*"

Richmond and Ségou have engaged in a conversation that will last many years and involve many people. Conversations have been developing between health and education professionals, artists and musicians, students and professors, journalists and radio stations, politicians and sportsmen and women, especially the women in Richmond who have been leaders of the sister city commission and Virginia Friends of Mali.

I visited Salim Coumaré's philosophy class at the Cabral high school, where we had a wonderful conversation about contrasting ideas. I talked to his students about American concepts of identity and society, democracy and individualism—all of which are a part of their Malian philosophy course. And how different our cultures are! America is focused on the individual: even nuclear family life has almost disappeared in America, where dogs and cats replace children for parents whose offspring now live in faraway Florida, Texas, Oregon, or Hawaii. In Mali, the individual is nothing; a child exists only as a part of his close and extended family. Unlike America, personal names have little importance in Mali. A man is Keita or Touré because his ancestors were Keita or Touré, and the praise-singer griots remind him constantly of his lineage. Keita and Touré and other women keep their identity and their name when they marry: they may marry a Coulibaly, a Traoré, a Konaré, but never will they be anything other than Keita or Touré. As for the first name, it is not terribly important in Mali: there are so many people called Boubacar or Mohamed, that a lot of Malians get by on a nickname and never use their given name at all.

In our discussions about identity, Malian students were astonished to learn that respect for age has vanished from American society. They were amazed that old people live in retirement homes—which do not exist in West Africa—and that a young Virginian would not automatically take his or her elderly parents to live with them in their house. Malian parents raise their children, and their children care for them in old age. The individualism of American society is unknown in West Africa; and the Malian students deplored it!

The Malian extended family includes the grandparents, married children and grandchildren all living around a family compound—and since the weather is always warm, people spend most of their time outside talking, eating or drinking tea under shady trees. Most mothers even cook outside in the courtyard. Some Malian men have two wives, who take it in turns to cook for their husband and for all their joint children. This Malian family structure resembles the American recomposed family, where divorced parents may remarry people who have their own children. American children are forced into proximity with "half-brothers" and "half-sisters" with whom they share no blood relationship, and whom they may not even like. Malian families easily take in cousins, or the children of old friends who join the family—so the "recomposed family" is easy enough for Malians to understand.

Our conversation broke down completely, however, when I explained that in America, it is now possible for men to marry men, or women to marry women. When I described two gay men adopting a child, who would therefore have two fathers and no mother . . . well, then the conversation collapsed into disbelieving hilarity. And who can blame the Malian students for laughing? Twenty years ago in Virginia, who would have believed that men would one day marry men and be able to adopt a baby? And how many Virginians can imagine a polygamous Malian household with one man having two—or even three—wives? Yet we all know American men who have had two or three divorces; this could be viewed as a form serial polygamy. Perhaps our families are not as different as we think?

We have probably had less success in engaging in deep conversation with Malian women, although close friendships between Richmond and Ségou women flourish, especially through homestays in both cities. The fact remains that Malian women are less involved in political and social leadership than American women. Women are seen as the leaders of Malian families, where the title "mother" is equivalent to "goddess"; but they are less well equipped to occupy the new municipal, regional, and national spaces that developed with colonialism and the nation-state. Participation in these new spaces requires fluency in the foreign French language and mastery of Western laws and institutions—skills that few Malian women have.

Malian women are of course a part of the Islamic world described by Theodore Zeldin. Islam came very early to Mali, arriving peacefully during the 800s with the trading caravans of camels from Morocco. Mali's Islam was strongly influenced by the humanistic intellectuals of Timbuktu's famous university, and by Sufi philosophical interpretations of Islam forged in the University of Fez, in Morocco. Mali's religion preaches Islam as Love, Islam as Caring, Islam as Giving Charity, Islam as Peace and Tolerance—very different messages from those of the harsh version of Islam found in the Saudi Arabian desert. To improve American understanding of Islam, and to start a conversation about Malian Islam, VFoM created the program "Teaching Timbuktu"—and this was the beginning of our sister city adventure.

Madame Koné and Monsieur Coulibaly: On Getting Women Involved

I have known Madame Safiatou Koné since I worked with her late husband Nazou in Gao in 1982. Nazou Douba Koné was the financial controller of the cooperatives I was funding.

By 1990, Nazou was near retirement and still making babies. We put a stop to the babies. His wife had borne six, and was caring for ten children. She told me she wanted to stop. My old friend Nazou was reluctant to sign the papers, but I sat him down in front of my wife's gynecologist friend, Dr. Fanta Diabaté, and he signed. Three years later, he died suddenly. His widow had six children of her own to feed, and four grown boys from his first marriage whom she had raised as her own.

Safiatou had been living in her elder brother's house when she was first told that her family had found her a husband. She was only seventeen at the time, and she fled when she was told that she was going to marry a thirty-four-year-old divorced accountant called Nazou Koné. She had seen him just once at the house, and had served him food. He must have fancied her, but she did not fancy him! Her uncle found her in the bus before it left town, and brought her back home. So she married Nazou. "My fat husband," she used to call him; but they got along very well, and their six children are all lovely. I know, because I educated them all, checking that they kept up with their studies and occasionally paying bills. There was no one else to do it: Nazou died and Safiatou refused to marry either of his brothers.

Marriage is the traditional social security system in West Africa: one of the brothers takes the widow as a second wife, and accepts the charge of the children. Technically known as "levirate," this provides a social safety net. But it is not an easy arrangement in the best of times, and Safiatou did not care for either of her brothers-in-law. One was a rigid civil servant, the other an underpaid teacher with only one arm—not a great choice—and neither really wanted to marry his brother's wife, let alone feed and educate his many children. Nor did Safiatou see herself as a second wife, reduced in status and forced to follow instructions from another woman. A strong personality and a leader of women, even when struggling to pay the bills and feed her children, Safiatou was determined to keep her independence.

After Nazou's death, her husband's family deserted her, the four grown boys driving off in Nazou's old car to take over his house in San, fifty miles away. Partly thanks to the help I was able to offer, Safiatou was able to keep going. I stopped by whenever I passed through Ségou on the way to visit one of my rural development projects. Sometimes I would sleep under my mosquito net in her yard, and spend the evening checking homework with Nazou's children.

Madame Koné made a modest living from the freezers that had been bought for her by Nazou. She and her daughters sold bags of cold water to thirsty shoppers and travelers in the market. They sold ice to bakers and butchers for their businesses. Sometimes they sold ice cream that they made in their kitchen. It was not easy to make ends meet. There was often an electricity bill to pay, or rent arrears that needed fixing. When one of the freezers gave up the ghost, I bought a replacement.

During elections, Safiatou also found work as a prominent vote organizer. Every political party in Mali wants to attract women voters, especially in important population centers like Ségou, Mali's second-largest city. With her warm and engaging personality, and her numerous daughters available to fetch their school friends and neighbors to attend political gatherings, Safiatou positioned herself as a valuable ally for any politician. She became skilled at bringing women to listen to party leaders, and arranged for her neighbors to dance at events for every candidate—with each one in turn paying her to run meetings and distribute their free T-shirts during rallies and other events. Party leaders offer these T-shirts and other free gifts, such as bags of sugar, to women who say they will vote for their party—so Safiatou prudently told candidates from each party that she would vote for them. In the end, members of each party contributed to Safiatou's budget, and thanks to the secret ballot, none of them knew for whom she and her friends actually voted. In this way, by hard work and creative cunning, Madame Koné fed and educated her children.

By 2007, all of Safiatou's children were married, or studying in Bamako—except Sali, who had been a babe in arms when her father died. A young widow with six children will never find a husband, but it is a different matter for an attractive woman with just one teenage daughter, especially if that daughter helps with the cooking. Madame Koné now became Madame Coulibaly.

Safiatou's new husband, Amadou Coulibaly, was a manager in Comatex, Ségou's cotton-spinning and weaving factory. Divorced from his first wife, he is an amiable man who enjoys Safiatou's boundless personality and conversation. We call her "the captain of Mali's national talking team," and she laughs cheerfully at our joking. Amadou especially admires the energy with which his wife has transformed his rice farm north of Ségou from a desperate failure into a profitable success.

She leads the workers into the paddy fields and herself bends down under the African sun, tirelessly planting seedlings in the mud.

Coulibaly—or "Kurubali" if you live on the Gambian coast—was the dynastic name of Biton, who founded the Bambara Empire in 1712. When the Moroccans conquered Timbuktu, and then Gao in 1591, they destroyed the Mali-Sonrai Empire. Small kingdoms sprang up all over the region. Biton Coulibaly (1712–1755) created one of the strongest, building a palace in Old Ségou, and Coulibaly is therefore one of the traditional Ségou names.

Madame Coulibaly was still Madame Koné, a widow with teenage daughters, when we took our first Richmonders to visit Ségou. Two years later, we were visiting the Mayor's office to discuss future project planning, and she had become Madame Coulibaly. I suggested that Monsieur and Madame Coulibaly might like to attend the meeting, since we were going to discuss community participation.

"That sounds interesting," said Amadou. "There might be something in it for Comatex. Perhaps I will join you at this meeting."

"Great," I said. "And maybe Madame can come too, since we will be needing people who can involve Ségou's women in the sister city movement."

"I will come," said Amadou. "Madame has to look after the household."

Safiatou looked disappointed, but she said nothing. Mali is not a place where women are crushed socially—especially in a prosperous urban environment like Ségou—and Safiatou is a major force among the women of her area whenever she wishes to be. Yet there was nothing to say in this case, for a woman is in charge of the household. While Malian mothers may be the goddesses who give life to their children and run their houses, Malian society has not yet worked out how to give women free rein in the public spaces of the modern state. In Richmond, at the 2013 VCU Women, War & Peace Conference, the Malian visitors were all men, while the five speakers at the opening ceremony were all strong American women.[1] So America is making progress in allowing women take social leadership roles. One of the questions we want to explore is how the sister city partnerships may be able to encourage not only American but also African women's participation and leadership. The answers are not obvious. We will search for answers to this question as we tell our story.

---

1 *VCU provost Beverly Warren welcomed the conference participants; VCU was represented by vice president for inclusive excellence Wanda Mitchell. Other co-sponsors were Ana Edwards, president of Virginia Friends of Mali (VFoM); Richmond Peace Education Center (RPEC) director Adria Scharf; and Richmond Sister Cities Commission (RSCC) chair Patricia Cummins.*

Richmond's First Visit to the Ségou Music Festival

Allan the Musician

I met Allan on the contra-dance floor in Richmond. He, like me, feels music and it moves him. Dance music enters my body through my skin, courses through my bloodstream, and exits through my feet. In Allan Levenberg, I found a great dancer who also plays that quintessential African and American instrument, the banjo.

Allan was the first Friend of Mali, and when we created the association, it was Allan who volunteered to be its treasurer—not a very arduous task, since we seldom have any money. He tells us in board meetings how many pennies we have left, and how much we owe the printer or the restaurant where we had our last party. Once or twice a year, he writes to thank some kind person who has sent us $200 or $1,200 as a donation. And if there is no money, he—or occasionally I or my wife or some other kind person—pays the association's debt with a tax-free donation of his own.

Allan once told us, "I had an easy life in business, coming in early in the IT revolution and being able to make a difference at a time when CEOs knew nothing about computers. So I sort of feel that I skimmed the surface. Now, with the sister city relationship and the Virginia Friends of Mali, I feel that I am working with things that are deeper and more meaningful than at any other time in my professional life. For me, this is truly inspirational."

It was Allan who set the tone for VFoM. To paraphrase an old proverb, "He who plays the music sets the tune," and so we vibrate to the sound of Allan's Old Tyme banjo. We believe in parties more than we believe in meetings—so we make every meeting into a party. Our executive committee meetings usually include an African stew with rice, perfuming the air with the fragrance of peppery peanut sauce or the onion and lemon scents of chicken *yassa*. Our board meetings consume more wine than effort, and our annual general meetings fit speeches and necessary reports between music and dancing.

It was also Allan who told us we must transform the Ségou friendship into an official sister city relationship. That was no easy task, for Richmond had no sister city commission at the time. Indeed, back then, Richmond did not even have a mayor—until Douglas Wilder was elected in 2005, in the first direct mayoral election. In 2006, we had to persuade the City to create a new commission, since the old one had been disbanded and forgotten. Then we had to get the city council to select a chairman and appoint members. Allan Levenberg was appointed the first commissioner. During their second meeting, the commission recommended that Ségou become Richmond's sister city, and the city council duly agreed. All of this happened thanks to Allan and his banjo!

The banjo is a derivative of instruments Malians still play today. Africans played the banjo on Thomas Jefferson's plantation, although he spelled it "banjar" in his diaries. It is the American descendant of the Malian *ngoni*, which has five strings stretched across a piece of carved wood covered with tight goatskin. There are three- and four-stringed versions as well and the leader of the famous Ngoni Ba Orchestra from Ségou, Bassekou Kouyaté, created a seven-stringed ngoni to give himself more flexibility. Bassekou and his band regularly play at the Ségou festival, and they were the undisputed stars of the 2011 Richmond Folk Festival.

Allan plays with various jam groups around Richmond, including his Sunday afternoon gig at the Cary Street Café. Some Monday nights, I join Allan at the Oregon Hill Old-Tyme group that meets at the house of Michael Gahan, the owner of the Pine Street Barber Shop. Michael strums the guitar, James plays the fiddle, Bill plays everything . . . and I sometimes play simple riffs on the *djembé*, the drum that Michael brought home from Ségou. But in those days, he had not yet been to Ségou, and I was content to listen, or to beat time on the spoons or beer bottle.

Allan is also a positive thinker. In no time at all, he had decided that he would come with me to visit Mali and discover the origins of the banjo. So, between playing versions of "John Henry" and "Country Roads," we discussed traveling to join the Ségou festival that had started just after the turn of the millennium. Michael and James decided to join us. We had a plan!

In Praise of Malian Lifestyles and Chicken Yassa

We landed in the airport of Bamako, Mali's capital city, in late January 2006, and were met by my adopted son, Kalifa Touré. He took us home to Daoudabougou, the modest part of Bamako where I own a house and where we were going to spend our first couple of days in Mali.

I always sleep outside, on a cotton mattress under a mosquito net. I find cement houses in Africa hot and airless; their walls absorb the sun's heat during the day, and give it back during the night— unlike mud brick, which makes for a better, cooler building material in a hot country. But the Oregon Hill folk chose to sleep inside, on three brand-new cotton mattresses lined up on the floor under three new mosquito nets, with electric fans to blow the air around. Luxury accommodation by my own Malian standards, but not exactly "American hotel" quality.

I need to explain that my wife and I raised our children in Mali during the 1980s and 1990s, while Michelle ran Save the Children in West Africa. When Michelle went off to work for the Christian Children's Fund (now called ChildFund International) in Geneva— and later Richmond—the house rent provided by Save the Children disappeared. I still had a US government contract, as I was working for USAID. I had to live somewhere, and so did the Malian children who had been born under our roof. Their father, our former gardener-cum-watchman, had died, and we did not want to abandon his wife Ami and their kids. So we purchased a small compound with two small houses: one for me, and one for Ami and her children.

Originally built by a man with two wives, the two houses suited my needs perfectly. Later, when our adopted son Kalifa got married, he took over my portion of the property, which has three small bedrooms. During this first sister city visit, one of these rooms was allocated to our traveling companion, Carol Warner, an adventurous retired lady and dear friend of mine who had been a math teacher at the Collegiate School in Richmond, and who joined our group for her first visit to West Africa. Naturally, the bedroom was not vacant; no Malian room is ever empty. Kalifa had to clear his mother and sister out of the house so that Carol could have her own space: a small room that boasted an actual bed, a private electric fan, and a mosquito net. It sat opposite a pleasant modern bathroom with pink tiling, a solar water heater—and a shower, the best invention America ever exported to the rest of the world.

"There is no toilet seat," Carol announced on coming out into the courtyard for dinner.

"Of course not," I replied. "Wooden toilet seats were an eighteenth-century invention for cold countries, because porcelain is chilly to sit on when there is snow on the ground. But wooden seats collect germs, and Mali has never seen snow. Even during January, the cool season, it will never get cooler than sixty degrees Fahrenheit, so porcelain never becomes uncomfortable, and we don't need unhygienic, germ-collecting toilet seats. And we have no need for hot water, either; most of the year, we crave cool showers in this hot climate. In fact, after you shower in the morning, you should fill a couple of plastic buckets with cold water to wash with later in the day. You'll appreciate it when the heat of the afternoon sun has made the water pipes and everything in them scalding hot!"

We sat around the yard in the cool of the evening, and Ami served us chicken *yassa*, one of the world's great dishes. A coastal dish from the lands of Mali now called Senegambia (a combination of Senegal and The Gambia), *yassa* is easy enough to make, provided you have enough onions: First, peel and chop about six to eight pounds of onions, and slow-cook them with a little oil for an hour or more to make a delicious sauce. While the onions are cooking, grill your chicken. Spice up the onion sauce with hot chili pepper, a touch of mustard, and some black peppercorns, and then add the smoky grilled chicken pieces. Leave the chicken to simmer in the sauce while you boil water for white rice, which should accompany the meal. When the rice is ready, add some squeezed lemon juice to the onion sauce, according to your taste, and serve with the chicken over the rice.

Ami has been cooking chicken *yassa* for me since her four children were small (her eldest daughter Nana is now over thirty, and the mother of two boys), and she knows how I like it. When I land at the airport, I usually call Ami and say, "I have landed in Bamako; it is time to prepare the *yassa* and the *gingembré!*"—my favorite iced drink, made with fresh ginger and fresh lemon juice. Ami laughs her pleasure into the phone, and gets busy.

Thirty-Plus Years Living in Mali

I have been in and out of Mali since the early 1980s, when I lived in Timbuktu, on the edge of the Sahara Desert. I ran a project helping to rebuild an economy and a society ravaged by drought. From 1973–74, crops failed, livestock died, thousands emigrated, and hundreds starved to death during a terrible drought in Northern Mali and the Sahel, the name given to the vast slice of Africa savannah land that runs along the southern fringes of the Sahara Desert. In fact, though I didn't know it then, the drought of that winter was the worst of a period of acute drought that the Sahel suffered from 1965 to 1990. This in turn was part of the gradual aridification of the Sahara Desert that has been continuing for three thousand years.

North Mali has a mixed population of farmers, herders, and nomadic fishermen. Most northerners wear a turban to protect themselves from the sun and the sand. The farmers are mainly black, and most of them live close to the Niger River, where access to water allows them to grow two or three crops of wheat, rice, and vegetables each year. The rest of Mali depends on thin crops of rain-fed millet or sorghum. Farmers living on the bend of the Niger mostly speak Sonrai, a composite language related to languages spoken in ancient Egypt and Carthage; but in some villages, people speak some of the other ten national languages of Mali that are mostly found farther south.

The herders are seminomadic traders who grow crops and trade animals. Arab (Moor) and Tuareg (Berber) merchants herd sheep, goats, and camels—and a Toyota four-wheel-drive (4WD) vehicle, if they can afford one. Another group, the Fulani, are Nilotic cattle herders who depend on rain-fed pastures and the Niger River floodplains, known as the interior Niger delta, to sustain their herds.

Finally, along the Niger River, Bozo fishermen follow the shoals of fish that they catch, eat, and smoke for sale. Nearly every woman in Mali uses dried and smoked fish in her family's sauce. Some fish may also be salted, but salt is not found around the river. It has to be imported from the desert, which was once an ocean, or from Senegal on the coast.

In the 1980s, I worked in rural Gao, Timbuktu, and Kidal as the director of ACORD, a nongovernmental organization (NGO) dedicated to digging wells and improving irrigation after the 1974 drought. We helped farmers improve crop yields, build cereal banks, and introduce seed selection. We helped nomads rebuild their herds of goats, sheep, and camels. We rebuilt the economy by organizing cooperatives of farmers, herders, and medical personnel in this vast northern region, which was less "governed" than surviving under a corrupt military occupation force.

For one hundred years, from the beginning of France's military colonization in the 1880s until the popular revolution of 1990 overthrew the military dictatorship in Bamako, Northern Mali was ruled by soldiers. Even after Mali achieved independence on September 22, 1960, it seemed to Northerners that they still lived under an army of occupation, for the Northern administrative positions of governor and *commandant de cercle* were held exclusively by Southern military officers. In those days of military dictatorship, Tuaregs and Arabs in the Malian army could not rise above the rank of captain.

Southern Malians hate hearing about the brutality and corruption of their army in North Mali; but I lived there when the regime of General-President Moussa Traoré was in charge, and I saw the army corruption firsthand. I fought to defend the peasant cooperatives against the theft of diesel fuel by soldiers—for if the diesel was taken, the motorized pumps could not irrigate their crops. I remember how bitterly the director of forest resources in Gao complained about corrupt colonels who flouted the laws on hunting game. These colonels would drive around the desert and shoot deer and ostriches from their army vehicles, using military rifles that could shoot multiple rounds per second. This was not hunting; it was massacring wildlife. After he filed a complaint against the army, the director of forest resources was transferred and demoted. No wonder there are no antelope or ostriches left.

Since the French invasion, military government was the norm, and North Mali knew ninety years of "negative peace." There was no actual shooting, but people lived in a permanent state of fear. Only when oppression is removed can people live under "positive peace" and start being able to relax.[2] No wonder the Tuaregs took up arms against General-President Moussa Traoré in June 1990, and against the military putschists in March 2012. No wonder North Mali welcomed the advent of democracy and the overthrow of military government.

Mali has a long tradition of democratic governance. A year after the Lion King founded the Mali Empire in 1235, he promulgated the *Kurugan Fuga*, which we may describe as a "written constitution" that laid down the rules for governing society. Although Sunjata Keita was

---

2 *I borrow this terminology from the 1996 book* Peace by Peaceful Means, *written by Norwegian professor Johan Galtung, the "Father of Peace Studies."*

the King of Kings, acclaimed *Mansa* by his peers, he was elected by West African chiefs acting rather like the Electoral College established by Thomas Jefferson and Co. to select the president of the United States. Democracy is not just a question of elections, but about listening to people and ensuring that have a say in decisions that affect them. After all, elections can be fixed, and often are.

The Mali-Sonrai Empire had a stable government for most of the time from 1235 until the Moroccan conquest of 1591. It was organized through what we now call "decentralized democratic governance." In each village, the chief, also known as the *chef de village* or *dugutigi,* was the most important official, and he was beholden to the people of his community. This was "democratic" both because the position was, and still is, elective (the Elders choose the most qualified person descended from the founding family of the village); because every family was/ is represented in the village council; and because women have always been consulted in Malian society before any decision is made. The system was not perfect: for a start, it was a gerontocracy in which old people were the bosses. Not everyone was equal. Founding families and wealthy families had the loudest voices, while poor people, recent immigrants, and people descended from "captives" often had little say in decisions. Nevertheless, it provided a better system of governance than the centralized military rule I discovered when I reached Mali in 1980.

These were some of the things I explained to my intrepid group of American friends as we sipped *gingembré* and digested our delicious *yassa* under a mango tree in my Bamako yard. I described how my wife and I had raised our biological children in Mali during the 1980s and 1990s. I explained how Ami Coulibaly had joined our household as a nineteen-year-old with baby Nana on her back. Kalifa Touré, a descendant of the Moroccan warriors who had conquered the Sonrai in 1591, told them how he had been in school with our son Edward at the age of fifteen when his father had died. And so Kalifa joined the household. Now it seemed that his widowed mother was ill, and she had come down from Gao to see the doctor. But since these distinguished Virginians were my guests, his mother had gone off to stay with some cousins. That is how things are done in the African extended family, which, in our case and at that moment, was composed of a courtyard with two houses and around seventeen people aged seven months to seventy-seven years—plus our four American guests, Virginian Friends of Mali.

Maha the Author, Baptizer-in-Chief of Ségou

I slept under the mango tree, enjoying the cool night air in my Bamako yard. Despite the electric fans, Allan, Michael, and James must have felt hot in the cement building, sleeping side by side on floor mattresses under three mosquito nets. Meanwhile, Carol had her own fan in the room opposite the bathroom with no toilet seat.

Since we were Richmond's first delegation to Ségou, our future sister city, the first people we visited were members of the Association of Ségoviens Living in Bamako. My Malian father, Mamadou Haïdara, a teacher and author known by his pen name "Maha," was the president of this association, which held its monthly meetings at the Colibris Hotel. This hotel is owned by Dr. Mamadou Fanta Simaga, a former mayor of Ségou who was also vice president of the association.

Around thirty members showed up to the meeting. My American friends were enchanted by their friendliness, as well as by the formality of the event. Each person in the room was introduced, in French, with myself serving as translator. When I presented my group, I also introduced their musical abilities. Immediately, the proposal was made to give each Amercian guest a Malian name—and since they were musicians, the names had to be those of *griot* families.

Griots are the musicians, poets and historians of Mali. Griots know the history of every clan, and this makes them intermediaries and diplomats, for peace, marriage, and business are all linked to ancestral tradition. Some clans are allies, or have had ancient rivalries, or even marriage taboos, and these things are known by the griots.

The most famous of all the griots was Balla Fasé Kouyaté, the thirteenth-century advisor, minister, ambassador, and praise singer to Sunjata Keita, the Lion King. Since Allan plays the banjo, a descendant of the Bambara ngoni, he was baptized Kouyaté.

James the violinist was awarded the second most famous griot name, Jobarteh (in English-speaking lands), or Diabaté (this is how the French-speakers spell it, since French has a soft "j"). Michael received the name of Africa's greatest guitarist and first Grammy winner, Ali Farka Touré. As he played his guitar around the Ségou music festival, we introduced him as Michael Farka Touré, and everyone loved it!

As for Carol Warner, her naming led to animated discussion between the competing clans. There were two people called Diarra in the room who claimed her for their own; and since Diarra was a dynastic name of Ségou, this would make Carol a princess. However, the Traoré clan would have none of it, and there were three of them. Traditional rivals and joking cousins of the Diarra, the Traoré men wanted to impose their name by rule of being more numerous. Carol was grinning happily at my chuckled translations, trying to make sense of the debate and the teasing laughter flying between the "little Diarras" and the "insignificant Traorés" when suddenly one of the women stood up, pointed her finger accusingly at the men, and claimed Carol for the women!

"I am Dembelé," she declared, "and I shall give her the name of my revered and departed mother. She shall be Saran Dembelé." And that was the end of the matter! No Malian ever challenges the status of a mother, and "mother" is a far more important title than "princess."

"And what about the translator?" demanded the audience. "He also needs a name."

"Aha," said Maha, "this man already has a name. Robin has been living in Mali for many years. He lives in the house of Barou Tall, president of the Chamber of Agriculture, and therefore he and his children are Tall. And he is also my son—not because I adopted him, but because he adopted me and my family, and this makes him Haïdara. He is Macky Haïdara Tall, and no one in Ségou will contest such an important name. By the name Haïdara he is—like me, his father—a descendant of the Prophet Mohamed—*asalala*, peace be upon him—and by the name Tall he is a descendant of the last kings who ruled Ségou. Ségou will know this man." And so everyone agreed, and my Malian pedigree was established.

Thus Maha, the author of biographies for adults and for children, presided over the baptism of our Mali delegation. And thence to Ségou, with its glorious river frontage, the rounded red-mud walls of its original fishermen's quarter, its mosques and trees and massive colonial administrative buildings with their broad balconies angled to catch the river breeze and cool the offices and apartments.

On the dock, surrounded on three sides by the river, a vast stage was being erected for the musicians. Ségou's Festival on the Niger River was about to begin. Artisans were crowding the streets, setting up stalls along the river banks to display their exotic carvings, colorful fabrics, wooden masks, articulated puppets, leather goods, and musical instruments for visitors to the festival. I had never seen the Ségou waterfront so lively.

It so happened that in January, Malian television had shown a one-hour film of the Malian prime minister's visit to America the previous fall. He had visited Richmond, and I—Macky Haïdara Tall—had been interviewed by a TV journalist about my love of Mali and about the fact that Michelle and I had raised our children in Mali. My name, my enthusiasm, my face, and my beautiful blue embroidered Malian robes had made their mark. When we reached Ségou, I was greeted in the street as "Macky Tall" by people I had never seen before, including policemen, shoeshine boys, and market women . . . to the amazement and amusement of my friends Allan Kouyaté, James Jobarteh, Michael Farka Touré, and Carol Saran Dembelé.

Mamou Daffé and Malian Fabrics: The Festival's Heart and Soul

We drove to Ségou in a car hired from Savane Tours to meet the company's owner, Mamou Daffé, founder of Ségou's Festival on the Niger River. From the road, we caught tantalizing glimpses of the lush vegetable gardens and orchards planted along the banks of the Niger, Africa's third-greatest river after the Nile and the Congo. Mamou has a very tolerant and interesting wife called Liesbeth, a Dutch woman who used to work with local women in the rice and cotton fields of Ségou.

Mamou Daffé also owns the Savane Motel in Ségou, where we ate supper under the stars. With other local hotel owners, Mamou had decided that a music festival would put Ségou on the tourist and cultural map of West Africa. Through a combination of dogged hard work and imagination, he has created in Ségou one of the most famous music festivals on the world circuit.

Mamou threw all his money into creating the first festival. Liesbeth told me how, for the first three years, she thought her husband had taken a mad, bad risk, putting their children's entire future in danger. But the gamble paid off. The festival is thriving. More than ten thousand people attend, mainly Malians; but two or three thousand European and African foreigners also come to Ségou for the festival every year.[3] Liesbeth is happy, and her children are growing bigger, because—contrary to her worst fears—Mamou's hotel and festival put food on the table.

Thanks to the festival, Ségou has also regained its traditional status as the artistic center of Mali, bringing fame and prosperity to artists, artisans, and musicians. In imitation of Ségou, a dozen more towns have launched festivals across Mali, creating a cultural surge of excitement. In Ségou, we found plenty of new workshops and galleries, where creative juices are flowing through the veins of the city's life and people.

In the elegant, mud-red Soroblé Center studio owned by the Coulibaly brothers, one can discover a mud-cloth workshop filled with beautiful fabrics. *Bogolan* (from *bog*, "mud"; and *lan*, "cloth") is a Ségou specialty that is now fashionable worldwide. It is the fabric that shows off Ségou's style, and its soul—for the designs have deep

---

3 *At least, they did, until the coup d'état of March 2012 transformed Malian into a security risk.*

spiritual meanings for the initiated. The cloth starts as hand-woven cotton which is dyed yellow with the leaves of the *ngalama* tree, also known as African birch. When the artist draws his patterns with fermented black mud from the Niger River—not such a sweet-smelling substance, this—a chemical reaction takes place between the dye and the mud, fixing the black color in the cloth. Bogolan cloth comes in a range of colors, from yellow and orange-brown ochre tints through dark brown to almost black. The geometric designs are strong, with symbolic meanings. With bleach, an artist can add white highlights. Surplus mud vanishes when the bogolan cloth is washed in the waters of the Niger and dried in the sun, leaving the fabric a splendid, sun-washed panoply of color.

My friend Mary Allen gave me a wonderful bogolan robe that everyone admires, and I once brushed my teeth while wearing it. Later I discovered a splash of discolored spots due, I suppose, to bleach in the toothpaste, and I had to get a bogolan artisan friend to re-dye my robe to remove the spotting. Bogolan is all-natural fabric, an ecologist's dream; and it is sensitive to chemicals.

We drank baobab juice on the studio terrace, enjoying a beautiful view over the Niger River while the Coulibaly brothers described how they create textile jobs in Ségou's villages. They sell their own art and crafts, and they also fill their store with the work of women from nearby villages, who produce products featuring Coulibaly designs for the international market: tablecloths and blankets, dining sets and elegant cushions, and curtains—all things that village women never thought of making in the past.

Many other workshops owe their existence to the Ségou festival. The workshop of Boubacar Doumbia's company, Ndomo, is a holistic and environmentally friendly mud-cloth factory where he trains young people in craft skills. Monsieur Doumbia loves to explain the meaning of the symbols used in bogolan designs, and visitors to his workshop can create their own bogolan fragment using these symbols. Ndomo is a statement of Doumbia's craft philosophy, where even the water from the natural dyes is recycled to sustain his garden plants.

His workshop smells sweetly of herbs. The beauty of Doumbia's studio buildings, and the prosperity of these workshops and that of the artisan community of Ségou, is tied to the success of Mamou's festival.

Mamou Daffé includes politics, philosophy, and economics in his festival, as well as music and culture. Every year during the event, a forum debates a subject of importance to Ségou and Mali. On our first visit, we were impressed that he had placed the Niger River at the center of his debates. Protecting the river and making good use of its waters is vital for Ségou and for Mali.

The Niger River flows down from the mountains of Guinea. For more than one thousand miles, it irrigates the fields and the cultures of Mali. The river is the lifeblood of Mali as well as the center of Ségou's economy. The name in Bambara, *Ba Djoli Ba,* can be translated as "Great Blood Mother," or the "Great Lifeblood Artery" of the nation. The Niger River is Mother Nature for Mali, the center of its economic life. Malians need to make good use of its water and to protect its ecosystem. Alas! pollution is increasing, the river's banks are eroding, and much of its water is consumed by thirsty sugarcane projects or lost through unproductive runoff from poorly managed rice irrigation.

Mamou wondered how Ségou might learn from the James River protection experience, and whether Chesapeake Bay watershed scientists might be able to advise Mali about river management and the protection of plant life. We Richmonders looked at each other in ignorance: accountancy, computer science, hair-cutting, and teaching were the only knowledge we had brought with us, apart from music. Mamou Daffé laughed and said that music was the center of his festival, friendship was the center of life, and as Friends of Mali, we could be content to play, listen, and share.

Daffé was the earliest Ségou partner of Virginia Friends of Mali and of the Richmond Folk Festival. He even spent several months in Richmond, living with Allan and Paula Levenberg as he worked to improve his English at VCU. As a child, Mamou was a victim of polio, which left him with a limp. If you meet him, you will be struck first by his smile, his charm, and the intelligence shining from his eyes. The limp you only notice later. It disappears when Mamou starts talking and you realize that you are listening to a visionary. "Ségou needs a new form of education," he enthuses, "to produce a new and modern Ségou citizen who understands business, can handle modern communications and is able to thrive in the globalized world where Americans speak English and force everyone else to listen to them. We need Ségou youths who can speak English and run businesses, and our sister city of Richmond is our door to modernity!"

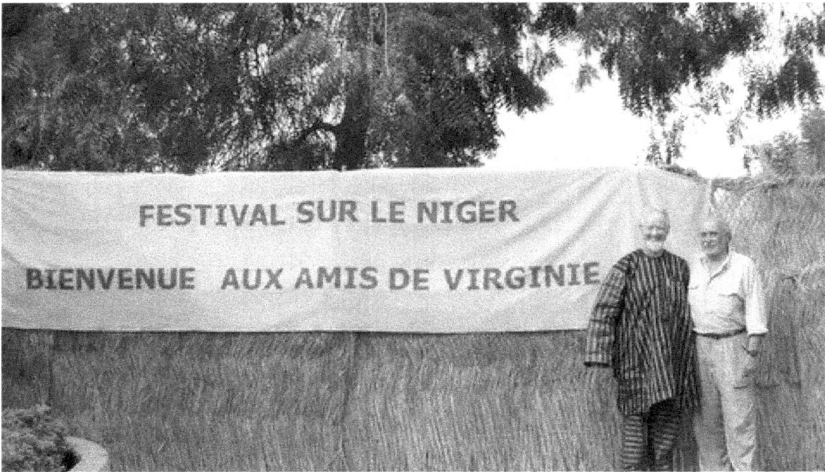

Fig. 2. Robin Poulton ("Macky Tall") and Allan Kouyaté pose with the banner created to welcome them to Ségou in 2006. Photo: VFoM.

Historical Epic Poems: A Ségou *Griot* Meets Old Tyme Music

Members of the Virginia Friends of Mali attended most of the first ten Ségou festivals, and I could write another whole book about those magical experiences. In Ségou, we have heard some of Africa's most famous musicians—household names of Mali's world music scene like Salif Keita, Amadou and Mariam, Khaira Arbi, Babani Koné, Bassékou Kouyaté, and Vieux Farka Touré, the son of my old friend Ali. The last two have also played at the Richmond Folk Festival. We have chatted with these international stars in the company of Mamou Daffé and Mayor Ousmane Simaga, and eaten from the same dish with Habib Koité of Mali and Baba Maal of Senegal.

One evening in February 2010, as we sat on benches in his yard and ate salad prepared by Simaga's wife, a Kouyaté griot stood up and announced that he would tell us the story of Biton Coulibaly, founder of Ségou. He had an audience of thirty. I translated for the Richmonders, from French into English. As Kouyaté began to speak, the women cooking our grilled chicken stopped chattering.

"When the Sonrai Empire was defeated by the Moroccans in 1591, chaos replaced the order of Mali-Sonrai," Kouyaté told us. "The Moroccan *arma* warriors in Gao and Timbuktu were foreigners: they took local wives, but they could not govern. The Bamana peoples—" Here, he used another name for the Bambara. "—began to emerge as a regional power in the mid-1600s, and the town of Ségou-Koro, or Sikoro—"Old Ségou"—became the center of two successor Bamana states: first the Coulibaly, then the Diarra. Their political model used social structures based on hunting, agriculture, and male age-grade associations called *tòn*. Originally designed for social and economic organization, the *tòn* became tools for dynastic rule and territorial expansion. Kalandian Coulibaly ruled Ségou-Koro; and after him, a new ruler emerged: the hunter-warrior Mamary Coulibaly, called Biton."

The salad dishes were collected, and smoky grilled chicken pieces were piled onto platters along our table. I grabbed a leg, bit deep into the juicy flesh, and inhaled the grilled meat as I chewed and translated. Mountains of fries arrived. I reached over from time to time, and grabbed a few fries while the griot intoned his story.

"Traditional Bamana society was a gerontocracy governed by a council of elders. The age groups called the *tòn* allowed young Bamana men to organize themselves into a workforce. An association of equals, the *tòn* elected their leader. Biton was selected to lead his *tòn* around the year 1700. He restructured his age group as warriors, and ordered others to cultivate the fields belonging to his *tòn* members. Biton and his *tòn* replaced the Elders and he installed himself as king in 1712. He also used the Bamana secret societies like *kòmò* and *kònò* to enforce his power; but mostly he used the *tòn* as strong and brutal warriors. If a village disagreed with Biton, the *tòn* would destroy the village."

When a griot speaks, he chooses his words with care. History from a griot has the sonority of an epic poem such as Homer and Virgil had written in ancient times. Old Testament stories are oral history, as is the Longfellow poem immortalizing Hiawatha, the spiritual chief of the Mohawk tribe who may have been a thirteenth-century contemporary of Sunjata, the Lion King. I fear that my English translations— delivered between mouthfuls of fried chicken—may not have reached the lofty eloquence of our Kouyaté griot.

"Ségou's rulers built imposing palaces. Bamana culture was vibrant, the verbal arts were refined: the historical epic poems composed and performed by court *jeli* or griots have lasted longer than the mud-brick palaces. Biton was not Muslim, but his complex of three mosques in Ségou-Koro became a place for Muslim pilgrimage. If you go to Sikoro village today, you can still see the mosque Biton built for his mother, and also his tomb and the restored palace with a tiny entrance door. Biton Coulibaly wanted his reluctant subjects to bow before him, but the Ségou people are too proud. Some Elders felt that Biton was an upstart. The king found a solution by building his palace with a door so small and low that everyone entering was forced to bow and do obeisance to the king as he entered the throne room.

"The spiritual power of Biton depended on his *boli*, or fetishes. There were four important fetishes in Biton's treasury. The names of two are known today: *Bakungoba,* "Big Forest Mother"; and *Nangoloko,* "Birth Business." The power of the sacred forest and fertility confirm these *boli* as sources of royal strength. The others are secret. The most important fetish is remembered in the name of Ségou, the "city of 4,444 acacia trees, plus one." The 4,444 acacias, or *balanzan*, you can count, although 4,444 is a sacred, symbolic number. But the *one* old tree you will not find, for that is the Great Fetish. Maybe it was destroyed by the jihadist El Haj Oumar Tall when he conquered Ségou in 1861. Or perhaps Tall was never able to find the Great Fetish, which still secretly protects Ségou today.

"Until his death in 1755, Biton expanded his control to include the great trading centers of Macina and Djenné. Timbuktu paid Biton tribute. Later, Timbuktu was conquered by the Diarra dynasty around 1800. Ngolo Diarra, who may have been a Coulibaly family slave, gained control of the kingdom after Biton's death, and Ngolo established the Diarra dynasty. That is a story for another day."

At this point, thirty greasy pairs of hands applauded the Kouyaté griot. His praises were called out, and some money changed hands, to keep the griot happy. My American friends were enchanted with this addition to their dinner. Who could imagine such spontaneous storytelling during dinner in Virginia? Malian culture is so rich.

Back to our very first Ségou festival! The Oregon Hill Old Tyme Band played all over Ségou: at the arts center, in the festival grounds, in courtyards, bars and restaurants and private houses. And of course, we were also griots. We played American versions of the griots' epic poems—for example, the timeless tale of John Henry, the African American hero with muscles of steel and a will of iron, who worked as a "steel-driving man," a man who hammered steel drills into the naked rock to make holes for the explosives that blasted railroad tunnels across America. John Henry worked on the construction of the Chesapeake and Ohio Railway in Virginia and West Virgina. According to the late nineteenth-century legend, John Henry's prowess as a steel-driver was measured in a race against a steam-powered hammer—a race he won; but his heart gave out under the stress. We played his song and we honored his memory, but without words—anyway, how many Malians would have understood our English? Mostly, we played them American Old Tyme tunes.

Allan Kouyaté led us on the banjo, while James Jobarteh created riffs on the fiddle and Michael Farka Touré played the bass on his guitar. I offered limited skill on the beer bottle—and sometimes on the Coke bottle, keeping the beat with two coins. The sharp *click-click* provided useful penetration for our beat, but we were no match for the power of Malian drums. We very quickly found that our music became inaudible any time a drummer began playing within two hundred yards of where we were sitting. Then our café audience could no longer hear us, and we could not even hear ourselves. Of course, there was no question in Ségou of our trying to use a *djembé* to increase our volume; among so many gifted professional drummers, we would have humiliated ourselves! Instead, Michael purchased a *djembé,* which he carried home to Richmond in a specially made cotton hammock. Jamming with the Oregon Hill Old Tyme Band on a Monday evening in Richmond, I sometimes play rhythms on Michael's Malian drum . . . but I would never dare admit that to a Malian drummer!

On one occasion, we pulled a surprise. As the Oregon Hill Old Tyme Band struck up a cheerful Scottish reel, I removed my voluminous Malian robe to reveal that underneath I was wearing a kilt, complete with sporran and woolen hose, and I danced a Scottish reel for the amazed Malian onlookers. They had never seen Scottish traditional dress, and they had almost certainly never seen a white man dancing wildly like a madman. Truly, they must have thought that Americans have no limits and no pride, in this region where the rule is that "Big Men don't dance."

In Ségou, a man is considered mature at age forty-nine, after he has passed through the seven cycles of seven years in the village initiation process. He is now approaching wisdom. Fourteen years later, now in his sixties, this African man—if he is still alive—will have completed his education and nine seven-year initiation cycles and reached the age of full maturity. A man—or woman—of this age incarnates wisdom; he dispenses judgments and advice to younger people, and issues edicts that govern the life of the community. And he certainly does not dance.

Madame Koné and Coulibaly: Breakfast on a Moped

Ségou's hospitality was rather hit and miss on that first visit in 2006, before Oumane Simaga became mayor. Though we were weary from travel, no one showed us our lodgings until 10:00 p.m. on our first night in the city. After dinner, which was generously provided by Daffé's Savane Motel and spent in the charming company of former mayor of Ségou Dr. Mamadou Fanta Simaga, our official host finally arrived. First Deputy Mayor Madani Niang had been named to this important position. We were excited to hear that we would be given our own villa, though I now suppose the reason for his lateness was that he had taken until 10:00 p.m. to find it.

By 10:30 p.m., we drove up to a house that seemed to be new. Monsieur Niang opened the door and switched on the electric light. It was then that we saw that he had literally arranged "a villa"—there were four bedrooms, but not a single piece of furniture. Nor was there any water. Mayor Ibrahima Thiero and his deputy Madani Niang had indeed found a villa, but they had given no thought to details like furniture, soap, towels, or food. Our official host had not visited the house, and had put no thought whatsoever into his hosting duties. We were the proud and tired occupants of an empty house.

There were half a dozen chairs on the porch outside, where my exhausted American guests rested in horrified disbelief while I started to get things organized. I sent Monsieur Niang away to find some beds while I knocked on doors to borrow buckets of water from the neighbors so we could at least wash our faces and flush the toilets. Five beds and five sheets appeared before midnight, and I somehow managed to string up the five mosquito nets I had purchased and brought with me from Bamako. There were still no towels, no soap, and no water in the pipes. I felt terrible for my American guests.

At 10:40 p.m., while searching for buckets, I called my friend Madame Safiatou Koné (as she still was then), the widow of my old friend Nazou, on my mobile phone and told her that my American guests needed breakfast at 8:00 a.m. the next morning. At 7:50 a.m., a breakfast motorbike arrived at the gate of our house; thirteen-year-old Sali was driving, while her mother, seated on the pillion, hung onto baskets, thermos flasks, and a cooler filled with food. Thanks to Sali and her mother, our first full day in Ségou began with fresh bread, butter and honey, boiled eggs, hot tea, and hot coffee—a feast. There was no sign of Monsieur Niang!

Safiatou had dropped everything to serve her American guests—and their happy faces told me that a good breakfast was more important than a lack of sheets and towels and running water. Meanwhile, I gave Madame Koné money to buy food, soap, linens, and chairs; that evening, we were more comfortable in our villa.

For a whole week, Madame Koné provided us with food and hospitality. The advantage of living in Mali on and off for thirty years is that I have a lot of friends, and there is no doubt that this has helped the success of our sister city experience. My Malian friends enriched our early visits until the Ségou sister city team was reconstituted under Ousmane Simaga, and Madani Sissoko took over leadership of the sister city relationship. Madani is an efficient organizer, and he and his wife Fati and the rest of the Sissoko family have become our greatest friends in Ségou—and nothing is more important than friendship in the matter of citizen diplomacy.

Madame Safiatou Koné is one such friend. When her husband died, leaving her with a babe in arms named Sali and five other children to feed, I followed the Malian tradition that your friend's children are your children. During one visit to Ségou, I discovered that Mariam, Safiatou's eldest daughter, had stopped her accountancy studies because of her eyes. I realized she needed a visit to Bamako's eye hospital and a pair of prescription glasses. Madame Koné didn't know about the eye hospital; she didn't even have money for the bus fare. But because I was there to take Mariam to Bamako and to buy the spectacles, Mariam is now a schoolteacher (she changed her mind about accounting); one of her sisters is a magistrate, and all of them are now married and comfortable.

If I had not been in the right place at the right time, Mariam would still be selling ice in the market. When her father died unexpectedly, her opportunities in life evaporated. That is what happens to people who are poor and unable to break out of the cycle of poverty—in America as well as in Africa, where there is no social safety net beyond the family.

Instead, I became the Koné children's extended family and their safety net. My reward is that I am called *Tonton*, "Uncle." Whenever I visit Bamako, the children come over to show me their babies. In the absence of my old friend Nazou, I have been a substitute father, and proud of it. That explains why I could call Madame Koné at 10:40 p.m. and order breakfast for 8:00 a.m.

We began to establish a small store of supplies in the Koné household for future Richmond sister city visitors to use. The alternative would be staying in a hotel and spending a lot more money, while removing the chances for social interaction with a family. And the arrangement was mutually beneficial: having a few more towels and chairs in her yard added prestige to Safiatou's social life, and our extra five mosquito nets provided the children with new defenses against malaria.

Nevertheless, life was tough for a widow with six children. Twelve years after her husband's death, however, when Sali, the baby in arms, had become a teenager and all the other children had moved on to study or live elsewhere, Safiatou remarried and became Madame Coulibaly—marrying Amadou Coulibaly, marketing manager for Ségou's textile mill. Amadou has the same name as Biton, the founder of modern Ségou. He took us to visit Biton's palace, his tomb and his mother's miniature mosque in Sikoro also known as Ségou-Koro or Old Ségou, one of Mali's most beautiful villages, nestled under ancient trees beside the Niger River.

Biton seized power by force. He was succeeded in 1755 by his son Dinkoro, who lasted only two years, and the Coulibaly dynasty descended into chaos until it was overthrown by a new dynasty: Ngolo Diarra (reigned 1766–1790), his son Monzon Diarra (1790–1808), and grandson Da Monzon (1808–1827), who was followed by his less-famous brothers Tiefolo and Kirango. Diarra became the royal family name, and the once-feared Coulibaly clan were now mocked all over Mali for having lost their power. "*i Coulibaly!*" is still a mocking greeting in Mali, used for someone you do not know, or for a friend you want to tease for having made a stupid mistake. "*i Tall!*" is the respectful greeting I expect to receive when I meet a Malian. For a man called Macky Tall, the greeting *"i Coulibaly!"* is an insult!

Amadou Coulibaly, Safiatou's new husband, calls himself a "real Ségovien" and is proud to carry Biton's famous name. He had divorced several years previously from his first wife, and was perfectly happy to assume responsibility for feeding and educating Sali, his wife's only remaining dependent. Sali lived happily with her mother and "Tonton Amadou" until she graduated from the *lycée* and got married. Over the past fifteen years, Amadou and I have discovered a happy partnership, caring for Nazou's children and saving his widow from undeserved poverty.

Fig. 3. The mosque that Biton Coulibaly built in Sikoro. Photo: VFoM.

Breakfast in Ségou with the Honorable Mountaga Tall

The delightful surprise of Madame Koné's delicious breakfast really bucked up the spirits of our American delegation after their exhausting journey and the confusion of an empty villa with no water. By the time breakfast had ended, we even had running water in our villa, so that we could all have cold showers. Believe me, a cold shower is what you need during the day in Mali. Again, I reminded my American friends, "You must not forget to fill up a bucket with cold water in the morning; by midday, the pipes will make the water too hot to wash your hands, unless you have some cold water to add." They had heard it before, and they nodded wisely.

The visit was looking up! In due course, we were taken to visit the mayor's office, up a steep flight of stairs above Ségou's city hall. It is a great colonial building, solid in construction, though in need of a coat of paint. Indeed, the paint may date from the independence celebrations in 1960. Mayor Ibrahima Thiero was reading a newspaper. We thanked the mayor for his invitation for Richmond and Ségou to become sister cities; but we had to explain that at that point, in February 2006, Richmond did not even have a sister city commission. We promised that our city would get itself organized and respond positively to Ségou's initiative. The mayor was courteous and welcoming. We had the impression that he spent a lot of his day reading newspapers.

Downstairs in the massive council chamber, we admired the portrait photographs of previous mayors. The twenty pictures showed us that only one woman has been mayor in seventy years. Much like in Virginia, women in Ségou have a tough time getting heard on the political stage. There were some large, signed documents in frames, attesting to the existence for the past twenty years of a "town twinning" between Ségou and the French city of Angoulême, although it seemed from what people told us that this relationship was fairly dormant. One spin-off benefit of Richmond's sister city relationship with Ségou would be the revivification of the energies of Angoulême, who did not want to be outshone by Richmond; seven years later, Allan and I would find ourselves sitting side by side with Madame Danielle Bernard of Angoulême at the formal inauguration of public latrines for Ségou's main market.

The next morning, as we ate Madame Koné's second delicious breakfast, we had an unexpected visit from Ségou's elected member of parliament, Mountaga Tall. An impressive-looking man, like many of the Tall clan, Mountaga is as tall as his name. I knew Mountaga; we are both "Tall," and I even called him "cousin" (he always laughed delightedly) because he was a regular visitor to my Old Brother, head of our enlarged Tall household beside the river in Bamako. A lawyer by training, attorney Mountaga Tall became one of the leaders of the democratic movement after the fall of General-President Moussa Traoré in 1991. As leader of CNID, the party that lost the 1992 elections in opposition to Adema, Mountaga had a complicated relationship with Mali's early democracy. He was even put in prison for a week or two for fomenting riots, and despite protests from Amnesty International, I thought he deserved it! But here he was in our breakfast compound, the elected deputy representing Ségou in Mali's parliament, honoring the Richmond delegation with a visit. Later, in 2014, we would take a group of VCU students to meet him in Bamako when he was minister for higher education.

Mountaga is always impeccably dressed—so much so that I have had to invest in several new and splendid Malian embroidered robes in order not to dishonor the Tall name in Ségou. Good clothes are essential to being taken seriously in Mali. The French proverb "Wearing a monk's habit does not make you a monk" is not true in Mali, where Big Men dress as Big Men. Once, at an African Day reception in Washington, DC, I turned up at the VIP door by mistake; but because I was magnificently dressed in embroidered Malian robes, I was treated as a VIP and ushered in to meet the ambassadors. In this land of wonderful fabrics and elegant embroidery, clothing is important.

Here, then, was the Honorable Mountaga Tall, standing in our modest courtyard dressed in such a magnificent gown of gleaming white lace embroidered with shining white silk thread that our friend Carol Warner audibly gasped in admiration. The rest of us, of course, were completely underdressed, as we had just come from sleeping. We were downing eggs and coffee on the terrace, wearing nothing better than shorts and T-shirts. I was mortified to be discovered in such a state of undress! I apologized in French for our lack of decorum. Mountaga

Tall smiled—he is one of the most charming of Mali's politicians—
and replied in flawless English that our dress was of no importance.
What mattered, he said, was the friendship that we represented with
Virginia, and the future friendships we would build together to bring
Malians and Americans closer. He learned each of our Malian names,
reminded me of my elevated status as his Tall cousin, greeted Madame
Koné and her daughter, wished us a pleasant stay, and swept out of the
courtyard, leaving us breathless. Safiatou Koné and Sali were speechless with admiration; to think that they had just been witness to a
meeting with the Honorable Mountaga Tall!

Beautiful Villages around Ségou: Sikoro and Kalabougou

When Scottish traveler Dr. Mungo Park reached Ségou in 1795,
during the reign of King Monzon Diarra, he became the first European
to see the River Niger. Europeans had heard of "the big river beyond
the desert," but they knew neither where it came from nor where it
went. Was it a branch of the Nile? Dr. Park was the first person to tell
Europeans that the Niger River at Ségou flowed eastward.

King Monzon Diarra didn't care to see this white Scottish doctor.
King Monzon Diarra was afraid of white magic. He sometimes sac-
rificed albinos for luck, and kept a group of unfortunate albinos in a
dungeon beneath his throne. In accordance with his orders, Dr. Park
was not allowed to cross the river.

Dr. Park did not see the Ségou that we see today. Ségou in 1795
was a small fishing town, now a village called Sikoro, some five miles
upriver from the bustling commercial city we know today. The Coulibaly dynasty, seen by Ségoviens as usurpers, had been overthrown and
scattered, becoming the joke of Mali. Diarra, by contrast, is an honorable Ségou name, and the new Diarra dynasty lasted until a Fulani
theological power arose in the mid-1800s and invaded the country
using firearms bought from the French. El Haj Oumar Tall was a
jihadist, a member of the Tijani Sufis who was using a religious label
to create his own empire. Tall moved his capital downstream to where
the city of Ségou stands today. The Tall reign was soon over, however,

as the French army conquered western Mali during the 1880s and invaded Ségou on April 6, 1890.

The beauty of Ségovien architecture can be seen in the old Somono fishing quarter beside the river, as well as in the elegant craft centers that reinforce Ségou's place as a cultural capital: notably the Centre Koré's art gallery and conference center, created by Mamou Daffé; Ndomo, the bogolan textile center of Boubacar Doumbia; and the Soroblé Center, built by the Coulibaly brothers for textile design and manufacture.

But the truest beauty of Ségou is the Niger River, Africa's third-greatest river, which flows gracefully, eternally past the river port of Ségou. I remember standing beside my friend Professor Christopher Brooks, a VCU anthropologist who had visited more than twenty African countries before coming to Ségou in 2013, and watching the river flow. "You know," said Christopher, his voice heavy with emotion, "This is one of the most important moments of my life. Imagine! At last, here I am beside the Niger, watching the lifeblood of West Africa, *Ba Djoli Ba*, flow past one of the great centers of world civilization." I put my hand on his arm, sharing the moment of reverence for the African ancestors on this mother continent from which Humanity is descended.

The next day, I headed across the river with Christopher and the rest of the VCU visitors in a twenty-seat wooden canoe to visit the village of Kalabougou, a couple of miles downstream. I was glad of my straw Fulani sun hat as the sun beat down on the parched, sandy paths that led to the village. We walked up the riverbank, between trees with tentacles; their hundred-year-old root systems had been partially uncovered as the annual river floodwaters receded in December, creating comfortable living benches on which we could sit and talk in the shade. Nearby, young men were loading fired pots into a canoe, called a *pirogue* in French, in which they would cross the river to visit Ségou on market day.

As we neared the village houses, we passed a huge pit in which another batch of clay water jars was being fired. Open pit fires can reach 1,112 degrees Fahrenheit—which is only half as hot as a modern kiln—so the finished pots are fragile; yet the rounded clay jars have a beauty that makes me enjoy caressing them voluptuously. The smaller, cuter pots are for food; perforated round clay fire-holders are for boiling tea or burning incense; the huge jars are for storing water. I have two of these water jars at my home in Bamako. Water seeps through the baked clay, and the heat is sucked away by evaporation, leaving a jar of cool water very different from the iced water beloved of Americans, but perfect for healthy drinking in a hot climate, provided you keep the jar disinfected. It is also good for storing mangoes or oranges if, like me, you prefer to eat cool fruit.

Fig. 4. Pottery firing in Kalabougou Village, near Ségou. Photo: Marco Bellucci, reproduced under a Creative Commons License.[4]

Needing a drink, and clutching the three plates that we had bought for three dollars each, we returned to our *pirogue* and its store of bottled water. As we were getting ready to depart, another *pirogue* came toward us, its wooden prow aiming directly for the side of our canoe. The boatman intended to beach his craft on the sand, but I

---

4 https://creativecommons.org/licenses/by/2.0.

realized he had lost control, and that the wooden beam on the prow was aiming directly for the head of my wife. "Duck!" I shouted, just in time, and Michelle did exactly what ducks do in a pond: she dived off her seat into the bottom of our canoe, just as three tons of wooden *pirogue* filled with three more tons of German tourists crashed into the side of our boat. Standing with his long pole at the stern of his *pirogue,* the boatman was laughing. Was it embarrassment, or humor? Perhaps the young man did not mean to mock us, but he seemed indifferent to the fate of my spouse, and to his own error. I climbed over two seats, put my hand to the beam of the aggressor canoe, and pushed it away; now that it was immobile, I could move the six tons sideways across the water, and Michelle reappeared unharmed.

Our canoe pushed off for Ségou, and I pulled out that marvelous modern device that has become indispensable for law enforcement: the mobile phone. I called the president of Ségou's sister city commission, Councilman Madani Sissoko, and denounced the bad steering of the other canoe. When the boatman returned to the port of Ségou three hours later, the gendarmes were waiting to arrest him—I suppose for bad driving.

At supper the following evening, Mayor Ousmane Simaga asked me, "Macky Tall, what do you want us to do with your boatman?" The young man had been in jail for twenty-four hours. I had forgotten all about him.

"I don't want to do anything with him," I laughed. "I know nothing about the rules of the river. I suggest you hand him over to the Fisherman's Committee, and let them decide." Which they did: he was suspended from the river for three months, on account of losing control of his canoe.

The Ségou Festival, in All Its Color and Excitement

Let me try to convey to you something of the magic of Ségou during the Festival of the Niger River. The sun is shining, and I have sought shade. After an hour of visiting artisan stalls and fending off street sellers, it is time for a drink. I have a fresh orange juice in front of me on a table in a shady hotel yard. This tangy taste of fresh citrus with ice is one of God's great gifts to Africa. Some people drink beer, but I keep off alcohol in this hot Muslim country, where the oranges, lemons, tangelos, papayas, watermelons, grapefruits, mangoes, cashew fruit, and ginger root, as well as the fruits of the tamarind and baobab trees, provide delicious fresh drinks.

Escaping the February heat of Mali's savannah lands, I am sitting in the quiet Savane, Mamou Daffé's spacious, cool oasis hotel where service comes from happy girls—festival volunteers wearing colorful uniforms. Or maybe I am with friends in the town center, sequestered inside the busy courtyard of the German-owned Djoliba Hotel, a yellow-painted two-story building named for the Niger River and situated on the corner of the street that leads down to the port and the festival plaza. Here, *toubabs* wander on and off their upstairs bedroom balcony, where washed clothes dry in one hour. More likely we have chosen the cozy old colonial gardens of L'Auberge, a century-old hotel owned by a Lebanese family, where ancient trees and beds of flowering lilies provide a sense of timelessness and old-world comfort beside the Niger River. Or we might have crossed the festival area, walking northeast along the river bank, past the music stages and the art exhibition hall, waving to friendly people running commercial and artisan exhibits, until we reach the riverside bar of Mayor Simaga's Esplanade Hotel, managed by an Italian. Here our feet are almost in the water, and I sip my fruit juice with a sleepy crocodile in a cage beside my right ear.

Out in the street after my drink, I am accosted ("*Bonjour,* Macky Tall!") by a shoeshine boy named Daouda. Of course, my shoes need some tender loving care; the leather is covered with dust, drying out in the heat. I sit on the hotel porch and allow him to remove one shoe, then the other. I never allow anyone to take both shoes at the same time, in case I am left sitting in my socks looking like a lemon. These kids really know how to buff up shoes. After washing with soap, the blacking is meticulously applied with what European cultures call a "shaving brush," used for applying soft soap to a face before the razor comes out. I chuckle, remembering the story of a *toubab* who asked his watchman to buy him a shoe brush. He was astonished to find a shaving brush, for Malians use cloths—not brushes—to polish their shoes, and they only use a brush to apply the polish. As Daouda (the Malian version of *Daoud,* which is the Arabic version of "David") finally whips his cloth to and fro across my leather shoes, the result is spectacular. I step out into the street with shiny shoes, leaving the happy shoeshine boy with half a dollar, which is twice the normal rate. I reason that if I am going to support child labor, I should pay a decent price.

There is my friend Bana with her sister Fanta Diabaté, walking down the street together in the most magnificent embroidered robes I have ever seen, except for the last time I saw them both. "Aha!" cries Bana. "My husband is here, and he is wearing the gray *grand boubou* I had made for him. And he looks good in it!"

Bana Sidibé—born Bantandian Diabaté—is married to my friend of thirty years and milk-brother, Hallassy; therefore, I am her co-husband. I embrace both sisters on both cheeks and breathe in the heady scent of frankincense with which they and their robes are infused. Fanta laughs. "And where is my sister, Michelle? Did you not bring her to Ségou this year?" Fanta Diabaté, a gynecologist and surgeon, is beautiful and brilliant and charming—unless you make a mistake, in which case she will tell you all about it! Fanta now works for USAID, and is also a key part of our VCU Richmond-Ségou AIDS and probiotics research project. Her younger sister Bana is the administrator and lawyer in charge of the festival's cash management. She has been managing the ticketing for Mamou Daffé since the festival began. The festival is buzzing, and she has a job to do, so they press on.

I turn into "artisan row" to look at the carvings. I want to buy a *chiwara* for the Teaching Timbuktu program in Richmond—not one of the huge and beautiful old village carvings that the woodsellers want to sell me, but a small version in very light wood that will slide into my luggage and will be easy to carry around Richmond's schools. I want a cheap tourist chiwara in soft white wood that has been stained black to look "genuine"—whatever that means. After all, what could be more genuine than a piece of wood carved by a Malian artist whom I have actually met, and seen in the act of carving my chiwara? I have never cared to buy antiques, for I do not wish to be a part of the rape of African history and culture. I do not want to own a mask that has been worn by villagers during dances half a century ago. Instead, I choose to buy modern carvings that help artisans make a living.

Among the magnificent masks and the heavy statues of elephants (*sama* in Bambara) and hippopotami (*mali*—yes, the country is named for its greatest river animal), I soon find my light-wood chiwara. It costs me five dollars, and will fit easily into my suitcase.

"Hey, Macky Tall, come into my shop!" cries the next stall-holder. "You have bought your chiwara from my neighbor Coulibaly, and because you are a Tall, you know that those Coulibalys are worthless. I am a Diarra, descended from King Monzon Diarra who threw out the false Coulibaly dynasty, so now you must buy from me." I laugh, and duck under the tarpaulin to look at his collection of carvings. Even covered with a layer of dust, every one of them is beautiful; but I refuse to add any more masks to my collection. I would love to buy one of his pieces in particular—a two-piece hardwood chair carved with tortoises—but it weighs one hundred pounds.

To make Diarra happy, I buy a small ebony crocodile (or *bama*— Mali's capital city, Bamako, means "the place of crocodiles") for my grandchildren. A drummer has started up down the street, so I head toward the *djembé* and the river. In the next stall, a young American is chatting in fluent Bambara about tie-dyed fabrics bearing the colors of twenty fabulous rainbows—she is probably a Peace Corps volunteer. I see a horseman in rich bogolan robes—maybe the festival's historical interpreter of King Biton Coulibaly, who founded the Bambara Empire. In fact, there are now three horsemen prancing around. But the drummers are far more intriguing, now animating some life-size animal puppets. There is a hippo, black and lumbering and menacing, eclipsed by a giant leaping fish with dangerous sharp fins, and a crawling, snarling crocodile that threatens onlookers by flashing and gnashing its gigantic teeth. I have seen real twenty-foot male crocodiles in the river, and they are pretty scary. This one, made of cloth, looks slow and overweight.

Puppets are a famous part of West African and Bambara culture. There is even a special puppet festival each year in the nearby town of Markala. One year, Ségou hosted giant wooden puppets from Burkina Faso. They took over the whole city as they strode down the streets on ten-foot legs, standing as tall as the *balanzan* trees that symbolize the city of Ségou.

As a representative of Ségou's sister city, I have a received a pass saying that I am a Very Important Person. Now, I enter the festival plaza through a triumphal arch built of red mud topped with charac-teristic Sahelo-Sudanian decorative turrets, and show my pass to the security guards. My namesake is there: Macky Tall is a square and muscular man in his forties, son of a former Malian ambassador, who has been working with Daffé and the Ségou festival since it started in 2005. He is now head of security. This used to involve watching out for pickpockets and keeping away young layabouts with no tick-ets. Since 2011, when NATO destroyed Libya and destabilized West Africa, security for a festival with ten thousand visitors is no small task. In these days of terrorism, frisking visitors and placing armed soldiers outside the main hotels has become a necessary part of the process. Macky tells me that armed police are patrolling the river, to ensure the festival's safety on all sides.

In the festival plaza, there are masked dancers from Dogon coun-try with more drummers. The drumbeat of the Malian soul leads instinctively to dancing. Malians dance for joy; they dance for sadness; they dance for pleasure; they dance for show; and, in the case of the Dogons, they dance for their ancestors. The Ancestors include grand-parents and great-grandparents; they include the founders of your vil-lage and the great hunters and warriors who inhabit your legends; they include the generations of mothers who birthed and nourished you and your forebears; and they include the Ur-Ancestors (a German expression) who lived in these ancient lands before humankind was born in Africa. Long before Charles Darwin and Alfred Russell Wallace introduced their concept of evolution and natural selection in a Linnaean Society paper presented in 1858, the Dogons knew that humanity's ancient ancestors included the crocodiles, lizards, turtles, and snakes that decorate Dogon houses and protect their owners from evil. Africans stand with arms outstretched and implore their ancestors to intercede with *Amma*, Dogons' name for the Creator (whom we call *God*)—a name that is curiously close to *Ana*, the name of the Earth Mother of Celtic religious tradition. One way to approach the ancestors is by dancing the masks that represent the world and the creatures the Ancestors have known. The masks of antelopes, birds, rabbits, and even the Original Eve (known in Dogon as the Fulani Woman) dance while I watch, stirring up the dust and stirring the blood of the onlookers. My feet and shoulders move in time to the drums, and my shoes are once again the color of Ségou dust. I am in total happiness . . . and when the formal music show starts around 6:00 p.m. on the giant Da Monzon Stage, life is going to get even better![5]

VFoM Stars of Film, Media, . . . and Donkey Carts

In February 2007, as I was drinking fruit juice one evening with a different visiting group of Richmonders in a hotel yard in Djenne, a beautiful medieval island city in the Niger River, we were hailed by an American voice coming from the corner of the yard: "I have to ask you guys, who you are and where do you come from?"

The voice belonged to David West, a charming Hollywood film photographer who was in Mali to shoot a film about peacemaking in Timbuktu, and who had become tired of sitting alone while I was enjoying the company of five intelligent ladies. I could not blame him: I was exchanging stories and laughter with Hester Lewis and Deedee Damschroder, highly professional women and art lovers who retired to Richmond after senior administrative careers in the nation's capital city. Their work with the Firehouse Theatre, among other activities,

---

5 *To get a feel for this marvelous festival in all its shades and liveliness, visit https://www. youtube.com/watch?v=iCW0qOoLOBc.*

has made them stars of Richmond culture; they once hosted a VFoM reception for Dr. Abdoulaye Sylla, a Malian museum curator and anthropologist who came to Richmond to attend the graduation of his son Omar Sylla, a University of Richmond basketball star.

The other three ladies at our table were equally delightful, even if they did cause me some anxiety. Sandra Leard was on her first "outing" after being recently widowed, and this was her first visit to Africa. Calm and unflappable, she had so enjoyed my lectures on Mali at the Shepherd's Center that she and her friend Gwen Westerhouse decided they would come to Ségou. At eighty-five years old, Gwen was worried that she might not be able to handle the journey, but I told her my Aunt Penelope was coming too, and that they were the same age. I called my aunt on the phone, and she and Gwen were soon chatting away, reassuring each other that everything would be fine and that they would have a great time together!

Actually, I was not too pleased about taking an eighty-five-year-old to Mali. It can be very hot, especially in February. The cool season starts in mid-November and runs until February, but you cannot predict when the cool will begin or when the heat will return. During some of the years I have spent in Bamako and Ségou, I wore a jacket or a light woolen cardigan every evening for a month; in other years, I have needed a jacket only three or four times, because the cool season has been shorter.

However, when it came to the question of bringing the ladies, I had no choice. During a visit to Penelope that summer, my cousin Nicola had announced that Penelope had not been to Mali for ten years, and wanted to come with me again this year. "Oh, yes!" enthused my aunt. "That would be lovely." I could not tell her "No!" in front of the whole family, so I was handed a done deal. The idea of having Gwen to support Penelope seemed attractive. I started imagining how I would manage them both.

Once we were there, things went well enough. Poor Hester had trouble with the dust, and I learned that anyone with even mild asthmatic tendencies needs to make careful preparations when coming to

West Africa. But the main problem was one that that the older ladies brought upon themselves: they simply did not follow my instructions to drink water every fifteen minutes. Sandra later told me that Gwen liked to have a cup of coffee for breakfast, maybe two cups, and she did not care for water. Penelope liked walking in the hot sun, even—or perhaps especially—when I told her not to. Old people's tissues do not absorb water as well as younger bodies, and both of the ladies ended up collapsing from exhaustion caused by dehydration. I rehydrated them with diluted Coke: I poured one bottle of cola into a 1.5-liter plastic bottle and filled the rest with water, creating a rehydration liquid that is well absorbed by the gut, rather like the electrolytes found in a UNICEF salt-sugar solution for infants. After that, I gave them some oranges—another source of indispensable minerals—to suck. The dehydration crisis was avoidable; they made it inevitable—but in any event, they each lost only one day of activity.

To handle the old ladies during the Ségou festival, I had a plan. I asked my friend Madame Koné to find me a reliable man with a donkey cart. Monsieur Tangara duly arrived, very pleased to be paid for three days of full-time work instead of waiting around in the market, hoping to be hired to carry loads. I gave him money to buy bamboo poles, rope, and some straw mats, and we constructed a simple awning over the cart to keep the sun off. We then roped two armchairs onto the cart, placed a carton of bottled water between them, and heaved Gwen and Penelope up into the chairs. Now I had the old ladies trapped! They could not move out of the shade into the hot sun, they would expend less energy, and I could make sure they were drinking water.

We led the donkey around the festival grounds, and my plan worked perfectly. I could show the old ladies whatever I wanted them to see—like the Tuareg musicians playing while seated in the shade of their tent, or Bobo masked dancers performing under a tree—and they were raised high enough above the crowds to have a good view of everything. Malians are extremely respectful to older people, and the Ségou crowds constantly applauded our grandmothers. Malians seldom see old white people, or even white children, because most foreigners in Africa are professionals of working age. Africans hear rumors of American and European families who lock away their elders in retirement homes, and they are shocked. The citizens of Ségou were thrilled to see the two grandmothers enthroned in splendor on their donkey cart, under a banner that read *"Les Amis du Mali en Virginie."* The Malians took dozens of photos of the grandmothers on their donkey cart. They loved our careful treatment of the elders, and the whole affair hugely enriched the sister city relationship.

Six months later, when I was working on a United Nations peace mission in Liberia following their civil war, I happened to stop by for a chat at a Malian corner shop selling carvings and other forms of art. "I know you!" cried a man who told me his name was Traoré. "You were at the Ségou festival! You are the man whose grandmothers were on the donkey cart. I was also at the Ségou festival. Look, I have their photo on my smartphone." And sure enough, there they were on the screen of his telephone: Gwen Westerhouse and Penelope Simpson, enthroned on their donkey cart, sun hats on their heads and water bottles in their hands, smiling like film stars and waving at the crowd like a pair of royalty!

Two weeks later in Bamako, after the festival and the departure of my American friends, I met film director Ashley Rogers and her producer, Jane Brinton, and became an advisor for their film, *333,* referring to the 333 saints who lie buried in the cemeteries of *Timbuktu La Mystérieuse.* I attended the world premiere of the finished documentary at the United Nations in New York, under the chairmanship of Michael Covitt, the executive producer and vice president of Sabatier Films. The Malian ambassador to the UN was the first speaker, who inexplicably began by telling the audience that he had never been to Timbuktu! Fortunately, I was able to talk about the city, as I had worked there during the 1980s. I talked briefly about the manuscripts and Malian peacemaking, and then I introduced America's foremost living film composer, David Amram, who had put together a delicate score for the film. Later I wanted to show the film to Richmond students and academics at the 2013 Women, War & Peace Conference held at VCU, but it was impossible because Sabatier demanded more money than an academic conference could ever hope to pay.

One day at the Richmond Folk Festival, I was hailed by a lady whom I did not know, but who recognized my Fulani hat and bogolan robe. "You are Robin! I'm Sherril Schlesinger. You don't know me, but I know you from editing Ashley Rogers' film on Timbuktu. I have pictures of you all over my cutting room floor!" Sherril had come to the festival from California to hear and admire her musician husband, Steve Weizman. Excited about the unused "stock film," I wrote to the film's executive editor, Michael Covitt—who has generously given us free photos to illustrate this book—asking him to consider making a charitable donation of the many hours of unused film his team had shot in Richmond and Ségou to VFoM, or to the VCU film department, in exchange for a useful tax deduction. A lot of film always gets left "on the cutting room floor," and that footage could be turned into another film. I happen to know that Sabatier's film crew was stranded in Ségou while their vehicle was being repaired, and they did what film crews do: they filmed for three days in Ségou, producing beautiful footage of Ségou, its people, and the river, that had no place in a film on peace and the Timbuktu manuscripts.

Ashley later came to Richmond with a photographer, and I gave her a whole day of my time for interviews, and for free. Seated cross-legged inside the mosque at the Richmond Islamic Center of Virginia (ICVA), Imam Shaheed Coovadia read the Holy Koran and explained on camera the meaning of the religious texts he had chosen with Ashley. There is even footage of the imam and his young family playing together in the mosque sanctuary. None of this was used in the film *333*. Perhaps one day, Sabatier will make a film about the sister cities of Richmond and Ségou.

Malian Storytelling in Books, Radio, Video, and Photography

Timbuktu is the subject of a beautiful photobook, *333 Saints: A Life of Scholarship in Timbuktu*, written by Alexandra Huddleston as the culmination of her Fulbright grant. Alex is the founder of Kyoudai Press and the daughter of my friend Vicki Huddleston, a former US ambassador to Mali whom I knew in Bamako. Vicki would later work in the State Department in Washington, DC, as deputy assistant secretary and head of African affairs, and then at the Pentagon. Her daughter Alexandra has become an international photographer and writer whose work has graced museum exhibits on Mali across the world.[6] I keep finding her photos in Washington, London, and elsewhere. How delightful is that!

This chapter is not intended to be a list of works about Mali; how boring that would be! Anyone who needs a book list can search the internet. Through Teaching Timbuktu, we do promote a few storybooks about Mali. I recommend Helen Cowcher's delightfully illustrated book *Desert Elephants,* telling the story of the annual elephant migration in Central Mali. I often use books written by griot artist Baba Wagué Diakité. On his website, where readers can also admire his art, Baba Wagué describes how he loved hearing stories told during his Malian childhood:

> My grandmother was truly inspired; her charismatic personality lit up the scene of her evening story times with us. The intensity in her face captured and pulled us in, impressing upon us the importance of the moment. Grandma's voice floated, swooping high and low and joining harmoniously with the singing chorus of nocturnal creatures surrounding us—frogs, owls, insects. This was more than simple entertainment. I felt connected, important and at peace. It's been forty years now, but in my mind, I can still hear the voices of storytellers; I can still see gestures in their faces and recall their personalities as they continue to inspire me. This is a gift I treasure from my elders. But a gift of stories is only valuable if shared and passed on to future generations. *Words must flow from the elders' mouths to new ears.* Help me make this happen![7]

---

6 *Discover Alexandra's work at http://www.alexandrahuddleston.com/blog.*

7 *You can see some of Baba Wagué's work and read some of his texts at https://igg.me/at/ bUW0AYKfM2U.*

These days, the internet offers instant bibliographies of more books and articles than anyone could read in a lifetime; but through Ségou, we have made special media friends that we should mention. One of the most colorful is Africa Sam, otherwise known as professional photographer Sam O'Selmou Keita, who keeps turning up in Ségou, Richmond, and New York, as well as in Paris, where I have also met him. Sam is a Malian with wonderful photographic skill and a magnetic personality, and once he starts talking enthusiastically about Richmond and Ségou, you know that you will have to miss your next appointment! Thank you, Sam, for donating photos to illustrate our sister city project. Mali—although not especially Ségou—has become a minor center for world photography—partly because of other famous photographers like the late Seydou Keita and Malick Sidibé, whose Bamako portraits were commemorated in a spectacular 2018 exhibition at the Cartier Foundation in Paris; and partly because Dr. Alpha Oumar Konaré, Mali's first democratically elected president, created a photography festival in Bamako called Bamako Encounters, or in French, *Rencontres de Bamako: biennale africaine de la photographie*. Ouagadougou, capital of neighboring Burkina Faso, is the home of African film, hosting the Pan-African Film Festival of Ouagadougou (FESPACO); and Bamako wants to be a pan-African center for photography. Ségou is the home of Malian (or Bambara, or griot) storytelling and the associated spectacular art of puppetry. And only Ségou has the Festival of the Niger River.

Other important photographer Friends of Mali in Virginia have been Felicia Shelton,[8] a gifted visual explorer of Virginian life and women and of the African American experience along the East Coast; Bob Pringle, a former US ambassador to Mali, whose magnificent photographic record of Mali is held in the Museum of African Art; John Moser,[9] whose photography is important for the Shockoe Bottom and Sacred Ground campaigns that seek to preserve Richmond's African (and therefore Malian) history; and the late Rudolph Hickman, a lovely

8 See *http://felicia-shelton.squarespace.com.*
9 See *http://moser-productions.com.*

man who was president of the Virginia Union Alumni Association and who acted as VFoM's "official" photographer until he sadly and unexpectedly died in 2010. I should also highlight the website archive curated by Michigan State University and Candace Keller, professor of African art history and visual culture, which contains thousands of photos from Malian photographers Mamadou Cissé, Adama Kouyaté, Abdourahmane Sakaly, Malick Sidibé, and Tijani Sitou.[10]

Radio is also important for storytelling. Mali has some of the best local radio coverage in Africa, thanks in part to a successful USAID project run by my friends Martine Keita and the late Dennis Bilodeau. On our very first visit to Ségou in January 2006, the Richmond delegation—Allan, James, Michael, Carol and myself—visited two or three local radio stations, including *Le Ségovien* newspaper run by journalist Moustaph Maiga, whose radio station is Radio Sikoro. We were offered a glass of Malian green tea while "on air" during a conversation with radio host Bandiougou Danté. I made everyone laugh by slurping my tea at the microphone—in Mali, it is polite to drink your green tea with a sipping noise, but not many people turn it into a radio performance.

Allan and James gave Radio Sikoro some music tapes donated by our local independent Richmond station, WRIR 91.3 FM. Ana Edwards and Allan Levenberg have hosted radio programs on this channel in which Mali, Ségou, and some of Richmond's other sister cities have featured regularly through interviews of members of the VFoM, my VCU students, and—each time he has visited Richmond—the mayor of Ségou. The latest plan, created following Mr. Maiga's 2018 visit to Richmond, is for WRIR and Radio Sikoro, under the leadership of Carol Olson and Mr. Maiga, respectively, to create "sister radio stations" run by young women. Our hope is that this venture will contribute to our shared sister city ambition to develop girls' education and women's leadership in both Richmond and Ségou.

We composed some Malian historical essays for Richmond's other NPR radio station, WCVE 88.9 FM, which broadcasts the popular

---

10 See *http://africasacountry.com/2017/05/the-archive-of-malian-photography*.

series *A Moment in Time* with Dan Roberts (who came to speak to my adult Teaching Timbuktu class at the Osher Institute and University of Richmond's Continuing Education Program). Our radio essays focused on trade in medieval Mali, the scholarship of Timbuktu, and the Lion King, researched by retired Richmond teachers Hilda Meth, Marilyn Hurley, Kent Skidmore, Bob Draben and Susan Wood. I edited these texts for Professor Roberts, although I am not sure how much he used them. These Osher students also researched two books on Mali for VFoM's Teaching Timbuktu project, the first of which has been published on Kindle: *Sunjata: Children of the Mali Empire, Then and Now: Stories about Malian Children (some of whom grow up) for Teachers and Students of Africa and America's West African Heritage.*"[11] It was written for teachers, but the stories offer a good read for everybody.

The VFoM website also features short videos designed to help teachers of students in the third, fourth, and sixth grades across Virginia teach the Mali SOL and describe Virginia's African heritage. Resplendent in African dress in my persona as Macky Tall, I give brief talks about Timbuktu, or camels, or the Lion King, and show gold Malian jewelry and pieces of desert rock salt while discussing the period when these two were traded at equal weights.[12]

When we travelled to Mali in 2007, our VFoM group included Karen Dorsky, an art curator from New York, and two ladies who introduced me to a new profession. Marilyn Geary and Carol Zuckert are personal historians: authors who write the biographies of cities, counties, families, and individuals who hire them for their research, design, and writing expertise. Who knew there existed such experts? It is partly thanks to their inspiration that this book exists, for it encompasses the personal history of ten years of the Richmond-Ségou sister city experience.

---

11 *This Kindle book can be ordered at https://www.amazon.com/Sunjata-Children-Teachers-Students-Americas-ebook/dp/B06Y2BRHHY.*

12 *See http://virginiafriendsofmali.blogspot.fr/p/videos.html.*

Working Women of Ségou: Mesdames Diao and Thiero

Ségou boasts several fine women leaders, of whom Fabété Tall and Djenéba Cissé are two. They are highly intelligent women, both involved in agriculture. Kadiatou Tall is married to a delightful banker called Diao, so her full name is Madame Diao, Fabété Tall. "Fabété" or "Bété" is a nickname, because there are too many Tall women called Kadiatou.

Naturally, because she is Malian woman, Fabété insists on keeping her Tall identity. Because she is a Tall, she is also one of my cousins; technically, she is my younger sister, since she is the younger sister of my Old Brother Tall in Bamako. (She is from a different mother, because their father had three wives—and I helped to bury two of them.)

Fabété Tall is a city councilor, a deputy mayor, and a member of Ségou's sister city commission. There are several mayoral suboffices around Ségou where deputy mayors serve their local communities, and Fabété runs one of these. Fabété oversees and registers a lot of weddings. She is most admired, however, for her farming skills: as president of the Ségou Women Agricultural Producers' Association, Madame Diao helps other women in Ségou to improve their farming techniques, develop their crops, and market their produce. People in Ségou say that "if she is not in a council meeting or marrying some young couple in her local mayor's suboffice, then you will find Fabété sitting on her tractor."

While Fabété is very small, Djenéba Cissé, who is also known as Madame Thiero, wife of the previous mayor of Ségou, is a very tall woman with a large voice. Djenéba used to lead a women's producer cooperative, creating added value by growing crops and then transforming them into secondary products. Groundnuts sell for more money if they are turned into peanut butter. Shea nuts sell at a much higher price if they are transformed into shea butter, which is prized for its potential use in cosmetics, medicines, and cooking. Rice sells at a higher price if it is dehulled. Maize can be sold on the cob, or it can fetch a higher price if packaged as grain in plastic bags or sold as corn flour. Millet and sorghum can be sold on the stalk or transformed into flour ready for use in the kitchen.

Djenéba was a cooperative member; but she was also their natural leader. Her powerful and commanding presence dominated the group. She led by her intelligence and her entrepreneurial spirit.

There was a donor project supporting women's cooperatives, but when that project stopped funding their efforts, many of her urban neighbors began to lose interest. Djénéba became tired of dragging a reluctant group of women behind her and decided instead to set up a family business making shea butter products. In the end, if she becomes an exporter of shea butter, Djénéba will probably help her former cooperative members earn more money than before. She quickly seized upon the commercial opportunities offered by the sister city relationship, and opened negotiations for exporting shea butter to Richmond for use in medicines and cosmetics. Her initiative illustrates what a presidential advisor told me one day at the Ségou festival while we were sitting in the VIP stands, waiting for Salif Keita to start singing: "The sister city relationship with Richmond will allow Malians to open many doors."

Djenéba Cissé illustrates some of the many ways by which women have been able to expand their horizons and increase their incomes in Mali's social economy since democratic governance replaced the military regime that collapsed in 1991. Early in 2017, she visited Richmond with her husband, and they were honored at a luncheon in the home of Mark and Monica Johnson, business people who are interested in shea butter. We will see where that leads. The Thiero parents were in the US for the graduation of their son Cheick Thiero, who later that year attended an African business conference VFoM coorganized at VCU in his new position as a journalist with Voice of America, reporting from Richmond, Ségou's sister city.

From 1968 until 1991, there was just one women's organization in Mali: the *Union nationale des femmes du Mali* (UNFM). It was run by Madame Traoré, Mariam Sissoko, the wife of general-president Moussa Traoré. Malians called her "Madame Ten Percent"—the cash commission she demanded on all foreign-funded projects. This illustrates just two of the many costs of dictatorship: institutionalized corruption, often orchestrated by the dictator's in-laws; and the suppression of personal freedom. In this case, women were not allowed to work together unless it was for the benefit of the "One Party"—ironically making the UNFM a pernicious obstacle to women's social development.

I remember one day in 1990, when two American women from Washington arrived in my USAID office to tell me about their work in Mali with the UNFM. "Oh, that is wonderful!" I cried. "I had always heard that there were foreigners who paid money to Madame Traoré, but I have never met any before!" My visitors squirmed in their seats. Then one of them said to the other, "Well, now you have heard straight out. That is what other people say when we are not in the room."

It would be unkind to mention the name of their organization, which was one of those Washington for-profit "beltway bandits" that spend US taxpayers' money without being worried too much about how the money is actually spent—so long as auditors approve the receipts. American auditors who want to see that recipients "buy American" seldom wonder if the American vehicles or computers have been taken over by army colonels, instead of being used for health or education. That is why I work with nongovernmental organizations. NGOs actually care what happens. I try not to work with government officials unless the project concerns security issues, which are clearly a government matter.

I felt guilty about teasing the two American ladies. As compensation, I promised that I would attend their reception, which was being held the next evening to celebrate the donation of health materials to the UNFM. I knew that no one else in USAID or at the embassy in Bamako would bother to attend. Since my wife Michelle was away supervising Save the Children projects in Burkina Faso, I persuaded her friend Dr. Fanta Diabaté, who was recently divorced, to come along with me. "It will do you good to get out of the house," I told her. "You work very long hours in your obstetrics clinic. Then you spend all your free time looking after your mother and caring for your younger sisters. Going to a party will be good for you."

Fanta is from a traditional griot family, and her mother comes from Ségou. She allowed herself to be persuaded, and stepped out of her house magnificently attired in a long blue gown of damask cloth embroidered with gold thread, with a matching headscarf adding six inches to her already stately bearing. I felt enhanced by Fanta's majestic presence, bewitched by the heady incense rising from her gown—before leaving the house, Fanta had burned frankincense on charcoal and stood over the small brazier to allow the smoke and the scent to infuse all her clothing. Malian women are particular about their selections and combinations of incense, much of which comes from the bark or sap of Sahelian trees, and which is known to us as gum arabic; and they always smell wonderful. Heavenly. Magical. Bewitching.

We arrived at the hotel where the reception was taking place, and stepped into a room filled with gorgeously dressed women. Fanta groaned. "I knew I should not have come! Look at them; they are all the wives of colonels or ministers. I know most of them because I am a gynecologist, and half of these women call themselves midwives. That means they have paid for a diploma, they take a monthly salary, and they never go near a pregnant woman or a clinic. This, Robin, is the one-party state at play. This is the beginning of a terrible evening."

Despite her assertion, I had a very good time, surrounded by the perfumed aristocratic women of the military dictatorship. Fanta was, of course, polite and charming to all of them. The American lady from Washington made a short speech and was flattered by her hostesses. I learned a great deal about how the UNFM worked, and how US embassies support corrupt political powers the world over.

I didn't waste any American government money in my projects. When I worked for USAID as a contracted project manager, I technically worked for the embassy, but my project gave money only to professional American NGOs that were committed to working in Mali for fifteen or thirty years, in partnership with grassroots groups and community-based organizations led by people of the quality of Fanta Diabaté and Djenéba Cissé and Fabété Tall. Even when I worked under the one-party state (and despite the UNFM), I was able to work with cooperatives and civil society activists. We identified real women's leaders, protected them from the military, and created space for them to build wealth; only they were not allowed to lead "women's organizations," and their development actions had to be approved by the local section of the party.

In 1991, the one-party state collapsed. Civil society leaders won power in the 1992 elections, and the country was liberated. The movement was led by Dr. Alpha Oumar Konaré, a former leader of the teachers' union and founder of the country's best-run cooperative health clinic, which had been created by the union to serve teachers and their families. A period of good governance began, and I suddenly found myself—for the first time in my life—living under a government with whose decentralization philosophy I was completely in agreement. Now, twenty-five years later, Richmond's sister city partnership follows the same principles of working with civil society leaders and strong women. We are helping Ségou train new women leaders, supporting teenage girls who will be able to function as community leaders and entrepreneurs in this new age of globalization and the internet. We hope and believe that one day in the future, the mayor of Ségou and Ségou's sister city commission president will both be women.

Fig. 5. Many manuscripts in Timbuktu carry messages of peace and reconciliation. This photo displays some such medieval manuscripts used in the film 333. Photo: David West, for the Malian Manuscript Foundation (used with permission).

Four Hundred Years of Historical Ties Between Mali and Virginia

The Malian History of Richmond, Virginia

Ana Edwards, coauthor of this book and vice president of the Virginia Friends of Mali, is also an artist and social activist.[13] Her interest in the links between Mali and Virginia is personal as well as philosophical. Ana's father is African American and her mother is Norwegian American—so the racial politics of Virginia is a part of Ana's life story, even though she was raised in California. Her family history runs deep into America's history of slavery and racial exploitation, and therefore into Richmond's relationship with the Mali Empire.

"I've always been told that one, possibly two of my great-great-great-grandmothers were sold out of Richmond, most likely in the 1840s," says Ana, referring to the slave trade that flourished in the city, especially in the east-side neighborhood of Shockoe Bottom, beside the James River.

"From the 1830s through 1865, Richmond's Shockoe Bottom was the nation's second-largest slave-trading center, second only to New Orleans," Ana continues. "So it was full of slave-trader offices, auction houses, jails, and all the many supporting businesses. If you were a grocer or if you were a dry-goods person, if you were a seamstress or

---

13 *As of December 2017, our new president is Mrs. Lydie Alapini Sakponou, a mother of five (including twins) and a teacher at Chesterfield Public Schools, who has French and Beninois (West African) nationalities. Former president Ana is now VFoM's vice president.*

if you were a blacksmith—and there were going to be lots of those—then you were involved with slavery. This was a slavery-based society."

As a social historian, Ana is the president of the Sacred Ground Project, a community effort to obtain recognition for and protect the site of the African burial ground at Broad and Fifteenth Streets, where historical researchers found a forgotten municipal cemetery used by Virginia's African American ancestors in the 1700s. Since 1959, that African cemetery had been partly covered by Interstate 95, and partly by a parking lot where VCU medical staff parked their cars. But in 2010, after much debate and several years of activism, VCU gave up the property, and in 2011, the city was persuaded to remove the asphalt from the parking lot and replace it with a grassy field. Now at least the ancestral burial ground looks decent, hosts a set of informative historic markers, and serves as the site of many annual commemorations.

One is bound to wonder why anyone of any color or religion would not immediately wish to respect a cemetery as sacred ground. The answer may be found in the response of one of my students at the Shepherd's Center of Richmond, an open university to which people generously donate their time and energy to provide free teaching to retired—mostly white—Richmonders. I was teaching a weekly course about the Mali Empire in a classroom at First Presbyterian Church. What most excited the elderly ladies in my class each week were the spectacular Malian costumes I wore to give a sense of atmosphere to my subject. I dressed in brown bogolan mud cloth when teaching about Ségou, and wore desert robes and a Tuareg turban when taking them to discover the wonders of Timbuktu.

At the time, the "Negro Burial Ground," as an old map of Richmond described it, had been rediscovered quite recently. I explained the links between Mali and Virginia to these wealthy middle-class ladies and a few men, and offered a petition. I explained that we were collecting signatures to ask the mayor to remove the parking lot and restore the Sacred Ground, out of respect for the Ancestors. To my amazement, one old white woman recoiled from the paper as if its existence was offensive to her, and turned away. "No," she said. "I do not want to sign that petition." I could tell from her body language that she would not—could not—bring herself to support the emancipation of blacks, even in death. Even after 250 years, she would deny African Americans their human status. Actually, they were Africans born in America, but not granted citizenship until the passage of the Fourteenth Amendment, after the Civil War.

Like Ségou, which is still struggling with the aftermath of French colonial rule, Richmond has found itself greatly affected by memories of its past, and particularly of the Civil War period—memories that serve to accentuate the problem of race that still exists in the city. When I first arrived in Virginia, I was told by friends, "Richmond is still fighting the Civil War, and [white] Richmonders are still not convinced that they lost that war." Richmond was the capital of the Confederate States of America, the thirteen secessionist states that attempted to leave the Union. The war was vicious. Improved rifle technology and outdated infantry tactics caused terrible slaughter. Malian society suffered a similar brutal impact from the arrival of Moroccan firearms in 1591, and then from modern rifles during the French conquest of Mali in the late nineteenth century. French colonial conquest imposed a form of enslavement on Mali. Who knows how many forgotten Africans were slaughtered by the French? Professor David J. Hacker believes that at least 750,000 died between 1861 and 1865, during the American Civil War—more than the total of 673,000 who died all other American wars. (These numbers are American deaths, ignoring the twenty million people that America has killed in its overseas wars).[14]

When Robert E. Lee sent word to Confederate president Davis on April 2, 1865 that he could not hold Petersburg in the face of superior Union forces, Davis gave the command for his government to evacuate, and for his troops to burn the army's warehouses of munitions and supplies. Southerners may tell you that the American Civil War was fought over power, economics, states' rights, freedom—even

---

14 See http://www.globalresearch.ca/us-has-killed-more-than-20-million-people-in-37-victim-nations-since-world-war-ii/5492051.

Celtic identity. As a Celt, I feel insulted! To find out what really happened, I have read, in original sources, many of the statements and declarations made by the secessionist states. No one should make any mistake about this: the underlying question over which the Civil War was fought was that of slavery.

The very first black people to arrive in British North America reached the colony of Virginia in 1619: twenty Africans who had been ripped from their homes in Angola, forcibly baptized on the shores of Africa, and then shipped to the West Indies. After British pirates captured the original Portuguese vessel that carried them, they eventually landed at Old Point Comfort, a spit of land on the Chesapeake Bay. The excellent historical museum at Jamestown offers a faithful reproduction of these slaves' Angolan homes and lifestyle, with an exhibit that looks exactly like rural Mali or the historic Senegambia region of the seventeenth century.

We know from the shipping records that most of the Africans who arrived in Virginia from the first century of English settlement until around 1720 came from the lands of the Mali Empire, shipped there by the slave exporters of Gorée Island off Dakar, or James Island in the mouth of the Gambia River.[15] These first Africans in Virginia, Christians in name at least, became indentured servants. The Virginia colony lacked a legal framework for slavery until forty years later; the great expansion of slavery did not start until 1700.[16]

Slavery is a very painful, complex, and controversial topic. Biblical references demonstrate that it has existed in human society for at least four thousand years. The inhabitants of the Middle East have used slaves for millennia, and some still do. Even Africans themselves had slaves. We cannot do the subject justice in this book, but I find this comment from GhanaWeb, the country's most popular news aggregator, helpful:

---

15 While Portuguese slavers may have exported slaves from Angola and Elmina (modern Ghana) to Brazil as early as 1482, the American trade in slaves from Ghana, Dahomey, and Nigeria became dominant only during the second half of the eighteenth century.

16 See http://www.virginiaplaces.org/population.

During the heyday of early European competition, slavery was an accepted social institution, and the slave trade overshadowed all other commercial activities on the West African coast. To be sure, slavery and slave trading were already firmly entrenched in many African societies before their contact with Europe. In most situations, men as well as women captured in local warfare became slaves. In general, however, slaves in African communities were treated as junior members of the society with specific rights, and many were ultimately absorbed into their masters' families as full members. Given traditional methods of agricultural production in Africa, slavery in Africa was quite different from that which existed in the commercial plantation environments of the New World.[17]

In 1800, it was descendants of South Africans who planned the famous slave rebellion against Richmond, known as Gabriel's Rebellion. A skilled blacksmith, Gabriel was able to travel around the state and earn money for his white owner, Thomas H. Prosser, whose plantation lay just north of Richmond at Brook Run. An historical marker stands along the nearby US Route 1, here also known as Brook Road, to remind travelers of Gabriel and his rebellion.

Gabriel was the son of a South African chief. He rejected captivity and slavery, and was able to organize his rebellion using a network of South African slaves who were distributed across the Virginian plantations of the tobacco magnate Robert "King" Carter. At age twenty-four, Gabriel organized the rebellion using a close circle of local co-conspirators that tapped a network of enslaved workers throughout the central Virginia region. But the rebellion was thwarted, first by a freak thunderstorm that prevented his troops reaching Richmond, and then by betrayal from within the rebellion's ranks. Gabriel and twenty-five others were tried and hanged, many on the city gallows at the Burial Ground in Richmond. They are remembered on a second

---

17 *See http://www.ghanaweb.com/GhanaHomePage/history/slave-trade.php.*

historical marker at Broad Street and Fifteenth. Every year at dusk on October 10, the anniversary of Gabriel's death, a memorial service is held at the Sacred Ground in Richmond.

At his trial—or rather, the kangaroo court of his lynch mob—Gabriel said nothing; after all, there were others who had not been discovered who might still aspire to success in a future attempt. But another of the men on trial eloquently explained their quest for individual rights and freedom, "I have nothing more to offer than what George Washington would have had to offer, had he been taken by the British and put to trial by them. I have adventured my life in endeavouring to obtain the liberty of my countrymen, and am a willing sacrifice in their cause: and I beg, as a favour, that I may be immediately led to execution. I know that you have pre-determined to shed my blood, why then all this mockery of a trial?"[18] Gabriel and his men were as much freedom fighters as George Washington. If George Washington had lost his war, he might well have been hanged by the British as a traitor. Africans, as much as Americans, value peace and democracy. Nelson Mandela, Nobel Peace Laureate and the world's greatest peacemaker, was once condemned by white politicians and jailed for twenty-seven years as a "terrorist" . . . simply because he demanded "One Man, One Vote."

The descendants of Malian slaves—including distinguished Richmond women like Ana Edwards, whose ancestors were sold in Richmond; Delegate Delores McQuinn, whose ancestors were Mende, part of the Malian diaspora living in Sierra Leone; and Viola Baskerville, who champions the Girl Scouts of Virginia at historic Ebenezer Baptist Church—are still fighting the battle for equality—equality of opportunity for women, and for black Americans. In Richmond as much as anywhere else, many black people struggle to get out of the poverty trap because so many suffer from low incomes and low self-esteem, from poor schools and poor nutrition, from low expectations, dim horizons and a degraded sense of culture. If they knew that

---

18 *Philip J. Schwarz, Gabriel's Conspiracy: A Documentary History (Charlottesville: University of Virginia Press, 2012), 238.*

they are descended from the Lion King, Richmond's black population might feel proud of their rich cultural inheritance. They might have greater ambitions for their children, and feel that the acts of voting and participating in the political process are more worthwhile. Like President Obama, they might believe that "Yes, we can!"

That is one huge benefit from the Ségou sister city relationship that we hope for Richmonders to realize: that they are descended from noble Africans who were free, whose culture was rich and sophisticated; and that they themselves can break free of poverty and depression. Yes, they can!

How the Lion King Founded the Empire of Mali

Every American has heard of the Lion King, but very few know that he was Malian. Sunjata Keita, the Lion King, was the founder and ruler of a great medieval empire in West Africa that lasted for hundreds of years. Created in 1235 on the foundations of the earlier kingdoms of Sosso and Ghana and Wagadou, the Mali-Sonrai Empire lasted until it was destroyed in 1591 at the battle of Tondibi, as the culmination of a Moroccan invasion that brought firearms for the first time in West Africa.

Virginia's schoolchildren know. In third grade, students learn about the Mali dynasty of the Lion King in Kangaba, and in sixth grade they hear about the final Sonrai dynasty in Gao. They know a lot more about their history than their parents do.

Sunjata of the Konaté clan was born around the year 1217, the son of Naré Maghan Fa Konaté, king of Niani (also known as *Maghan Kon Fatta,* meaning "the handsome prince"). Sunjata's mother was the king's second wife, Sogolon Kondé or Koné, also known as Sogolon Kédjou—"Ugly Sogolon". Legend says she was a hunchback from the southern land of Dô. The fourth son of this marriage was Prince Jata. Known as "Sogolon's Jata," his name became shortened to Sonjata, or Sunjata. The Moroccan explorer Ibn Khaldun called him *Mari Jatah*; "Mari" meaning "Amir" or "Prince," and "Jatah" meaning "lion."

Prince Sunjata Konaté was prophesized from birth to become a great conqueror. His father's totem was the all-conquering lion, and his mother's totem was the strong and fierce buffalo. The griots and seers proclaimed that this prince, born of a lion father and a buffalo mother, was destined for high achievement. The prince did not have a promising start, for oral tradition says he dragged himself on his arms until he was seven years old. However, once Sunjata gained the use of his legs (probably thanks to the use of iron calipers to compensate for his being crippled by polio), he became a fine horseman, showing huge upper body strength. When his father died, Dankaran Touman—the much older son of the senior wife Sassouma Bérété—seized the throne and forced Sunjata into exile along with his mother and two sisters. Before Dankaran Touman and his mother could enjoy their power, however, Sumangoro Kanté, the wicked sorcerer-blacksmith-king of Sosso, invaded Niani and forced Dankaran to flee. Sumangoro may have killed Sunjata's father in battle, for legend says that his throne sat upon the skulls of the nine kings he had defeated and whose strength and power he now controlled.

After a decade of exile at the court of Wagadou and then at Mema, Sunjata was approached by a delegation who begged him to free the kingdoms of Manden or Manding from Sumangoro's despotism. Now a powerful young man, Prince Sunjata returned at the head of the combined armies of Mema, Wagadou and other rebellious Manding city states whose fellow-princes he had impressed during his years of exile. The combined forces of northern and southern Manden defeated the Sosso army at the Battle of Kirina (or *Krina*) in 1235. Sunjata's sister Nana and his griot Balla Fasé Kouyaté had infiltrated the court of Sosso and discovered the secret of Sumangoro's magic: he could be killed only by an arrow tipped with the spur of a white cockerel. When the aging Sumangoro saw the spur-tipped arrow aimed at him from Sunjata's bow, he knew he was beaten, turned, and fled from the battlefield.

King Sumangoro the sorcerer transformed himself into a rock in the hills of Koulikoro, and the Manding armies captured the remaining Sosso cities. Sunjata was declared "*faama* of *faamas*" with the title "*Mansa*," which translates as Emperor. The twelve allied princes in his cortège drove their spears into the ground in sign of homage and cried, "*Kay Ta*," "he has taken it" or "take it!" This became Keita, the name of Sunjata's new dynasty (which is why Malians say that Konaté is equivalent to Keita). Crowned as Mari Jata Keita at the age of eighteen, he received authority over all the twelve kingdoms and became the founder of the Mali Empire.

The following year, in 1236, Sunjata promulgated the *Kurugan Fuga*, which is known as the "written constitution of Mali," although it was mainly transmitted orally by the griots. This Malian constitution was born just twenty-one years after King John signed the *Magna Carta* in England, guaranteeing, among other things, that the king would never again lock up prisoners without presenting them to a judge. This important principle is known as *habeas corpus*, or "we have the person," and it remains fundamental to the rule of law inherited by every citizen in Britain and in the United States of America.

The *Kurugan Fuga* Charter was reconstituted in the 1990s by Mali's griots and published as forty-nine articles that make for fascinating reading. They codify the lifestyle of medieval Mali. Roughly 540 years before the American Declaration of Independence, Mali had a constitution stipulating that women should be heard in council. American women obtained the vote only in 1922, nearly seven hundred years later.

African Women Farmers Produce Milk, Not Spare Ribs

"Women are the backbone of Africa," said world music diva Angélique Kidjo on September 20, 2014, in an interview on the TV channel France 24. Yet foreigners do not see it! Even today, Western and Arab development agencies are guilty of neglecting women. Foreign experts favor cash crops grown by men, mostly sold to bring profits to foreign companies. There is a permanent bias in bureaucracies everywhere against the main food farmers of Africa, and in favor of their husbands.

Angélique Kidjo, who comes from Benin in West Africa, also raised the Jewish legend of Eve and the apple, the Judeo-Christian creation myth, in order to dismiss its interpretation as making women guilty of sin. Malian women have no time for sin: they are too busy being the managers of their households, the farmers and food providers, the traders and negotiators, the educators of their children, the finance and food organizers and cooks who tell their husbands what to do, and reward them with food if they do it! Guilt, the apple and the serpent have been used for centuries by Jewish, Christian, and Muslim men to control and denigrate women. The West African creation myth is different: it puts women in the center of economic production as well as reproduction and keeps mothers ahead of men (fathers) by showing them to be the heart and soul and backbone of Malian society. Women in the African creation myth are not the product of Adam's spare rib. Not at all!

The Fulani creation story begins with God the Creator, who is called *Guéno* in the Fulani language—although these days many Fulani use the Arabic name *Allah*. Death holds no fear for Africans. Destiny has already determined when we shall die. If it is our day, we shall pass over and our spirit shall be reborn in another member of the clan. Modern science confirms that this is in fact a very accurate description of what happens. The DNA of my son and grandson is virtually indistinguishable from my DNA. When a grandson is born, I am very literally reborn in his DNA. But first of all, the Fulani story of creation reminds us that we are alive thanks to our mothers, and thanks to the milk we drank from their breasts when we were babies.

"In the beginning, there was the cow," say the Fulani. "Guéno the Eternal created the World from a drop of milk. First Guéno created the cow. Next He created a woman. Finally, Guéno created a Fulani man. He placed the woman behind the cow. He placed the Fulani behind the woman. Thus was created the first cowboy. Glory be to Guéno, the Eternal Creator of all things, to Him who created chaos and light. From a drop of milk, He created the universe. From the act of milking a cow, He created speech. That is why children are able to talk, and to tell stories. You must always tell the truth and take care of the cattle who give you milk. You have just heard the truth from my mouth, the story of how Guéno created the World. *Allah-o akbar!* God is great."

I like to tell this story to the third graders in Virginian schools, to boost the self-confidence of girls and to offset the "phallocracy" of macho American society. There is something rather horrible about the Jewish story that Eve was created from Adam's spare rib. This creation myth puts women below the status of men, founding a pattern of discrimination against women and their manipulation by the Judeo-Christian churches—and I include in these the Muslim mosques that follow the same legends and the same prophets, and impose the same male control over women. Americans often forget that Jesus was a Jew; and Mohamed was a Christian who took Unitarian Christianity to Arabia, in order to reform the corrupt and pagan society that he called derisively *jahiliya*. Only later did Mohamed have revelations from the archangel Gabriel (*Gibril*) that evolved into Mohamedism, or Islam. Contemporary travelers in the Levant like John Moschos and his pupil Sophronius the Sophist who wrote a wonderful seventh-century travelogue, considered early Mohamedism to be just one of many Christian subsects.

The legend of "Adam's spare rib" is a real put-down for Middle Eastern and European women. If you add the guilt that afflicts women who are blamed for Eve having accepted an apple from the serpent, you realize that Christian women are born into a position of permanent repression by men. No Christian or Jew ever blames Adam. We do not ask why Adam accepted the apple. Eve's greedy, gullible, thoughtless consort showed no better judgment than his wife. And the serpent—was he not also male?

Instead of these Old Testament stories demeaning women in nomadic Jewish tribes, I prefer to dwell upon the importance of women and mothers in Malian society. I relish the fact that—when He created the world from His drop of milk—Guéno the Creator (who is called *God*, or *Nga*, or *Ngai*, or *Dieu*, or *Allah* in other languages) placed the Woman before the Man. To the eight-year-olds in my Virginian elementary school teaching, I say, "This story shows why mothers are considered goddesses in Mali. Malians know that your mother gives you life. And she gives you life twice over: once when she births you, and a second time when she feeds you as a baby with her milk. Without your mother's milk, you would die; but with it, thanks to that milk, you have grown strong and healthy. So now, kids, I want you to promise me this: when you go home tonight, you will hug your mother and say, 'Mom, I discovered in class today that you are a goddess.' Will you do that for me?"

One day, when I had finished entertaining a class of third graders, preparing them for their SOL exams about Mali, I heard a nine-year-old girl say to her little friend, "So I am going to be a goddess when I grow up." Smart girl!

Another time as I waited in line for the cashier in the Kroger supermarket, an unknown woman said to me: "Dr. Poulton, I just wanted to thank you. After your visit to her third-grade class, my daughter came home and told me I was a goddess, and it made me feel great!"

Mothers of Richmond: Ana, Lydie, Oumou, Haoua, and Dana

Our sister city story is based on the strength of our Richmond women. Allan and his friends are the musicians, but it is the women who organize us and make things happen. After we first met on the dance floor and I told him about Mali, Allan said he would bring some people to meet me. We spent a happy afternoon in my sitting room, drinking tea on a thick Ségou carpet with two lovely women: Lauranett Lee, anthropologist at the Virginia Historical Society; and Ana Edwards of the Richmond Defenders.

At the exhibit on Mali presented by the Richmond Public Library in 2005, we met cheerful, smiling Dana Wiggins. Dana was raised in Chesterfield County and works for poverty alleviation in Richmond. She was excited about Mali because she had been a Peace Corps volunteer in West Africa, living in a small village. Every day for two or three years, Dana had used the very same weird African cooking implements we were exhibiting to third graders. Dana is the only person in Richmond who can talk about rural West Africa in intimate detail and understand our lifestyle of twenty years. Also, Dana is a great teacher, and she is funny!

Then at the house of friends one evening, we met Francis and Lydie Sakponou, a couple from West Africa who had just moved to live in Virginia at about the same time that my lovely wife Michelle came to Richmond to become the vice president for International Programs of ChildFund International (Christian Children's Fund) after many years working in Mali as West African director for Save the Children. In the villages of southern Mali, Michelle had earned the Malian name Oumou Koné. Later we would become firm friends with a chuckling VCU French professor from Ivory Coast called Brahima Koné, who was born across the colonial frontier about fifty miles from the Malian villages where my Oumou Koné used to work. I used to call her "mother of twelve million children" for her amazing work with village schools, refugees, and early childhood education. Her great friend Lydie Sakponou was a French attorney who moved from Paris to Chesterfield County when her husband Francis came to the US with Oracle Computers; she chose Chesterfield, because it has the best schools in America. Since she could not practice law in Virginia, Lydie began teaching in the public schools. For Lydie, Mali is a surrogate for Africa: she wants Americans to learn more about West Africa, where her parents come from—and whence most African American ancestors came.

I cannot say exactly how it happened, but we all became firm friends: the *de facto* (and later the *de jure*) executive committee of Virginia Friends of Mali, which is run—as it should be—by mothers. Ana went to Ségou, fell in love (with Mali), and became VFoM president. Allan is the treasurer who did the work to get us the tax-free status as an IRS-approved 501.c.3 association, charming on the telephone some federal agent in Texas who very kindly expedited the process before the VFoM's next annual meeting so that Ana, our president, could announce the good news. But since we never have any money, why would we ever pay any taxes? The main rule we have established was that every meeting must be a party. We eat lunch while we laugh and talk. Our official annual meeting is usually a concert for Mali's national day on September 22 each year, with speeches in the music breaks, and a signed sheet to show who turned up for the dancing and the food. Often the Malian ambassador in Washington, DC comes to make a speech, but he and his staff seldom dance.

Lydie and Francis Sakponou have five children. When the Jamestown Foundation called to ask if VFoM could provide an actress to play the role of Angela, the first African woman in Virginia, we sent them Lydie's elder daughter Johanna, who was eighteen. This was a part of Virginia celebrating in 2007 the four hundredth anniversary of the founding of Jamestown, with the arrival of sailors, soldiers and artisans from the Virginia Company of London in three ships: *Susan Constant* (captained by Christopher Newport), *Godspeed,* and *Discovery.* Jamestown was Virginia's capital until 1699, when it was replaced by Williamsburg.

The first Africans arrived in 1619, people who had been brought from Angola on a Portuguese slaving ship that had been captured by privateers. Of the twenty Africans who landed at Jamestown, one was a woman, and written records show that she had been forcibly baptized Angela. Johanna Sakponou, dressed in a comely seventeenth-century bonnet, read a text for the Jamestown website that described her life as Angela. I don't know if the website still shows "Angela" describing her journey from Angola, but Johanna was perfect! Later Johanna, by then our VCU student committee member, and her sister Laetitia of William & Mary College joined our Teaching Timbuktu team, and then they joined the VFoM board.

Our first vibrant link with Ségou was musical. Richmond runs a magnificent folk festival every year in October. Very soon we were receiving in our homes, Malian guests attending the Richmond Folk Festival. The first to come were Ségou festival organizer Mamou Daffé and other members of his committee: his sister Ina Daffé and his manager, Mohamed Doumbia. Then members of the Ségou sister city committee started arriving: Madani Sissoko, Mayor Ousmane Simaga, and others. The Richmond Folk Festival became our first "event," and here we discovered Madame Haoua Cheick Traoré, a business woman and promoter of Malian art and handicrafts who became another of our important VFoM Mothers.

Haoua was born in Ségou, where she often visits her own mama. Now she was living in Northern Virginia, vivaciously wearing colorful turbans and flowing fabrics, designing and importing arts and crafts from Mali. Haoua is a social entrepreneur who has worked with craftsmen and women in Mali, Benin, Ghana, Ethiopia, Swaziland, and Lesotho. She has participated in trade fairs in Florida, California, New Mexico, Maryland, and Connecticut, as well as in NOVA and DC. In 2002, Haoua won the Verizon Capital Award for best entrepreneur from the Women Business Center. For several years Haoua was the beating heart of the Virginia Friends of Mali, running her craft stall at the Richmond Folk Festival, in partnership with Richmond's fair-trade craft business Ten Thousand Villages, and joining us in Ségou each February. People who wanted to find Friends of Mali in Richmond, would find Haoua Cheick Traoré at the folk festival. We would arrive early and help Haoua set up her stall. When we travelled to the Ségou festival, Haoua was often there before us—and sometimes Haoua led the Richmond sister city delegation.

And then Haoua got married to Andrew, a delightful American who lives in . . . Portland, Oregon. Sadly, Oregon is far from Virginia; these days we mostly see her in Ségou.

Fig. 6. Haoua Cheikh Traoré and Dany Bernard of Angoulême, Ségou's sister city in France, speaking in Ségou about women and private enterprise. Photo: Madani Sissoko, VFoM.

Djita: A Malian Girl Born in Virginia

It is easy enough to create a new school course; but in 2003, when the Mali Standard of Learning (SOL) was created, how were teachers supposed to teach this new subject of Mali, about which they probably knew nothing at all? There were no books. The internet offered educational materials produced by the excellent education centers at James Madison University's Madison Museum in Harrisonburg, Virginia; and the Museum of Fine Arts (VMFA) in Richmond, which houses a fine collection of African and Malian art. Five Ponds Press came out with the very good *Mali: Land of Gold and Glory*, by Joy Masoff; and soon after, Melanie Stanley produced an even better book: *Mali: Today and Long Ago*. But more were needed. Especially, we thought Virginia needed a book that would bridge the gap between learning about medieval Mali and linking this new knowledge to the rich African American culture that Virginia inherited from Mali.

Since there were so few materials, I decided I had better write the book that teachers could use at several levels. The actual inspiration came when I was visiting the real Djita and her mother in their apartment. We were discussing Djita's class project. Djita had to show the class how a music teacher works. We talked about her lesson plan, and seven-year-old Djita raced off to her room to search for musical instruments. She came back with a xylophone and a small drum. We decided that Djita should present her various musical instruments: first the *balafon*, the wooden ancestor of the xylophone that features small gourds hanging below the wooden slats as soundboxes; and then her drum. Then she would demonstrate Malian dance, making clickety rhythms with the beads in her hair. Djita would then get the children to clap or tap out Malian dance rhythms. Finally, she would play a CD and get her classmates to dance while listening to the instruments and the beat. Djita's class went so well that later, I wrote it up as a story. "That is a lovely story," Djita's mother smiled. So the story became a small book.

I realized that Djita's life story, even by the age of seven, encompassed more than just one class project. With her dual nationality, Djita represented both American and Malian children. Her life is different from a typical seven-year-old Malian girl's, and different from a typical American girl's; yet she is both Malian and American. So "the Djita book" became the true story *Djita: A Malian Girl from Virginia,* which can be bought from a bookshop or online for under ten dollars. Djita attends an international school where most children speak two or three languages, which is a story in itself for Americans who typically speak only English. As Patricia Cummins, who is a French professor, likes to say, "Someone who is trilingual speaks three languages. Someone who is bilingual speaks two languages. Someone who speaks one language is American!"

Djita's story supports the sister city relationship between Richmond in Virginia, and Ségou in Mali. *Djita* is a "flipbook" combining drawings and photos, with English in one direction, and French if you flip it over. So the book can be used by teachers on both sides of the Atlantic Ocean, in Malian schools as well as in Virginia. Djita's story also reverse-mirrors that of the triangular slave trade: teachers can draw parallels between Djita's travels and those of the African American ancestors. The book offers a way to change perceptions and grow history away from the slavery-dominated narrative of relations between Virginia and Africa, toward a contemporary narrative about the importance of respect for the Empire of Mali, based on cultural understanding.

Djita's mother had prepared dinner. We ate *wijila,* one of my favorite dishes from Timbuktu. The apartment was filled with the aroma of rich cooking and sweet spices. Djita's parents both have northern roots, and desert perfumes filled my nostrils. The dish known as *wijila* is a combination of wheat-based dumplings and a very specific sauce flavored with the incomparable spices of Timbuktu. Wheat is grown beside the river around Timbuktu where the climate is more suitable than in Bamako or Ségou, because the Tuaregs' Mediterranean ancestors were wheat-eaters. As well as the dumplings, Tuaregs eat unleavened bread. The tasty round loaves, made with brown flour, are cooked either in an oven or on burning hot stones set over a desert fire.

The *wijila* sauce is famous because it contains pulled lamb suffused in the "twelve spices of Morocco." Moroccan influence remains strong in Timbuktu, from the architecture, to the scholarship, to the food. In southern Morocco, near the town of Zagora, there is a famous signpost pointing south that reads "Tomboctu 52 days"—in case you are planning to cross the desert on foot or by camel in heat between 100 and 110 degrees Fahrenheit. If we had been eating our *wijila* in Timbuktu, of course, we would have been enjoying "thirteen spices," as Ségou Malians like to joke: the extra spice being the grains of sand that infiltrate desert cooking, desert water, and everything else in that City of Sand. Only an ample turban can keep the sand out of your mouth and nose and ears—but you cannot use a turban to protect cooking pots from sand. Ségoviens joke that you can tell a man from Timbuktu by his small teeth, worn away from grinding the sand grains in his food.

More often when I visit Djita's family, we eat a southern Malian peanut sauce *domoda* with rice *kini*. Ah! the joys of tasting that rich fusion of cabbage and bitter tomato (actually a form of aubergine) with okra and peanut and lamb meat, tinged with just the right amount of hot chili pepper. We eat with our right hands from the common dish (never the left hand, which is kept for washing your feet and other places). The hot pepper is taken out of the pot and placed on the side of the dish, so that we can rub its juice with our fingers to add nonburning flavor before scooping up a ball of the rice and sauce and dropping it into our mouth. Sometimes we start the meal with fruit juice and a plate of *akra*, delicious balls of black-eyed pea flour (*niébé* in Bambara) spiced with hot peppers and fried. These are the ancestors of the hush puppy found in America, a recipe adapted by Africans who found no *niébé* in Virginia or Mississippi and had to make do with cornmeal. So much Southern American cooking comes from Mali. None of the dishes that follow came from England or Scotland or Ireland or Italy or Germany: the cola nuts used in Coca-Cola's famous soft drink came from Africa, and so did ginger beer; fried chicken is African, and so are fire-grilled meat, sweet potatoes, peanut soup, peanut sauce, iron-rich dishes of vegetables or turnip greens, rice served with chicken or fish sauce, *akra* and hush puppies, okra soups ("okra" is the Ghanaian name for the vegetable that Gambians call *gombo* and Malians call *kanja*), and even donut holes, which were an African breakfast staple long before Columbus was born—and many of the Louisiana recipes that have created the fame of Creole cooking. Jambalaya is African cooking with an American flavor, and a French name taken from the old Provençal language. What could make a more perfect or more delicious fusion than West African and Southern French cooking?

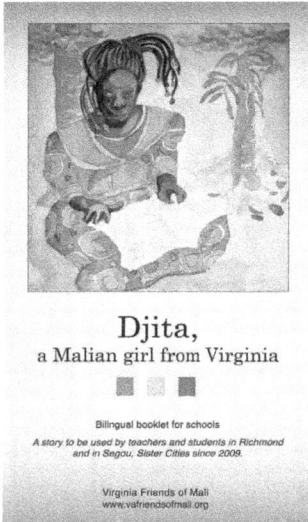

Djita,
a Malian girl from Virginia

Bilingual booklet for schools
A story to be used by teachers and students in Richmond and in Segou, Sister Cities since 2009.

Virginia Friends of Mali
www.vafriendsofmali.org

Fig. 7. Djita: A Malian Girl from Virginia was written for children and their teachers. It tells the story of Mali through the eyes of Djita, and can be ordered at any bookshop, or online at AuthorHouse or Amazon.com. Illustration by Rebecca Brinton.

Reclaiming Afrika for Its American Descendants

In the Spring 2014 newsletter of the West Africa Research Association (WARA), a dynamic high school teacher called Dara Bayer wrote movingly about her high school teaching experience. It is so relevant to our mission that she gave permission to include her article here. She is a high school humanities teacher at Boston Arts Academy and can be reached at dbayer@bostonartsacademy.org. Thank you, Dara!

During the first week of my freshmen high school humanities course, I ask my students to conduct a short community survey on how they and others imagine Afrika. Their task is to ask themselves, family members, and friends the following prompts:

"When I think of Afrika, the first thing that comes to my mind is . . ." and "If I went to Afrika, I would expect to see . . ." The day after my students complete this assignment, they write their responses on poster paper around the room. We then take time to reflect on what we notice about our community's perception of the continent. Recurring words/phrases that always arise are: poverty, desert, dry, jungle, animals, starving children, disease, huts, tribal dances, gold. Through examining these words, we begin to unpack the pathological images of Afrika deeply embedded in our collective consciousness. This activity opens space for my students to explore how a Eurocentric perspective has shaped our worldviews.

Thus the course becomes a journey of seeing the world through Afrocentric lenses. To do this, we contrast our status quo images of Afrika with Nikki Giovanni's poem "Ego Tripping," which personifies Afrika as a powerful woman, the mother of humanity; we spell Afrika with a "k" to symbolically represent a reclaiming of the name; we interrogate how perspective and bias connect to the creation of secondary historical sources; we study a precolonial Afrikan civilization to understand the complexity and sophistication of societies that existed over a thousand years ago; we explore literature of the Afrikan Diaspora; and we examine the anti-apartheid struggle in South Afrika as a case study for liberation movements on the continent.

Over 85% of the young people I teach are of Afrikan descent and represent a broad array of national and ethnic identities from the Diaspora. In addition to "Afrikan Americans,"[1] many are first-generation Dominican, Puerto Rican, Jamaican, Trinidadian, Brazilian, and Haitian. A large majority of these students do not identify their ancestors as Afrikan. In fact, many students initially see no connection between themselves and Afrika. Even after demonstrating an intellectual understanding of the concepts of Afrocentrism and Eurocentrism, my students say that they wish they had "soft" hair or light eyes. Some of my current students made these exact comments during a recent reflective Circle about our family trees. As with the monolithic, one-dimensional images of Afrika highlighted during the community survey activity, many of my students hold deeply embedded notions of beauty and self-worth that are based in Eurocentric norms. My goal is to engage my students in critical and creative work that supports them in unearthing these notions, so they may embrace all aspects of their cultural and ancestral identity.

However, I am not only an educator of students of color. My white students are also part of our classroom community and are also on the journey of learning about themselves through the lens of Afrikan history and culture. It is just as important for them to understand how Eurocentric perspectives of the world have shaped their understanding of themselves and others, and, most importantly, that they have the ability to take on a different perspective. It is certainly a challenge to create both an inclusive and critical space to interrogate how histories of oppression connect to our current understanding of identity. Yet taking an Afrocentric approach to my teaching practice—creating opportunities to honor all of our ancestors, telling our stories, and collaborating— allows for each individual to feel honored. Though I have dealt with defensive white students who do not want to address race, the modes of learning within the classroom support all students in (hopefully) recognizing the unique gifts [2] they bring to the collective.

Despite the challenges, pride and passion do slowly emerge through the course. When we study the Kingdom of Ife, and Yoruba influence on the Americans, my Caribbean students—especially the Puerto Rican and Dominican students, who rarely identify as black—begin to see direct connections to their culture. When we read poetry and short stories from writers of the diaspora, we discuss the complexities of Afrikan American (in the most expansive sense) identity and how white supremacy ideology has cut us off from certain parts of our roots. Both students of color and white students struggle with making meaning of their social identities and the goal is for them to hold the tension of embracing their membership in a common human family—in the end we are all children of Afrika—and also recognizing the history and current realities of racism that privilege one group over others. When young people begin to unpack how relationships of power and oppression have shaped their cultural upbringing and how they see the world, they gain the agency to decide how they want to consciously position themselves in relationship to structures of power; they have tools to confront and challenge the status quo.

I believe that building solidarity among peoples of Afrikan descent must start with education. I see the high school classroom as a space to strip away the mental blindfolds that centuries of colonialism and slavery have inflicted on all people, but specifically black and brown people; I see understanding the roots of our common humanity and the power of our original homeland as a healing remedy to the deep scars of ideological white supremacist warfare waged for centuries on all of our psyches.

Ultimately, I hope that my students leave my course with a more nuanced understanding of Afrika and their own identities; my hope is that their understanding will only become more complex as they continue to learn and grow. Working with the hearts and minds of young people as they are in the midst of solidifying a more permanent identity, and defining how they want to relate to themselves and others in the world, is a great privilege: one that must be at the forefront of our vision for positive transformation.

[1] In this particular paragraph, I use "Afrikan American" to refer to the group of people whose ancestors were enslaved in what is now the United States. I have chosen to put this label in quotation marks because I do not want to uphold the United States imperialist practice of claiming the term "American" as a singular national identity. In truth Afrikan Americans are people of Afrikan descent of the Americas (North, Central, South, and the Caribbean).

[2] I often use the metaphor of "gifts" when describing the unique perspectives, talents, experiences that each individual brings to the classroom. This language comes from a quote by Sobonfu Somé, a healer and spiritual leader of the Dagara people. She writes: "Community is the spirit, the guiding light of the tribe, whereby people come together in order to fulfill their purpose, and to take care of one another. The goal of the community is to make sure that each member of the community is heard and is properly giving the gifts s/he has brought to this world." I share this quote with my students on the second day of class, and incorporate several different rituals into my teaching practice that focus on building an interconnected culture within the classroom.

VFoM Annual Meetings, Guests, and Cheick Hamala Diabaté

Virginia Friends of Mali organize musical meetings, with food and drink. Conviviality is a key part of who we are. A meeting in Mali has a formal Chair, and often there is a two-hour wait before the work begins, while the audience waits for some government administrator to come and read a boring opening statement. And then he (it is seldom a she) goes away again, having learned nothing about the people he has addressed. It is certainly not an American system for holding meetings. Richmond's sister city commission—like its Ségou equivalent—holds formal sessions around a conference table in city hall (although the RSCC does not suffer tedious speeches from ministers or governors). VFoM prefer to hold our meetings around a dinner table, preferably while listening to the music of a griot.

In Northern Virginia, we are fortunate to have our own resident Malian griot, Cheick Hamala Diabaté. He phones us regularly to remind us that it is time to hire him to play for another meeting. A typical annual meeting starts with music and dancing, and glasses of *bissap* (red hibiscus) or *lenburuji* (lemon ginger *gingembré*) juice. We have spare *djembé* drums for volunteers who want to support the band. Reports from the president and treasurer are slotted in between the music and the food, and attendees sign the attendance sheet as they arrive in order to get a drink. Occasionally we remember to put out a collection box for cash donations; usually, we forget. VFoM members are better at friendraising than fundraising.

Peanut stew for committee meetings may be cooked in the kitchen of that month's host, but food is often provided by Mamusu's West African restaurant, run by a Liberian American woman called Ida Daniels, who makes great dishes. She has restaurant on the corner of Main and Second Streets, where Mamusu (from *ma*, "mother," and *musu*, "woman") feeds her customers and also teaches young Richmond girls to cook delicious and clean African food—not the unhealthy fried chicken of Southern cooking, but tasty onion-flavored greens and okra dishes; not oily cornmeal hush puppies, but the original African *akra,* balls made from the peppered flour of crushed black-eyed peas. We organized several of our early VFoM meetings at Mamusu's restaurant, until the space became too small for our membership. Then we held parties elsewhere, and ordered West African food and juices from Ida.

Another source of good West African food has been our friends in the African Community Network, an association of expatriates from various African countries. The chief organizers are Jean Bosco Mfogham from Cameroon and Abdoulaye Niang from Senegal, who became an alternative source of catered food when he and his wife started the Gorée restaurant and catering business. There are very few Malians in Richmond: Kakotan Sanogo, a businessman who used to work in biostatistics at VCU; Ibrahim Bah and Abdoulaye Coulibaly, who drive trucks and sometimes drive our Malian visitors; a small floating population of mechanics and hairdressers who have often moved on before we hear about their arrival in Richmond; and occasional students at VCU, for whom we have often supplied free accommodation when they first arrive. Liberians, Guineans, Ghanaians, and Nigerians are more numerous and better organized, but these groups have expressed little interest in us or our links to Mali.

Life is not all parties and dancing! In 2013, we worked with VCU to organize the Women, War & Peace Conference, which doubled as the VFoM's annual meeting. Eight hundred Richmond students attended our conference, giving Cheick Hamala a bigger audience than usual to play for. Sometimes we invite a guest speaker, often from another university; JMU, GMU, VUU, VCU, Virginia Tech, and the Embassy of Mali have all sent us exciting speakers. In 2007, in celebration of the fiftieth anniversary of Ghana's Independence, we invited JMU history professor David Owusu-Ansah, a distinguished Ghanaian, to talk about African independence. In 1957, Ghana became the first African country to take independence. Since we were then still a fairly small group, we held the Ghana AGM inside Mamusu's restaurant. But mostly our AGM is a celebration of Mali's national day, September 22, 1960, and we celebrate with Malian music.

Cheick Hamala has a number of music students in and around Richmond, so there are often Richmonders who play along with him. Tim Harding and his world music/jazz group Hotel X are regular partners of Cheick Hamala's band. Charles Kerwath is an enthusiastic Malian-trained guitarist who plays when Cheick Hamala comes to Richmond. Our biggest treat comes when his star ngoni pupil Seth Swingle (a.k.a. Waraden Diabaté) visits from Charlottesville, bringing his Bambara-speaking dad Craig (also known from his Peace Corps days as Waraba Doumbia). If Seth is playing with Cheick Hamala, the music takes first place in our annual meeting, and we do not waste too much time on speeches or financial reports (quickly done—whenever we get some money, we send it to Mali).

One year, we took out a group of Malian guests for a special American meal. There was no music, but we spent a great evening at Buz and Ned's, the best barbecue joint in Richmond. Malians normally love grilled meat. Our Muslim guests could not eat pork ribs, of course, but we ordered enough beef ribs and coleslaw for everyone to enjoy. More than enough, as it turned out! Some of our guests liked the meat: dry bones were piled up in front of their plates. Other Malians ate almost nothing. I was surprised. When I made inquiries, they said the barbecue sauce was too sweet for their tastes.

"I have learned something this evening," commented Dr. Sanogo, head of the Ségou hospital. "I have discovered that Americans like to eat their beef with sweet barbecue sauce, and this explains why there are so many obese Americans. In Mali, we like to eat our meat with salt, which explains why we have so many heart attacks."

After that experience, we went back to African food for Malian guests, cooking peanut stews or chicken *yassa* in our homes, or buying rice dishes from Richmond's Liberian, Senegalese, and Sudanese restaurants. These restaurant meals, as well as tasty chicken stews from the Iranian restaurant on West Broad Street, are popular with our guests, but much more expensive than home cooking.

Fig. 8. Our griot resident in Washington, DC, Cheick Hamala Diabaté, holding his ngoni. Cheick played at the Richmond Folk Festival from 2012–2017, as well as at the 2018 Ségou festival. Photo: Cheick Hamala Diabaté.

Music: Mali's Greatest Gift to America

In the beginning was the Word. It is the Word, *kuma* in the Manding languages, that distinguishes Man from other mammals. It is the Word that makes us who we are, not the fact that we walk on two legs instead of four, nor that we groom our hair and wash our bodies or take up simple tools such as a rock to break open nuts to eat, for other animals also do these things. No; it is speech that makes us human beings. Ultimately, it was the Word *kuma* that gave men magical power, allowing humans to create families and clans, villages, and towns.

With the gift of speech came the possibility of articulating needs, then wishes, then affections, and finally developing new thoughts and ideas and beliefs and philosophies. Without words, men are not men, women are not women, and babies cannot become children. The power of the Word is magical, and mystical and that power in West Africa belongs to the griots. The European word "griot" comes from a Portuguese word meaning "troubadour," but that is not what the griots are. The Malinké word *jeli* is close to the word for "blood," *jeli* or *djoli,* depending on the dialect. Griots are the lifeblood of culture, the historians and guardians of oral tradition, and it is through their words and music than the clans of the Mali Empire learn who they are and what their ancestors achieved.

The Mali Empire, one of Africa's great medieval kingdoms, was founded by Sunjata Keita, the original Lion King. Sunjata Keita's tutor and advisor and chief ambassador was Bala Fasé Kouyaté, the griot whose stories of Sunjata's prowess made the Lion King so famous that even Walt Disney couldn't ignore him. Kingship requires distance and reserve. An African king speaks softly to his griot, and the griot proclaims the word of the *mansa.* The king's griot is both a minister and spokesman. A king will give instructions to his griot, and the latter will depart on whatever diplomatic mission is required, be it to see a local troublemaker, to carry a message of approval, or to visit a distant ruler to negotiate peace—or war.

So griots are not mere singers—in fact, some never play music at all. The greatest griots are revered as saints, because they are also high initiates in the secret initiation societies of the *komo* and the *koré,* which gives them power of the word they exchange with the ancestral spirits who may intercede (if they will) with Ngai, the Creator. I have seen old women crawl forward to stroke the hem of the robe of the late Kela Bala Diabaté, head of the griot initiates of Kangaba, in the hope of being blessed by his touch, his presence, his spirituality.

In the beginning was the Word. Then came the Music. Music whispered through the reeds that rustle along the Nile River and the wind made music with leaves brushing together on trees that grew alongside streams, while cool water contributed a burbling, musical note that created harmonies and allowed Man to discover Music.

Probably the flute was the first musical instrument, for shepherds and goatherds heard the music of the reeds, and cut a reed to imitate the wind—and long before men had learned to raise domestic herds, ancient hunter-gatherers heard the music of the reeds and made their own musical imitations of wind and water. Then they tied twisted wheat or millet straw across a calabash and made the first one-stringed instrument, the precursor of the Fula *dili*, the Malian ngoni, the lute, the guitar, the banjo, ancestor of the multistringed *kora* of the Manding and the *sithar* of India and the European harp, and the distant ancestor of violins, violas, and cellos.

Yet even before music, there was rhythm. Music as we know it combines the notes that began with whistling reeds, and the rhythms that come from the sonority of the drum. Africa is a continent of rhythms. The drumbeat of the African soul is rooted in the rhythms of wood and trees and the thunder that echoes around the mountains of Ethiopia during a storm. The quintessential foundation of the African being is a sense of rhythm. Africa's rhythms infuse the music of America: original jazz, pop, rap, and hip hop are direct descendants of the rhythmic sonorities of Africa, while traditional or "trad" jazz, reggae, Cajun and soul, blues, bluegrass, and swing evolved from the harmonies built by the drums and strings and songs of West Africa and the griots, and then by the descendants of the griots in America. As Peter Szego writes in "Searching for the Roots of the Banjo," an article in the *Old-Time Herald* dedicated to old-time music, some black banjo players in the Deep South trace their musical heritage from their fathers unbroken to their great-great-great-grandfathers in Africa.[19]

It was the griots who took the Word, joined human speech to the rhythms of the drums and the *balafon* to the music of reed pipes and strings: the single string of the *dili bo* guitar from which jazz musician Bo Diddley took his stage name; the three or five strings of the ngoni—direct ancestor of the banjo; and the twenty-one strings of the *kora*, the West African harp which ripples like cool water running across pebbles. With these tools our griot ancestors created the songs and choruses and responses that form the basis of our human, ancient, musical tradition, the underpinning of culture. The special place of griots in West African society resides in their mastery of these essential gifts—elements that transformed a biped mammal into a human being.

---

19 Szego, Peter. "Searching fot the Roots of the Banjo." Old-Time Herald 10, no. 4 (April-May 2006): 14–23.

The magic of the Word belongs to the griots. To the magical power of speech, they add the poetry and the music that makes their magic unforgettable. The Word has the power to express love and hate, yet it becomes more magical still when it is transformed into song. The greatest poets of our modern era are the musicians: Bob Marley, Bob Dylan, Joan Baez, John Lennon are the poets whose words moved the twentieth century. Poetry, that supreme achievement of human development, was created in Africa, by the ancestors of modern griots.

Elegba and Omilade Promote the Memory of African Identity

Omilade Janine Bell, founder and artistic director of the Elegba Folklore Society (EFS), has done more than anyone else in Richmond to explain the West African origins of Virginia's African American population. When she came to live in Richmond, after a childhood of music and dance in North Carolina, Omilade was struck by the city's confusion over issues of race.

A visit to Richmond Public Schools is all it takes to see the truth of the data: the black population of Richmond lives with higher levels of poverty and lower levels of privilege that the white population. The Greater Richmond population in 2015 was 976,000, of whom only 218,000 lived in the City of Richmond. Richmond has been grow-ing blacker and poorer as middle-class and white families move to the wealthy counties of Chesterfield, Hanover, and Henrico. Far from happily integrating, Richmond's communities seem to be growing further apart. Poverty, like wealth, is inherited. So is the alienation imposed by slavery.

"Our people lost everything," says Omilade. "Coming to Amer-ica through the channel of slavery, we lost our names, our languages, our families, our identities, our religions and our spirituality . . . our roots. A new identity was imposed upon us. We became like a vase of cut flowers: they look beautiful when you first see them, but they are doomed to wither because they have been cut from their roots. Like plants, people cannot survive if they have no roots."

Omilade articulates the issues of African American society with eloquence. Back in the 1980s, she created her Ẹlẹgba Folklore Society as a "cultural bridge to Africa" to help heal Richmond's confusions. Researching African spirituality and culture, Omilade discovered that among the Yoruba people of Western Nigeria, Ẹlẹgba is the *orisa,* or intercessor, who brings clarity out of confusion. Other trickster spirits cause confusions, but Ẹlẹgba opens paths to solutions. Omilade is what sociologist Belinda Robnett calls a "bridge leader"—people (often women in the Civil Rights Movement) who bring different groups together behind the scenes, without demanding formal titles. The RSCC and Virginia Friends of Mali are two of the groups that have become partners of the EFS. Omilade has welcomed the Ségou delegations on several occasions to her cultural center with food, African music and Malinké dancing.

Richmond is still recovering from Jim Crow—the post-Civil War reimposition of white dominance through unjust laws. In Richmond, the civil rights struggles were led by the lawyers Oliver Hill and Spottswood Robinson, sometime partners of future Supreme Court Justice Thurgood Marshall, at the time when he led the legal division of the NAACP. They finally persuaded the United States Supreme Court to destroy the pernicious doctrine of "separate but equal" that condemned the African American community to inferior schools and other facilities. Professor Shawn Utsey, a psychologist who leads VCU's department of Afrikana Studies, says from his own childhood experience: "To be born a black male in America is to be born with a huge burden that weighs you down from the very beginning."

Shawn, of course, has achieved huge professional success, although much of Richmond's black population remains mired in poverty. Shawn works with urban youths, to help them find paths toward personal progress. Black descendants of Virginia's savage past carry not only the burden of their slave history, but also scars from the Civil Rights struggle in Virginia, the home of "massive resistance" to integrated schools, which led to the famous *Brown* decisions of 1954 and 1955:

The *Brown* decision of 1954 was actually a judgment in five different lawsuits that had been consolidated because the principle to be decided was the same—the constitutionality of laws establishing separate schools for whites and blacks. One of the five lawsuits came from Virginia—*Davis* v. *Prince Edward County, Virginia.* On April 23, 1951, sixteen-year-old Barbara Johns led a student strike against inadequate facilities at grossly overcrowded Robert Russa Moton High School in Farmville, where science classes lacked even a single microscope. The NAACP took the case, only when the students—by a one vote margin—agreed to seek an integrated school rather than improved conditions at their black school. Then, Howard University-trained attorneys Spottswood Robinson and Oliver Hill filed suit.

A state court rejected the suit, agreeing with defense attorney T. Justin Moore that Virginia was vigorously equalizing black and white schools. The verdict was appealed to the U.S. Supreme Court . . . . On May 17, 1954, the U.S. Supreme Court unanimously declared that "in the field of public education the doctrine of 'Separate but equal' has no place." [. . .] *Brown* II, issued in 1955, decreed that the dismantling of separate school systems for blacks and whites could proceed with "all deliberate speed," a phrase that pleased neither supporters or opponents of integration. Unintentionally, it opened the way for various strategies of resistance to the decision.

In 1954, the political organization of US senator Harry F. Byrd, Sr., controlled Virginia politics. Senator Byrd promoted the "Southern Manifesto" opposing integrated schools, which was signed in 1956 by more than one hundred southern congressmen. On February 25, 1956, he called for what became known as Massive Resistance. This was a group of laws, passed in 1956, intended to prevent integration of the schools. [. . .] The linchpin of Massive Resistance was a law that cut off state funds and closed any public school that attempted to integrate. In September 1958 several schools in Warren County, Charlottesville, and Norfolk were about to integrate under court order. They were seized and closed, but the Virginia Supreme Court of Appeals overturned the school-closing law. Simultaneously, a federal court issued a verdict against the law based on the "equal protection" clause of the 14th Amendment. Speaking to the General Assembly a few weeks later, Gov. J. Lindsay Almond conceded defeat. Beginning on February 2, 1959, a few courageous black students integrated the schools that had been closed.[20]

This is the harsh legacy that Omilade tries to address through the cultural and spiritual programs of her Ẹlẹgba Folklore Society. She herself was baptized Janine, a name she chose to complete with the African name Omilade. She offers road-opening experiences, as African Americans—and American Africans—discover that they are descended not from 150 years of enslavement, but from 40,000 years of survival and success on the African mother continent. The Lion King and the Mali Empire are a part of their history. Their inheritance is not only the sociopolitical struggles of America, but also the creativity and spirituality of their African Ancestors. The Ẹlẹgba Folklore Society, "Richmond's cultural ambassador," brings to America's schools and festivals the West African culture and dance traditions that help students to embrace the Spirit! Omilade's website proclaims, "Together, let's explore the richness of Mother Africa's gifts to us through interactive artistic, cultural experiences. Her influences are many. Come with your family. Let's learn, let's affirm, let's enjoy."[21]

While Ẹlẹgba is the messenger god of Yoruba tradition in modern Nigeria, the spectacular drummers and dances presented by the EFS derive from the Manding cultures—from the lands of the Mali Empire.

20 *Quoted with the kind permission of the Virginia Historical Society from http://www.vahistorical.org/collections-and-resources/virginia-history-explorer/civil-rights-movement-virginia/massive.*

21 *To contact the Ẹlẹgba Folklore Society, visit http://efsinc.org/, or call 804.644.3900.*

Our Manding griot friend Cheick Hamala Diabaté is a regular visitor not just to VFoM and the Richmond Folk Festival, but also to the EFS, where he is a cherished partner in Omilade's work. She is convinced that African Americans will feel more rooted in themselves and in their history when they realize they are proud descendants of great African civilizations like Mali and Yoruba. "There is a lack of knowledge in the community," says Omilade. "When we teach, we are careful to start the story in Africa." Africa and America are related: today's colonial frontiers have imposed artificial barriers on Africa that the ancestors would not recognize.

Back in 1993, a new initiative began in RVA called Hope in the Cities, which organized a conference to launch their work of bringing people together. Their Facebook page says: "For nearly 20 years, Hope in the Cities has supported citizens working to build more just and inclusive communities by creating conditions of trust where people of different racial and social backgrounds, or divergent political or religious views, are empowered to speak honestly about their experiences and find common interests where once there were divides."[22]

Omilade led conference participants on a walk along the "Trail of Enslaved Africans," starting from Ancarrow's Landing in Manchester, a former independent city across the river from what was then Richmond on the north shore of the James, and that used to be the bigger trading center. Everyone placed their hand on the shoulder of the person in front and walked with their eyes shut—emphasizing the powerlessness of the newly enslaved people who had just been pulled off a small, stinking, wooden ship that had brought them, tossed and chained together on the ocean for six weeks. Omilade led them across the river on foot and through the slave market area of Shockoe Bottom, where thousands of slaves were imprisoned, abused and sold. Not for nothing was this area known to Africans as "the Devil's Half-Acre."

The City of Richmond picked up Omilade's initiative, and created a commission to develop awareness of the slavery heritage, under the leadership of city councilman Saad Al-Amin. Omilade became

---

22 See https://www.facebook.com/hopeinthecities/about/.

vice chair. The commission is chaired currently by Delegate Delores McQuinn, who has leveraged new resources from Virginia's General Assembly. Hope in the City still organizes an annual Anniversary Walk along what is now called "Richmond's Historic Slave Trail"— enriched since the 1990s by historical markers; by the Reconciliation Monument that stands near Main Street Station as one of three statues placed at the apexes of the Triangular Trade (the others are in Liverpool and Benin); by archeological discoveries at Lumpkin's Jail, just one of twenty slave jails that existed in Shockoe Bottom; and by deeper awareness and historical research that has revealed, among other things, the site of Richmond's eighteenth-century African cemetery.

"We need to decide what Richmond should do with this precious history," says Omilade. "You do not want to trivialize the story, by thinking we already know what the story is. You want to make it the biggest story you can make. You think you know about Lumpkin's jail; but who was Mary Ann Lumpkin? What do we know about her? You have to allow the research to lead the decisions, not the presuppositions."

She puts her finger neatly on the fact that most of the plans for Shockoe Bottom have been promoted by men—especially the absurd idea that City money should subsidize the building of a baseball stadium bang in the middle of the city, stretching across the center of late eighteenth-century Richmond in a zone notorious for flooding. If historic Shockoe Bottom could become the "Ellis Island" of African American history, it would bring huge income to the city. Richmond needs to establish a community conversation, where women obtain an equal space and where short-term corporate interests are offset by vital cultural, historical, educational, and community interests.

"It is ironic to think," says Omilade, "how many times I drove through Richmond on Interstate 95, traveling to Washington, DC, as a student from Chapel Hill in North Carolina . . . driving through the slave markets of Shockoe Bottom without knowing their history, crossing the Sacred Ground where our African ancestors lie buried, without knowing that it was a cemetery. Then one day, I turned off and discovered Richmond. I believe the African presence drew me off the Interstate. And I accepted the assignment."

Fig. 9. Dances of the Manding, presented by the Elegba Folklore Society of Richmond. Photo: Elegba Folklore Society. Used with permission.

Elizabeth Kambourian's Historical Research in Richmond

Elizabeth Cann Kambourian came to Richmond because her Armenian brother was in business here. After undergraduate studies at VCU, she became interested in Richmond history after she and her family bought a house in 1974 that included a title search from 1918, tracing her plot of land back to 1745. Out of curiosity Kambourian went to the Henrico County records one day, and found a plan of the Quincy Plantation that included her own plot. Describing her history adventure, she told reporter Aram Arkun, of Richmond's *Mirror Spectator* in December 2011 that, while in college, she had skipped American history . . . but it caught up with her! "I knew already that a slave rebellion had taken place in this neighborhood. I thought that surely my house would have had participants, since it was adjacent to two other plantations where slaves participated. And I did find a slave,

George Smith, who was involved. He was a conjurer. It was fascinating."

The slave rebellion, called the Gabriel rebellion after its leader, was planned for the summer of 1800. Kambourian's research led her to locate the gallows where Gabriel was hanged, along with his fellow conspirators. They were buried in a nearby site that was now a parking lot on Broad Street. On a Richmond map dated 1807, she found this plot described as "Negro Burial Ground." No one in Richmond was very interested in Elizabeth's discovery, until she gave a lecture in the Black History Museum and Cultural Center in Jackson Ward. The *Richmond Defender,* a newspaper published by the Defenders for Freedom, Justice, and Equality, began to cite her discoveries, and "The Defenders" then led a struggle to memorialize the burial ground. VFoM became involved; Mali's prime minister raised the matter with Governor Mark Warner during his visit on November 5, 2005; and later, after the parking lot had been transferred to VCU ownership, Ousmane Simaga, the new mayor of Ségou, wrote to VCU's president, Dr. Michael Rao, in support of reconsecrating the Sacred Ground in which Richmond's Malian ancestors lie buried.

Elizabeth Kambourian's historical research identified where the Sacred Ground lies, and she also revealed the full extent of Richmond's Shockoe Bottom slave industry—including the locations of as many as twenty slave jails. The infamous "Devil's Half-Acre" (Lumpkin's Jail) has been excavated as an archaeological site, but the history of early Richmond and of Shockoe Bottom (where the Shockoe stream flows into the James River; only these days, it flows through an underground concrete pipe) are mostly hidden beneath asphalt parking lots and ugly storage buildings of no commercial or aesthetic value.

There is a potential here, which greedy developers are keen to cash in on. The previous mayor of Richmond, Dwight Jones, proposed using subsidies from the city council to build a baseball stadium in the middle of the city, with no obvious road access, no easy parking, and in a zone that is so liable to flooding that the stadium might have been unusable. The triple hidden agenda seems to have been to make millions from demolishing the existing baseball stadium beside I-95, building and selling luxury apartments, and wiping Richmond's slave history from the city map—all with guaranteed public funds that would remove risk from the developers and make them rich. When they used Kambourian's map as a part of their argument, she objected, and became active in the movement to "Stop the Ballpark in Shockoe Bottom."

This public scandal has been blocked, at least temporarily, thanks to the awakening of furious Richmond citizens demanding a "public conversation" about the future of Shockoe Bottom: an area that has untold spiritual, historical, archeological, educational and tourism potential. Developing the historical story of Shockoe Bottom could enrich Richmonders in multiple ways—including financially. Using such a resource could turn VCU into America's center for African and early African American research.

In 2004, the Sacred Ground Project established a state historical marker at the corner of Fifteenth and Broad Streets to mark the site where the burial ground lies. The marker states that this was the place where, on October 10, 1800, the great slave rebellion leader Gabriel was executed for the capital offense of fighting for freedom. Gabriel's slogan was "Liberty or Death"—recalling similar words used by Patrick Henry in the famous speech he delivered in Saint John's Church in Richmond, on March 23, 1775, arguing for American independence from Britain.

Thanks to Kambourian's research, Gabriel's death was commemorated in 2002 by a resolution of the City of Richmond, and in 2006, Governor Tim Kaine pardoned Gabriel and his collaborators in recognition of their struggle to end slavery and promote equality for all people. To quote Richmond historian and photographer Jeffrey Ruggles, "The Burial Ground for Negroes is probably the oldest site in Richmond, Virginia with a specific African-American association. In use from the 1700s to about 1815, it is overlooked by the standard city histories and was largely forgotten until recently.[23] Now the Burial Ground has become a matter of public discussion."

Fair Trade, Village Cooperatives, and Ten Thousand Villages

One of the most interesting organizations in Richmond is Ten Thousand Villages, part of a fair-trade chain with 140 stores across America. Fair trade supports producers, reducing the "cut" of the middlemen: so that a cocoa farmer, for example, gets more than 2 percent of the retail price of a chocolate bar. There are many beautiful gifts on sale in the Richmond store, all of which come from cooperatives in Asia, Africa, and Latin America. These cooperatives all respect strict ethical standards that include sharing profits, ensuring equality between men and women, and never employing child labor. If Ségou craftsmen and women were able to sell their goods through 140 stores in America, they might make a lot of money.

In 2003, Ten Thousand Villages hosted an Oxfam visitor from Mali. Monsieur Traoré was a cotton farmer from the southern region of Koulikoro. He was aware of the tragic nineteenth-century stories of Africans picking cotton in America; but he and his village were beneficiaries of a very successful, twenty-five-year-long USAID project to develop the economy of the Upper Niger Valley in Mali. The US government had paid for roads and improved cotton cropping systems, introduced maize and turned this corn crop into a new Malian staple food, provided functional literacy and built up cooperatives, and generally helped transform the region into a prosperous agricultural zone, proving that US aid can achieve good results when it lasts for twenty-five years—which is the real length of a project cycle in rural Africa.

Our Oxfam visitor, Monsieur Boubacar Traoré, was about forty-five years old. He described the economic success of his village, which I had once visited when I worked for USAID in Mali. Their

---

23_The city of Richmond proper was not "created" until 1747, yet English immigrants had farmed here for one hundred years: the "first Thanksgiving" took place on Berkeley Plantation in 1619. Many Malian ancestors were probably buried beside the Shockoe stream during the 1600s *(see* http://www.scribd.com/doc/42051809/Burial-Ground-Ruggles-12-09).

cooperative is now run by people of Boubacar's age group, who had learned the skills of reading and writing and basic accountancy in their Bambara language. The community Elders, both men and women, had agreed to share economic decision-making with Monsieur Traoré's age group; the Elders were promoted to the role of "advisors," and the gerontocracy no longer held back the community from trying new ideas. Cooperative marketing of cotton had improved both quality control, and prices. The community had built their own school, which in 2002 had six classrooms and six teachers, all paid by the village.

Cotton is Mali's biggest export crop. Malians call it their "white gold," and they grow it for personal profit—not for slave owners in the New World, as was the destiny of their unlucky cousins in America and the Caribbean. But in the fall of 2002, just when they were about to bring in the biggest and most profitable cotton harvest in their history, the villagers learned that President George W. Bush in faraway America had just signed something called a "Farm Bill" that awarded huge subsidies to American cotton farmers. The price of cotton fell 50 percent overnight. Mali and America are part of the same world market for cotton; when US cotton prices fall, so does the world price. Instead of a healthy profit from a bumper crop, Monsieur Traoré (speaking in French with a translator) told us that his cooperative had made a big loss on their 2002 cotton harvest. They had already paid for and used their seeds, fertilizers, and pesticides, all priced in US dollars and imported from the world market. The sales value of their record cotton harvest was now less than the cost of the inputs. Cotton farmers in Ségou region suffered the same financial losses that year.

Monsieur Traoré's community was forced to fire three of their teachers, causing class sizes to increase to seventy students per class. With one stroke of his pen, President Bush erased twenty-five years of hard work and development, destroyed the positive results of a successful USAID agricultural program, ruined millions of villagers, and halved Mali's national dollar earnings from cotton, its biggest export crop. And that was the damage done in only one country!

After the meeting with Monsieur Traoré, we had a conversation with Karin Taylor, the manager of Ten Thousand Villages. I told her about the Mali SOL and about our Teaching Timbuktu campaign. Later, when we started the Richmond Sister City Commission, I suggested that she might like to become a commissioner and support our work in Ségou. What could be better, I thought, than offering the artisans of Ségou the chance to sell their products through Ten Thousand Villages? Allan and I went to visit Karin, who told us that five of the American stores were located in Virginia. Even selling crafts through the Richmond store would be a great start, and Karin had the option to seek her own sources for up to 10 percent of her products, with the rest coming from central buying.

It turns out, however, that organizing artisans is difficult. Getting them sufficiently organized to work with American retail outlets is even more complex, especially if they have to comply with the fair-trade or *commerce équitable* concept, which requires certification about gender equality (difficult if you are running a women's cooperative with no men, or vice versa!), no use of children (which may not seem very sensible to Africans running a family business), fair sharing of profits, absence of commercial intermediaries, and a number of other constraints. The rules are not difficult to respect, but they require close cooperation and complex certification. Filling out printed forms is tricky for artisans who may not speak French or English, may not be very good at reading, and may not have access to a computer or the internet. From the floor of a craft workshop in Mali, fair trade seems like an American bureaucratic nightmare.

On numerous occasions, we have discussed the fair-trade opportunity with artisans in Ségou. Some of them claim familiarity with *commerce équitable*, . . . but not one of them has ever come back to say they want us to help them follow up with the idea. Perhaps it is not for them. Or maybe we are sowing seeds, and they will grow to blossom in the future.

Inside Ten Thousand Villages in Richmond, Karin Taylor introduced us to her deputy manager, Amber, who had previously worked in Cameroon and who speaks French. We were excited! Amber had all the skills needed to help a Ségou cooperative get online, fill out the forms, and qualify for fair-trade exports. We discussed the possibility of Amber traveling to Ségou to discuss fair trade with the artisans. But VFoM would have to find the money to pay for her travel. We would need to hear a great deal more enthusiasm from the artisans than we have yet found. So here is one of many small sister city initiatives that is stillborn . . . at least for now!

2006- 2007

Teaching Timbuktu to Virginia

Teaching Timbuktu to Virginia

Teaching Timbuktu to Seven-Year-Olds

In the 1990s, Virginian children learned about ancient Egypt, ancient Greece, and ancient Rome, and heard plenty about King Henry VIII of England and his six wives. A well-known rhyme describes the fate of each: "Divorced, beheaded, died, divorced, beheaded, survived." Only the sixth wife survived marriage to King Henry. Virginia was named after Henry VIII's daughter Elisabeth I, the Virgin Queen. Her mother was Anne Boleyn, Henry's beheaded Queen Number Two.

Such stories from European history are highly entertaining—but a number of Virginia's teachers felt that students descended from African cultures also needed to learn about the African motherland whence their ancestors came. They wanted to create a curriculum about West Africa.

One of these innovators was Ms. Thelma Williams-Tunstall, a social studies and history teacher. At the turn of the millennium, a state commission of educators recommended that students should study the Empire of Mali, as many Virginians have Malian ancestors. Thelma was a key member of this commission, and her triumph came when a Standard of Learning (SOL) on the Mali-Sonrai Empire was established for Virginia's elementary schools. By the time I arrived in Richmond, Thelma had become the specialist advisor for Richmond Public Schools, supervising teachers of history and social studies. She was certainly surprised to receive me one day in her office in Richmond's city hall, offering free teaching for third and sixth graders and their teachers as an expert on Mali.

Soon after my meeting with Thelma, I received an email from a teacher in Fairfax County, Melanie Stanley, who was writing a book on Mali for the new SOL. Melanie was a distinguished writer for children, but she had never visited Mali. Would I read her text and correct any errors? I was happy to correct and enrich her text, suggesting a few stories only I could know. The resulting book, *Mali: Today and Long Ago*, published in 2003, is excellent.

One day in 2003, I received an email that Melanie was visiting Richmond. We met in the Virginia Historical Society, and Melanie had a shock: she was expecting to meet a black woman called Robin, but she found a man with gray skin and gray beard! Thereafter, I decided to call myself "Robin Edward Poulton" in Virginia, to warn Americans that I have blotchy pinkish skin and a white beard.

In the fall of 2003, Thelma invited me to speak at her annual Conference of Social Science Teachers from Richmond Public Schools. This was a great honor. I was not sure how my enthusiasm would go down: how would three hundred Richmond teachers react to a white man from West Africa wearing African robes, telling African Americans about the glorious history of Mali and suggesting techniques for teaching Mali in their classrooms? But I need not have worried; half a dozen teachers came down to the front at the end of the session to thank me and shake my hand. One teacher threw his arms around me and said that I was doing exactly what was needed to make people understand the African motherland. I felt wonderful! It takes only one person saying something so warm and encouraging to give you energy and confidence for another five or ten years.

Within a few weeks, still dressed in magnificent Malian robes, I was entertaining seven-year-olds in Richmond's public schools with stories about the Lion King and Mali. "In the Bambara language," I cried, "'Mali' means 'hippopotamus,' so Mali is named after the *biggest* and *fattest* and *strongest* animal in the Niger River. Waaah!" At this point in my narrative, a picture of a huge hippo would flash onto the screen, its mouth agape with huge, dirty teeth, menacing the audience of children whose own mouths were also wide open with amazement.

I made the students laugh with tales of cows and elephants eating lettuces and cabbages in Malian women's vegetable gardens—not something that Malian farmers find amusing! I told stories of lion hunting, and the children gasped. I explained that lions are the totem of the royal Keita clan; the Keita do not hunt lions, and they claim that lions never eat livestock belonging to a member of their clan. I had the students chant in unison the name "Sunjata Keita, Sunjata Keita, Sunjata Keita," so that they could speak the musical Manding language and hear equally accented syllables in their own heads; I wanted to challenge the American tendency to overaccentuate just one syllable—usually the second—at the expense of the others.[24]

The learning did not stop at stories. We explored the foods from Mali that have found a place in Virginian cooking: okra and gumbo, fried chicken and donut holes, peanut butter and peanut stew, and hush puppies inspired by *akra* from Mali. We also examined other ways Malian culture has influenced life in the South, effecting such practices as building porches, lying in hammocks, venerating grandmothers, drinking Coke, and playing great music. Especially the music!

Music is so important in Africa that I developed a separate lesson plan for teaching African rhythms to students. For this lesson, I ask that each child bring a stick and a box. For the box, students may substitute plastic buckets, but nothing metallic, for this would immediately change the sound from African to Caribbean. I sit in lotus position on the floor, in a circle with the cross-legged students so we are all on the same level, and together, we beat out a one-two, one-two, *tam-tam, tam-tam* rhythm on our boxes. Then we try a new rhythm: *tam, tam-tam; tam, tam-tam; tam, tam-tam*. Next, we create a third, more complicated rhythm: *tam-tam, tam-tam-tam; tam-tam, tam-tam-tam.*

---

24 *I have met Virginians whose pronunciation of "Mali" is so distorted that they sound like they are talking about Malays from Malaysia, on the other side of the globe. In "Mali," the first syllable is accentuated.*

Having discovered three different rhythms, we now divide the class into three, and try playing the three together, at the same time. This creates a polyrhythm, which is the sort of thing you hear when the Mandingo drummers get going on their *djembé* drums.

This is the moment when I put on a CD and allow the students to listen to African rhythms, which are often played on several different drums at once. Some students are able to pick out different drumbeats underlying the music of famous Malian musicians, like Salif Keita or Vieux Farka Touré, and I encourage them to play along with what they hear. Not being a musician myself, I often find students who can hear more detail than I can, as they listen to "the drumbeat of the African soul."

Finally, I try to teach the students to follow the rhythms with their bodies. African nomads play and dance while seated under the shade of their tents to avoid the sun, so dancing while sitting is an art form of Northern Mali. While they are still seated like Tuareg nomads in their tents, my young American students try to dance with their arms and shoulders. Americans often confuse their shoulders with their elbows; young white men especially seem to think that pumping their fists and knees up and down is a form of dance. When you move your shoulders, however, you are dancing with your whole upper body. Africans dance with their whole bodies. Sometimes their knees sway and their feet barely move. At other times, their feet and legs move with frenetic speed, but their whole body is involved in dance.

I play the music of the late Ali Farka Touré, telling the students to listen for the rhythms of a camel caravan in his album *Niafunké*, and to move their arms and shoulders in imitation of a camel plodding across hot desert sands. Sometimes they ask me if this is blues. I always repeat the words of my old friend Ali, who won two Grammy Awards for his guitar magic: "Americans call me the Blues Man of Africa. But I do not play the blues. I play the music of my region. I play the music of Niafunké and Timbuktu. That is where the blues came from. My people brought the blues to America."

Taking Timbuktu to Newport News and Harrisonburg

I began teaching about Mali by emptying the contents of my sitting room into museums and libraries and schools. I cannot remember how I contacted them all, but within six years, the founders of VFoM had recorded twenty-five thousand students and teachers and parents passing through more than a dozen exhibitions, enjoying my collection of mats and hats: especially the great round Fulani cow herders' hats. These "cowboy hats" have a diameter of two or three feet, and they really keep the Sahara sun off a man's face and shoulders. Naturally, museum exhibits must not be touched; but when I was giving tours of the Mali exhibits, I would unhook the hats from the wall (after all, they were my hats!) and place them on the heads of the children I was entertaining.

To adults I would explain how the straw and leather design of the Fulani hat mirrors the shape of a woman's breast—illustrating the importance of milk in the Fulani creation myth. I confess that I took secret pleasure from the embarrassment of certain prudish American adults who reacted as if no one had ever told them that women have breasts, or that breasts produce milk! I like to show teachers how the different colors on the hat's brim represent the periods of the year when Fulani cattle are grazing the savannah (brown) or crossing the river to feed on the rich *bourgou* grasses (green) left behind as the Niger River floods recede every year from December onward. The sight of cattle swimming across a branch of the Niger River is unforgettable. One time in the region of Timbuktu, when traveling in a canoe visiting rice fields, we turned back to save a couple of young steers that were nearly drowning, pulling them by their ears toward the shore. One calf was reckoned too far gone, so the herders decided to cut its throat and feast on grilled meat. Their blade was so dull that I produced my Swiss pocketknife. Thanks to my trusty blade, the calf had a quick end. Their rusty blade was then used to cut up the meat and hack off the hide.

After the hats, schoolgirls are always drawn to our jewelry exhibit, while the boys' eyes fixate on the knives. Both sexes are interested in the jagged lumps of rock salt draped with delicate gold necklaces. From their class teachers, third graders learn that in Mali during the 1300s, desert salt and forest gold were traded at equal weights; in those days, salt was literally "worth its weight in gold"—gold that went via the camel caravans to Morocco and on to Europe. Two-thirds of medieval Europe's gold came from Mali. That is why "Timbuktu" became a mystical name synonymous with wealth and distance—the unattainable city of gold beyond the vast, sandy ocean of the Sahara.

Third graders know that Timbuktu was a great city of Muslim scholars, with a great medieval university situated on the edge of the Sahara Desert. They learn that Mansa Musa, the grand-nephew of Mansa Sunjata, built a great mud-brick mosque there in 1326, which is still Timbuktu's main Friday mosque today. They know that Timbuktu is the capital of North Mali. Many of their parents, on the other hand, think that Timbuktu is near Kalamazoo, in Michigan.

At our exhibit, children learned that gold was exchanged for salt dug from ocean deposits deep under the sand of the Sahara and carried to Timbuktu, because Malians needed salt for cooking and for preserving fish. Salt is also important for health reasons in this hot country, where it is in short supply. These days, salt comes into Mali by train from Senegal, and Timbuktu's trade in rock salt has been reduced to a few dozen camel caravans each year. Unfortunately, unlike the salt deposits under the desert, left from when the Sahara was an ocean three hundred million years ago, the salt pans of Kaolack in Senegal are lacking in iodine. Iodine is important for health, and Mali's soils contain very little. As a result, many Malians develop thyroid problems and goiters, and children born with severe iodine deficiency may be deformed or have attendant mental development issues.

One of the children in my household in Bamako developed a goiter around the age of twelve. I purchased iodized salt for her mother to use, and within one year, the swelling had vanished. Now I am constantly reminding her to buy iodized salt for home use, to ensure that her own children do not develop a goiter.

The very first Mali exhibit we organized was in the community center at McLean, Northern Virginia, where the exhibitions curator Deborah McLeod put together a wonderful combination of paintings, ceramics, sculptures, and photographs of Mali. Huge oil paintings of desert figures by Fousseiny Kelly of Timbuktu provided a backdrop to Mali-inspired sculptures by American artists, including a great metallic model of a characteristic Dogon meeting house: the *toguna,* which is built intentionally low so that you have to crawl into its shade to rest and take part in community discussions. That way, any Elder who loses his temper in a discussion will hit his head on the beams when he tries to stand up! The exhibition detail came from Baba Wagué Diakité's stunning ceramics, many of them tiles used as illustrations for his colorful children's books. I provided a photo exhibit of Tuaregs on camels witnessing the burning of rebel weapons at the Peace of Timbuktu in 1996, as well as a selection of Malian fabrics and leatherwork (and the hats, of course—always the hats!).

Later we held two important exhibits in the Peninsula Fine Arts Center in Newport News, where thousands of schoolchildren came to see the hats and jewels and Tuareg knives—as well as household and kitchen equipment such as wooden spoons, stirrers, brooms, buckets made from recycled rubber tires, and wooden pestles and mortars for producing flour or grinding herbs. We keep the knives and jewelry in locked glass cabinets, of course; but young kids need to be able to touch and feel and smell things. That is why I insisted upon reserving a corner where the children could roll around on a leather carpet of antelope hide, stroke the antelope fur, and bury their faces in dark blue fabrics to inhale the bewitching scent of the sweet-smelling indigo plant that has provided their color. West Africa is famous for its fabulous clothing and woven blankets, and we dressed up tailor's dummies to show off elegant embroidered Malian robes and dyed fabrics.

The success of the Mclean and Newport News exhibits encouraged us to move forward with a mass of smaller exhibits in Richmond schools and an exciting exhibit featuring musical instruments at James Madison University in Harrisonburg, which coincided with the inauguration of museum curator Dr. Kathleen Monger's new exhibition galleries. Our Malian and American drummers entertained a thousand JMU students on the university lawns during their lunch break. But it was the two major exhibitions at the Richmond Public Library that really set us up with Virginia's schools, and also with the Embassy of Mali in Washington, DC. We invited the Malian ambassador to open the first exhibit in 2005, which also happened also to be the first big event for Richmond's new librarian, Ms. Harriet Henderson.

The Richmond Public Library and Ambassador Abdoulaye Diop

Kelly Kyle is a lovely woman, and was, before her retirement, a generous bookseller. I used to buy Malian books from her store on Richmond's Kensington Avenue. Kelly supported our teaching program on Mali. As a generous Friend of Mali and president of the Friends of Richmond Public Library, Kelly proposed a Teaching Timbuktu exhibition for the library.

We went to First Street in Richmond to visit the library building, which hides its elegant art deco foundations behind ugly, Soviet-inspired cement frontage imposed upon it in the 1950s. Beside the children's section is a noble marble court, and here RPL exhibitions expert Sharon Fuller mounted our 2005 exhibit on a theme of four corners: one corner was for music and featured instruments to look at, drums to bang on, and a music tape to listen to and enjoy; one had a leather carpet and cushions for kids to lounge on; Timbuktu Corner featured decorated camel hides, clothing, and a camel saddle stool for the kids to ride beneath a magnificent, colorful woven Fulani wedding blanket that hung down from the balcony above; and the fourth corner featured a Malian kitchen. To help recreate the kitchen, I added some wooden Sonrai kitchen utensils around a cooking hearth composed of three stones and three pieces of wood (but no fire!). To complete the recreation, I drove to my wife's office and borrowed the colossal red wood Malinké pestle and mortar, made of African mahogany (also known as *bois rouge* or *kaya senegalensis*), that I had given her for one of her birthdays. The piece was too heavy for her slender arms, but it served as a powerful reminder of women's work in Africa, where the act of cooking often begins with the difficult task of grinding cereals.

I read stories to children on the leather carpet. I also visited every one of the nine city branch libraries to read storybooks to Richmond's children, using well-known books written and illustrated by Baba Wagué Diakité, a talented Malian artist and storyteller who married an American and lives in Oregon. My renditions of his stories *The Hunterman and the Crocodile* and *The Hat-Seller and the Monkeys* keep small children spellbound. I even enjoy hearing myself acting out these stories!

The highlight of the Richmond Public Library exhibit, however, were the storyboards we borrowed from the 2003 Smithsonian's Mali Folk Life Festival on Washington's National Mall. I called my friend John Franklin, the Folk Life organizer, who told me he had passed them on to Howard University's Department of Architecture. Dr. Victor Dzi agreed to loan them to us for two months. I had to hire a van big enough to transport them from (and back to) Washington, DC. Along with the classy design work from Sharon Fuller, the size and professionalism of the Smithsonian's photographic storyboards made the RPL exhibit exceptional. The square marble court looked so wonderful, we decided to invite the Malian ambassador to come down and inaugurate the exhibition on the first Friday of October 2005. We did not know him, and he did not know us, but he agreed at once.

It is fascinating to watch children at an exhibition that you yourself have created. I consider our Teaching Timbuktu exhibits gender-neutral, but as might be expected, the boys all stopped to stare at the Tuareg knives. The girls moved on to the jewelry, showing medieval trade beads of imported Italian glass and Russian amber, local Malian clay, seeds, and fishbones. We even showed a necklace of stone beads dating back some five thousand years, loaned to us by the Yorktown bead collector Anne Cipriano; and other valuable beads from Barbara Pringle, a founder of the Washington Bead Museum. Teachers leading their groups of students emphasized the (locked) exhibit cabinet containing salt and gold: the lumps of rock salt sat with gold rings and a gold necklace, illustrating the famous trade that made Timbuktu wealthy, exchanging desert salt for the forest gold that was carried up the Niger River from Mali's secret imperial gold mines in the southern forests. When you hold a small lump of salt and a handful of gold rings, it is difficult to believe that these two commodities once traded weight for weight. How values change!

But the boys kept coming back to stare at the Tuareg knives, gaping at their elegant leatherwork and incised steel blades kept safely under locked glass. Once, many years ago, before Toyota took over the vehicle market in West Africa, a Tuareg blacksmith in Timbuktu tried to sell me a Tuareg sword on the basis of the excellent quality of its steel. "It is the very best," he cried, "made from the steel springs of a Land Rover."

His Excellency Abdoulaye Diop turned out to be very tall, very elegant, and very charming. He charmed all the women. He charmed all the men. He was delighted to discover, just two hours from his embassy, a small group of enthusiastic supporters of Mali. In the car that evening, driving homeward to his historic residence on 'R' Street (the house where F.D. and Eleanor Roosevelt lived before he was elected president), Diop reflected on how he could take advantage of Richmond to promote Mali. Four weeks later, he brought us the prime minister, the US Secret Service, and an invitation for Richmond to become the sister city of Ségou.

Mali's Prime Minister Meets Richmond Third Graders

Prime ministers mostly visit America for trade talks and financial meetings. Ambassador Diop wanted to end the PM's week of finance with a spiritual adventure. "I would like to bring Prime Minister Ousmane Issoufi Maiga to Richmond, to see your Mali exhibit and to meet Virginian children who are learning about Mali."

A prime ministerial visit takes a lot of arranging. I asked my wife: "Where shall I take him for lunch? There will be twenty or twenty-five people in the Malian delegation, and the embassy will pay." Michelle looked at me in amazement. "The prime minister? You have to take him to the Jefferson Hotel, of course, which is the most beautiful building in Richmond."

Umar Kenyatta agreed. This African American teacher at Richmond's Nubian Village Academy had become my friend after a lecture I had given about the Malian heritage. He came down to the front of the lecture hall and told me, "Robin, you are changing the African paradigm for Richmond. It is wonderful." Such encouragement to a white West African new to Virginia was especially valued coming from a senior African American citizen. Umar would become the founding vice president of VFoM, invested especially in the Malian and Muslim heritage of Virginia's ancestors. Many slaves were Muslims who were denied the chance to practice their religion when they reached America. Umar had returned to the Muslim faith, wanting to correct the course of history. "Michelle is right," Umar told me. "The Jefferson Hotel is the place for a prime minister."

The Secret Service called me. They approved of the Jefferson, because its security system is good. The PM approved too. He had his photo taken beside the statue of Thomas Jefferson in the Palm Court lobby, beneath a colorful domed window. Our party then swept down the grand staircase (claimed by Richmonders to be the centerpiece of a famous scene in the Civil War film *Gone with the Wind*) into the magnificent Rotunda Library, with its rich marble columns and leather sofas. The Jefferson Hotel was built in 1895 to be Virginia's premier five-star hotel, and it still is.

Le Maire's dining room is named after Thomas Jefferson's French chef, and he would be proud of its cuisine. We sat at round tables. I placed Thelma Williams-Tunstell and Umar Kenyatta beside the PM, with Ambassador Diop and the ministers of investment and agriculture (a Thiam and a Traoré) who were part of the impressive Malian delegation—including Moussa Ouattara, with whom I would later work on Ségou rice irrigation for the Millennium Challenge Corporation. Thelma's amiable husband cheerfully accepted that he had to join the journalists and accountants at a lesser table. It was the embassy accountant who most interested me: I did not want my credit card to cover lunch for forty at the Jefferson Hotel.

Before lunch, I asked the prime minister, "Would you like to wash your hands, Excellency? The washrooms are over here, through TJ's bar." As I moved forward to guide him, a heavy hand landed on my shoulder, pulling me backward. A voice of authority in my ear murmured, "When the prime minister moves, Dr. Poulton, it is Agent Lee who leads him, and you stay back." The Secret Service was in charge.

I had contacted the governor of Virginia, who named the secretary of state for education, Mr. Peter Blake, as the state's official host. After the meal, Mr. Blake had arranged a brief visit to Governor Mark Warner, who had been lunching in the company of the presidents of four universities. We shook hands with all of them. "Make sure you shake the governor's hand," somebody muttered in my ear. "One day he may be president of the United States." I was only there as the translator, although I admit that I had prepared the PM's talking points, and also written his speech for that evening. Future president or not, I was very happy to shake Mark Warner's hand, for he was an outstanding governor. He would not remember me, even though I was the only white person in the delegation dressed in embroidered Malian robes—my vestimentary gesture to honor the prime minister and the culture of Mali.

Peter Blake was a charming host. His own kids were attending the J.B. Fisher Elementary School, so that is where we now drove in a convoy of fifteen cars. Head teacher Charlene Brooks ushered half of the twenty Malians into a third-grade classroom. Twenty-two seven-year-olds were waiting for us, bright-eyed and excited.

"Have you been to Timbuktu?" asked a small girl. There was an easy answer. "Yes," said Monsieur Ousmane Issoufi Maiga, who was born in North Mali.

"Does the prime minister own a camel?" asked a boy in a blue shirt. I raised an inquiring eyebrow at the PM, who told me he did not. That was obviously not the answer the children were hoping for.

"Yes," I mistranslated cheerfully. "The prime minister owns a camel, and its name is Timbuktu." The children clapped their hands in delight. Ambassador Diop laughed out loud and observed in French that my translations were more pertinent than the PM's answers. Monsieur Maiga smiled tolerantly.

"Does the prime minister's camel have one hump, or two?"

The prime minister said that his camel had two humps, and that you sit on the front hump. Now I was really in trouble, because every American student knows that Asian Bactrian camels have two humps, and African dromedaries have just one hump. This did not mean the PM was wrong, of course; it meant that the PM knew a lot about dromedaries (a lot more than I knew). He knew that the hump stores up to eighty pounds of fat, which a camel can break down into water and energy, allowing these amazing animals to travel up to one hundred miles through the desert without water. But the PM also knew that the shape of a full, fat dromedary's hump included a small ridge in front of the main hump. That is where you sit to ride on a camel, and that is what the PM meant when he answered, "Two humps." All of which I had to translate into language accessible to third graders.

And then we were out of the classroom, posing for photos, exchanging gifts (The school now owns a magnificent mud cloth blanket showing a nomadic encampment complete with camels, which hangs in the entrance hall), and moving on to the next event, which was a speech to Virginia Commonwealth University and a "*shakehand*" (this is the French expression) with the PM's fifth university president of the afternoon, Dr. Eugene Trani. The student government association, led by Eddie O'Leary, Jessica Lee and Ali Faruq, had put a major effort into promoting the visit of the prime minister. It is not every day that a prime minister visits VCU, of course; but arranging a "standing room only" conference with an audience of six hundred people at 5:00 p.m. on a Friday was quite an achievement.

We filed onto the stage, led by professors Mckenna Brown and Peter Kirkpatrick, the VCU "official hosts"; and I handed the prime minister his speech. I had sat up well past midnight, amending the boring French text drafted by his civil servants in order to produce a more interesting English version. I now gave him my text in both languages. Yet how should I handle the translation of his speech, I wondered, if Prime Minister Maiga chose the French version? Should I interrupt him after each paragraph? I could not ask six hundred Americans to sit in silence for twenty minutes, listening to a foreign language.

At the time, my aunt Penelope was staying at our home in Richmond; and in Mali, an aunt is considered as important as one's mother. "I have a message from my mother," I told the PM as he proceeded to the podium. "She says you must read your speech in English."

To his credit, the PM did as I asked, and then we had thirty minutes of questions and answers in French and English. Ambassador Diop asked me later how I had convinced the PM to use English, and I told him about my mother's message. He laughed. "Only Macky Tall would understand the cultural fact that a Malian can never refuse the request of his mother!"

Prime Minister Maiga's Speech at VCU, November 5, 2005

Honorable Secretary for Education in Virginia, Mr. Peter Blake; distinguished members of the faculty of Virginia Commonwealth University; students and friends of VCU; ladies and gentlemen:

Let me start by saying how delighted I am to be standing here today, in this distinguished university, to talk about my country of Mali. A Malian proverb says that "It is difficult to speak about yourself, and it is bad to boast about yourself." Even so, I shall try to tell you about my country, to tell you why it is adored by historians and fêted by people of culture the world over. Modern Mali has become a famous tourist destination, a magical land for explorers, and a world-renowned laboratory for building peace and democracy.

In America, you have an expression, "as far away as Timbuktu," evoking an imaginary land, a mirage, or a myth. Well, no: Timbuktu really exists! Timbuktu is a town and a province in the country of Mali, *a crossroads for civilizations.* Mali is a land filled with history and culture, where the Arab and Berber peoples of Northern Africa have mingled and traded with the peoples of black Africa since the beginnings of time. Trade flourished here for centuries, and Timbuktu was its commercial center.

We are a landlocked country: we are dependent on the ports of Dakar in Senegal and Abidjan in Ivory Coast, 1,200 kilometers—750 miles—away from our capital city of Bamako. Although we are far from the ocean, we have West Africa's two largest rivers: the Senegal River; and especially the Niger River, which flows through the whole length of Mali for 1,700 kilometers—1,063 miles. The Niger River is the lifeblood of Mali, and irrigates 350,000 square kilometers—135,000 square miles of our land. The Niger River is truly God's gift to Mali.

In size, Mali is the ninth-largest country in Africa, more than twice as big as Texas. We have an immense land to cultivate, and even greater spaces for pasturing our cattle and sheep and goats. Mali is already Africa's biggest cotton producer. We could become the breadbasket of West Africa if we manage our land and water resources successfully. In recent years, cotton has been overtaken as our most important export by gold, of which Mali is now the third-biggest African producer, after South Africa and Ghana. Gold made Timbuktu and the medieval Empire of Mali famous. Well, it is true; Mali produces lots of gold!

Mali's history is rich and wonderful. Seven thousand years ago, men lived here. The famous French archaeologist Theodore Monod discovered a seven-thousand-year-old skeleton in the mountains 190 miles north of Gao, where I was born. That proves that people have been living in Mali for a very long time. You might have read about Djené Djenno in *National Geographic* magazine. This was an ancient island city in the Niger River, near the modern and beautiful city of Djenné. The American archeologists Mr. and Mrs. MacIntosh excavated this ancient riverine civilization, which dates back to three hundred years before the birth of Jesus Christ.

During the Middle Ages, these lands around the Niger River saw a succession of glorious empires. The Ghana Empire grew for seven hundred years before reaching its peak between 950 and 1050. The Mali Empire was founded in 1235 by Sunjata Keita—the original Lion King. His empire lasted stretched from the Atlantic Ocean as far inland as Lake Chad . . . from Richmond to California. In those days they did not have cars: Sunjata Keita and his contemporaries travelled on horses, on foot or by camel. Then came the Sonrai Empire, which lasted from 1460 until 1591. I know this one best, because most Sonrai prime ministers were called Maiga—they were my ancestors.

More and more people are talking about the Atlantic crossing of Malian Emperor Aboubacar around the year 1312. Did the Malian king's fleet succeed in reaching the coasts of Brazil, 180 years before the epic journey of Christopher Columbus? That is what the American archaeologist and historian Ivan van Sertima says in his book *They Were There before Columbus*: that a Malian Emperor crossed the Atlantic Ocean first. The competition between Columbus and the Emperor Aboubacar is a subject of intense scientific debate. Some of you might like to carry out your own research on this issue so that the truth may one day be known.

Mali is a country where black, sedentary farmers from the forest lands of the south mingle with brown nomadic herders from further north—and the places they meet are great river trading centers like Timbuktu and Djenné. This mixing of people created a Malian nation before there was a modern Malian state, which explains the harmony and cohesion of which we Malians are so proud.

On September 22, 1960, Mali gained independence from France. In 1991, Mali entered the new era of liberal democracy based on the rule of law and a system that guarantees multiparty and multiunion negotiations. Our media are very active: in addition to about twenty private newspapers, we have around 250 private radio stations that cover the whole country. The justice system is independent and is one of the pillars of the state.

All these attributes of a liberal democracy are enshrined in the Malian constitution, approved by a universal, national referendum in 1992, when Mali's first multiparty elections also took place and Dr.

Alpha Oumar Konaré was elected president. In 1997, he was reelected for a second and final term. In June 2002, Amadou Toumani Touré was elected president after another round of free and fair elections, in which there were no fewer than twenty-four candidates. Sixteen political parties are represented in the National Assembly. We also have more than three thousand associations, which are part of civil society—another strong pillar of the state, and a rich source of ideas and decisions. Let me also mention that Mali's constitution ensures the separation of church and state. Citizens of every religion live and worship happily, side by side, although 95 percent of Malians are Muslims.

Mali is a great place to invest your money! Our resources and our facilities—and the charm of our people—should encourage private investors. Private investment in Mali will help us create a prosperous Mali for our children to inherit.

Before I end, I want to say how wonderful it is that Virginian students are learning about Mali. I have just visited an elementary school! to meet with third-grade students and teachers who are studying Mali. This will equip the future leaders of Virginia to understand Africa. They will be able to develop mutual relations to the benefit of Virginians and Malians alike. To pursue this idea further, I would like to suggest that we should establish a partnership between the University of Bamako and some of Virginia's universities. We could exchange professors, students and joint research. We could agree to recognize each other's courses and programs.

And I also bring with me a letter, from the mayor of Ségou, Mali's second city, beside the Niger River: it is an invitation to the mayor of Richmond for Ségou and Richmond to become sister cities. Both cities are ancient capitals, Ségou of the Bambara kingdom and Richmond of the Confederacy; both are important agricultural trading cities beside great rivers, the Niger and the James; and both have a famous music festival. Let these two great cities help each other to grow together!

Thank you all!

Teaching Timbuktu and Terrorism to Undergraduates

Islam came peacefully to Mali, arriving with the trading caravans traveling southward from Morocco around 800 CE. Malians in Mansa Sunjata's capital city were impressed by the calm demeanor of the Arab traders, their communal solidarity, their five-times-daily cycle of prayer, and by the fact that they all prayed to God as a group, bowing down shoulder to shoulder in "peaceful submission" (which is the meaning of the word "Islam"). Praying in the mosque is powerful because of the community feeling it develops. The solidarity engendered by communal prayer movements creates an almost military sense of joint action, a bit like marching does—or at least, that is how I experience communal Muslim prayer. I used to take groups of undergraduates to the Islamic Center of Virginia to meet Muslims and to watch the process of prayer. They found it a very enriching experience and they learned that Muslims are like everybody else: nice folks.

I found the peaceful history of Malian Islam to be especially helpful in teaching my Virginia Commonwealth University and University of Richmond undergraduate classes in the aftermath of 9/11. When American bombs started falling on Afghanistan in October 2001, most Afghans, who had never heard of the World Trade Center or of New York City, thought that the Russians were attacking. The Red Army had withdrawn from Afghanistan in 1989 after a decade of bloody fighting. Were they back again? Why were they bombing us this time? Certainly Afghans did not expect an attack from the US. Afghans hated Osama Bin Laden and his arrogant Arabs. They hated the aggressive Arab form of Islam. Saudi "literal" Islam is not Afghan; instead, most Afghans are spiritual and mystical Sufis who love music and enjoy dancing—rather like Malians. Saudi Wahabbism is not Afghan Islam—just as it is nothing like Malian Islam. Afghans did not like the fact that Osama was protected by one-eyed Mullah Oumar, head of the Taliban and Osama's father-in-law. In addition, the Afghans had nothing to do with 9/11. Most of the hijackers were Saudis, and Osama Bin Laden was a Saudi citizen.

Why the Republican Party decided to bomb Afghanistan in October 2001 has always been a mystery to me. The Taliban were not their enemies. The Taliban were an Afghan political party supported by Pakistan, mainly composed of Ghilzai Pashtuns who had ousted their rivals, the Durrani Pashtuns. The Durranis had seized power in 1747, taking it away from the Ghilzai Pashtuns of Kandahar. Of course, George W. Bush and Dick Cheney knew nothing about Afghan history—but Afghans have long memories.

Misunderstandings about Afghanistan and Islam were important, because as I was organizing the first exhibits on Mali from 2003 to 2006, I was also teaching undergraduate courses about Central Asia, the Middle East, and terrorism at VCU and UR. In each of these courses, radical Islam emerged as a theme, along with Salafism, an interpretation of Islam based on a religious and political desire to recreate the conditions of seventh-century Islam as the Salafists believe it existed under the Prophet Mohamed—peace be upon him.

Osama Bin Laden's Arabs preached a Saudi version of "purified" Islam originating from an eighteenth-century Yemeni reformer, Abdul Wahab. Considered a troublemaker due to his efforts to enact reform, Wahab was threatened with hanging. He was saved in 1744 by the al-Saud tribe, who gave him refuge in their mountain castle. In 1927, after that tribe defeated the al-Rashid tribe, the British, who controlled the region after World War I, recognized the al-Saud tribe as rulers of Arabia. To confer legitimacy on their new kingship, the Saudi family revived the ideas of Abdul Wahab, and "Wahabbism" became their creed.

Now, the weak and corrupt Saudi royal family clings to power partly by making claims of the "purity" of Wahabbist ideology, and partly because their fabulous oil revenues allow them to pay off the Wahabbist preachers who might otherwise revolt against them. The 1973 oil crisis increased the price of oil and brought them limitless funds. Saudis have been promoting "checkbook Wahabbist imperialism" across the world, including in Mali. The Saudi royal family keeps power partly by paying off their opponents, and partly because Western armies keep them in power. While American troops protect the Saudi royal family today, it was French troops who saved their regime in 1979, putting down a coup d'état led by Juhayman al-Otaibi in Mecca and killing his armed followers with poison gas injected into the basement of the Great Mosque of Mecca. After allowing foreign troops to invade the Holy of Holies in order to kill Muslims, the Saudis were considered pariahs by many Muslims, including Osama Bin Laden.

These are things that my undergraduate students discovered as they studied the history of Islam, African colonial history, the peace agreements that followed World War I, the rise of political Islam, and the creation of the modern Middle East during the 1920s—mainly by British and French politicians. Saudi Wahabbism is Islam-militant, angry and military. Malian Islam has always been peaceful, Sufi, and spiritual.

Teaching Americans about Terrorism and Religion

As all Americans were confronted daily by news reports that confused politics and religion without discrimination, Timbuktu proved to be a valuable teaching tool. The spiritual Sufi Islam of Timbuktu offers a refreshing contrast to the harsh desert Islam of the Salafists. I brought Timbuktu into all my university courses. I delivered an honors seminar at VCU on the difference between spiritual, mystical Sufism, which I described as circular, and Salafism, which I likened to a straight and pointed spear. Their confrontation in the Sahara would explode onto the news pages in July 2012, when Salafists claiming a link to Al-Qaida (though their main leaders were Algerian drug smugglers) took over North Mali, imposed their strange version of sharia law, and destroyed eight medieval tombs of Sufi saints in Timbuktu—monuments under UNESCO World Heritage protection—because "they were more than eighteen centimeters high!" Where in the Holy Koran does it say that the height of a tomb should not exceed eighteen inches? Nowhere of course; but very few of these fanatics can actually read, let alone understand, the classical Arabic of the Koran.

French troops arrived in January 2013 and saved Mali from becoming a Salafist state. In September 2016, the Salafist head of Timbuktu's Moral Police, a young Koranic teacher called Ahmad el-Mahdi, became the first man ever to be convicted by the International Criminal Court in The Hague for war crimes associated with the destruction of UNESCO-protected monuments.

Unlike Salafists, Sufis seek the truth, and seek to find God. The greatest scholar of Timbuktu was a humanist peacemaker called Ahmed Baba al-Sudani who was teaching at Sankoré University when the Moroccans conquered Timbuktu in 1591. Like other Sufi scholars, he studied the wisdom of one thousand years of Islamic theology and philosophy, interpreting the Holy Koran and the teachings of great Muslim holy men. Such research is known in Arabic as *fiqh,* and scholarship is revered in Islam. Salafists have no time for such nonsense. They know what the Koran means, and they impose their own interpretation of the Koran on everyone else. Since few of them know how to read, they have little respect for books and scholarship.

Of course, Salafism is not a religious project; it is a political project. Terrorism is not "religious"; it is political. Whether they are in Mali or Nigeria, Afghanistan or Pakistan or Syria, Salafists use Islam as a tool (alongside other very modern tools like Kalashnikov automatic rifles, internet propaganda videos, Toyota Landcruisers, and satellite phone technology) to seize power and gain control of oil wells. Terrorism—the creation of fear—is also a political tool. Most victims of modern terrorism are Muslims. The attempted takeover of Mali by Salafists was an attempt by one small group of armed Muslims to take over a Muslim country and turn Mali into a Salafist state.

Mali is not threatened by "Islamic terrorism," but by criminal terrorism: most of the Algerian, Tunisian, Mauritanian and Malian leaders of the Salafist forces in 2013 became wealthy through smuggling cocaine, hashish, cigarettes, firearms, and people. Their religious label is useful for recruitment and fundraising. During the Irish troubles, so-called Catholics and Protestants did the same: many of the Irish armed groups were criminal gangs smuggling heroin and alcohol for profit. It is convenient for criminals to adopt a political cause, but smuggling heroin is not Christian. Smuggling cocaine is not Islamic. These are criminals and opportunists. I believe there is no such thing as "religious terrorism"—just terrorism by criminals who adopt a religious label.

While most Virginians know very little about Islam, all of Virginia's third graders learn about Timbuktu, the holy city of Islam; and so did my graduate and undergraduate students. While most Africans are Muslims or Christians, both these religions were colonial imports to Africa. Jesus Christ taught peace. "Islam" means "peace and submission to God"—so it is also a religion of peace. How many Virginian parents understand that? Young Virginians know more about Islam than their parents. Some parents, I have discovered, know rather little even about Christianity.

Both Jesus and Mohamed were religious reformers. It was other people who, after their deaths, gave their teaching new names: Christianity and Mohamedism. Judaism is a monotheistic religion that gave birth to both Christianity and Islam. Judaism is based around the Torah, the first five books in the Old Testament that are also venerated by the other two religions. Christianity, however, is about the message of Jesus told in the New Testament. Some "Christians" in the United States spend more time on the books of Judaism than on the Gospels of Christ. Many Americans follow the Old Testament God of wrath, more than they worship the qualities of love, compassion, and peace that Jesus emphasized. In Islam, Allah is primarily compassionate and merciful.

Like Judaism and Christianity, Islam is also a "religion of the book"—in this case, the Holy Koran. Muslims venerate the prophets Abraham, Moses (whom they call *Musa*), David (*Daud*) and Jesus (*Isa*), all of whom feature in the Koran. Jesus ranks as second-most important prophet, after the Prophet Mohamed (pbuh). His mother Mary is mentioned thirty-four times in the Koran—more times than in the Bible—and the Sura XIX is named for her. The three religions are so close, they should really be seen a single religion with separate branches that follow the advice of different (completing, rather than competing) prophets.

Mohamed emphasized that his followers should respect the teachings of both Jewish and Christian philosophers, but Islam seems closer to Christianity. Mohamed was a seventh-century merchant who adopted the Unitarian Christianity he discovered on the shores of the Mediterranean Sea. Jesus and Mohamed both emphasized a personal relationship of women and men with God. This was a challenge to Africa's traditions, which perceived God as too powerful for mere humans to address. "If you go too near to the sun, you will get burned." Therefore, Africans have always asked their ancestors to intercede with God, rather like Catholics pray for saints to intervene for them.

When the Malian ambassador in Washington, DC, first visited Richmond in October 2005, Imam Shaheed Coovadia, the spiritual leader of the Islamic Center of Virginia (ICVA), invited him to speak in the mosque after Friday prayers. Ambassador Abdoulaye Diop spoke about Timbuktu, called the "city of 333 saints" for the many revered Sufi teachers who lie buried there. He explained that 90 percent of Malians are Muslims, mainly following the Tijania, Sufi, Malekite Sunni interpretation of Islamic law that originated in Fez, Morocco. Richmond's Islamic community was thrilled with ambassador, and they pleaded with him to come again. That was the same day that Abdoulaye Diop imagined twinning Richmond with Ségou.

Later the president of the board of ICVA thanked me for arranging the ambassador's visit. He confessed, "I did not even know that there were Muslims in Mali." How little Americans know about Islam, and about Africa! Our Teaching Timbuktu campaign aims to change ignorance into understanding.

Imam Coovadia, Annette Khan, and the Islamic Center of Virginia

Imam Shaheed Coovadia led the mosque community on Buford Road, in Richmond's Bon Air district. He also taught part-time at VCU; later he moved on, becoming a full-time professor of Arabic and of Islam at Virginia State University in Petersburg. When I first visited the mosque, I was struck by the beauty of the Imam's Arabic. He speaks prose with the cadences of poetry, and with a perfect Arabian accent. I assumed he had been born in Mecca. It turned out that Shaheed Coovadia was actually born in South Africa. Before his PhD in comparative literature in Manchester (UK), he studied Arabic and theology in Saudi Arabia at the University of Medina, and it is there that he became so skilled in the language. This did him no favors in Richmond, where some Arabs in the congregation (people from Egypt or Sudan or Jordan or Palestine) were jealous of his eloquence and resented the fact that an erudite and spiritual African of Indian descent was able to speak their language so much better than they themselves. In fact, of course, each country has its own dialect. British people think that Americans "speak funny," while Americans tell us "We love your accent!" These Arab Americans were simply jealous of the Imam's perfect Arabian accent and his mastery of classical Arabic.

Arabic, like English, has many regional variations. Each is as valid as the next. Arabic—like Persian, and perhaps like French and Italian—is a language of poetry. Spoken Arabic is sometimes more atmospheric than literal, and this is certainly true in the mosque, where the beauty and poetical flow of the original classical Arabic of the seventh century requires careful thought, discussion and analysis before its relevance to the twenty-first century can be determined and its guidance understood. Many of the Muslim faithful hear the words as spiritual music, somewhat like the Latin Mass in the Roman church, which most of the faithful did not fully understand.

Imam Coovadia is an academic, a scholar of Islam. He loved my Teaching Timbuktu program, and I found his spiritual explanations and his weekly sermons of great value. So did my VCU and UR students, when they came with me to visit ICVA on a Friday. They would first meet with one of the mosque's Elders in the ICVA library, to hear about Islam and to ask questions about the practice and beliefs of Islam. They would learn about the Five Pillars of Islam: faith (belief in one God), prayer five times per day, alms (generous charity), fasting (during the holy month of Ramadan) and hajj. The hajj is the pilgrimage that should be made once by every Muslim who can manage it: reversing the *Hegira* or *hijra*, Mohamed's flight from Mecca in AD 621. The Prophet Mohamed was born in Mecca, where his neighbors did not want to hear his preaching. He had to flee to the nearby city of Medina, where his preaching was appreciated. From this *Hegira* comes the well-known proverb "A prophet is never recognized in his own country."

ICVA and its elementary school were managed by a smart and spiritual American Muslim called Annette Khan, a pillar of Richmond's InterFaith Council and the organizer of excellent after-prayer food sales. I used to buy tasty and aromatic Mideastern pastries in the women's section of the mosque after Friday prayer. I ate them with my students at the mosque, or carried them home for supper.

Annette's husband Malik Khan is a charming and gentle man, an intelligent and much-missed former ICVA president. I found the governance of ICVA rather un-American. There were nine members of the committee, all men and all elderly—rather like a Malian or a Pakistani village council. Each year, the next in line moved up to become ICVA president (even if his temperament was quite unsuitable for this position), while a new man was elected to the elderly committee. In nine years' time, he would become president—by which time he would have been exhausted by nine years of the internal bickering. As a result, ICVA had some very bad presidents, and it was difficult to introduce any new ideas. I used to think, "Down with gerontocracy! Down with all-male clubs! ICVA needs to bring in some young people, and some women." I kept silent, even though I thought that

Annette Khan would make a far better ICVA president than any of those conservative old men.

One reason I felt comfortable at the mosque, was that it was filled with outsiders: minorities, mainly first-generation Americans, people like myself who had arrived with a different culture. America has plenty of Muslims, mainly African Americans, but in Richmond they have done nothing to make these foreigners welcome. American Muslims in Richmond keep to their own mosques. Louis Farrakhan's Nation of Islam—a political and moral movement that most Muslims do not consider to be a part of Islam—also keeps itself very much to itself. So ICVA was a place filled with foreigners.

Driving around Richmond, I was struck by the number of notices I saw suggesting that Christian immigrants are in much the same position: "Korean Church" and "Vietnamese Church" are indications of separateness . . . of linguistic and cultural commonality. These signposts confirm the words of President Barack Obama that "Americans are never more separated, than on Sunday mornings" (or Fridays for Muslims, Saturdays for Jews) when the American nation seems to fragment into its enclaves of separate identity.

Teaching Timbuktu with the Rotary: Oumou and Aissata Daou

The Rotary organization is just one of many American charitable networks, but it happens to be the main one that has thus far supported VFoM's work in Africa. Ken Hodge in Newport News liked our Teaching Timbuktu exhibits, and his Rotarians—together with Rotarians in Richmond—sponsored two young Virginians to visit Mali. And they did more than visit! Rachel Davies and Virginia Vassar each spent a whole year living in the home of the Daou family in Bamako and attending a Malian high school. Later, one of the Daou sisters spent year in the Vassar household while attending VCU.

Ken Hodge called me: would I invite Rachel and her mother over to answer questions about Mali and to reassure the mother? Well, what mother would not feel worried about her daughter of seventeen flying off to West Africa for a year? I invited Rachel and her mother around for tea. I have seldom been more impressed with a young girl than I was with Rachel. Her questions about Mali were so pertinent that I found myself howling with laughter as I described to her the minutiae of Malian kitchen and bedroom and bathroom habits, imaging the shocks she might have to confront in the complex structures of Malian families that she would soon be discovering for herself. Rachel's enthusiasm was so great that I ran upstairs to bring down a Malian woman's three-piece embroidered outfit in glorious purple damask. After I showed her how to wear the skirt and how to tie the headscarf, Rachel whirled around my sitting room in excitement, rather as Peter O'Toole whirled around the sand dunes in David Lean and Sam Spiegel's film *Lawrence of Arabia* when he first put on Arab dress. So I gave Rachel the damask outfit, telling her how impressed her Malian mother, Madame Daou, was going to be when she unpacked the suitcase in Bamako and discovered this four-hundred-dollar, magnificent, top-quality embroidered *bazin* dress. Which is exactly what happened.

Virginia Vassar went to Mali the following year, replacing Rachel in the Daou household. Monsieur Ousmane "Babalaye" Daou and his family have proved to be extraordinarily kind and generous Rotarians. Rachel had been baptized Oumou; Virginia became Aissata Daou, and her Malian siblings welcomed her as generously as they had welcomed Oumou. Meanwhile, one of the Daou sons had moved to study in Pennsylvania—Aissata only met him the following year, back in the US. Different girls have differing experiences, naturally, and the two had different adventures. In both cases, I admired their pluck and imagination. I gave the girls some minimal support during their year in Bamako, calling occasionally by phone to remind them that I knew how tough it can be living in a foreign country. Not surprisingly, there were occasional tears; when you are plunged 24/7 into such a strange environment, living and sleeping and speaking French without a break, simply the relief of being able to talk to someone in English can be enough to set the tear ducts in motion.

On one occasion, while Madame Daou was away, Oumou decided to invite one of her classmates back to the house for tea. Her Malian mother was horrified when she returned. By chance,[25] I called the same evening, and Oumou was in tears. What had she done wrong, and why was her Malian mother shouting at her? The following afternoon, she found out: the boy arrived with his father, to request Rachel's hand in marriage! Oumou was sent to her room, while Madame Daou explained how impossible this would be and how cross-cultural mixed messages had led to misinterpreting the meaning of a cup of tea. In Mali, a girl who cooks for a man is making a declaration of love, and the man who eats the food must accept the risk that it might be poisoned (unlikely in this case), or that it may contain a love potion purchased from a marabout—a charlatan. On the one or two occasions when unexpected dishes have arrived on my table in Mali, I have always fed them to my dog: I do not mind if the dog falls in love with an amorous lady, but I am not going to let it happen to me.

Virginia-Aissata had different excitements. When we talked, she explained how difficult she had found entering the Lycée Koronso in the Korofina district of Bamako. She spoke poor French when she arrived, and she discovered that all the eighteen-year-olds already had their established networks of friends. Of course, she was placed in the top class for English—where the teacher was stupid enough to criticize and correct her English. This depressed Aissata, and she withdrew from the class. Wise language teachers do not correct native speakers; instead, they use them as a teaching resource to benefit the rest of the class.

Because of her elementary spoken French, Aissata joined ninth-grade classes, where younger kids in their new school were in "friend-making mode." She made friends with some of them. A lot of Malian teaching is done by dictation: "Write down my words, and learn them by heart"—a style of teaching that suited Aissata very well in her ninth-grade classes and helped her French, although she found the system very old-fashioned. Indeed, the whole *lycée* was old-fash-

---

25 *Of course, it was not by chance. Nothing in West Africa is "by chance," because everything is determined by God. Therefore, it was a spirit that moved me to call Rachel on the very day of her crisis, when she most needed comfort.*

ioned, shabby, and ill-equipped by American standards. Aissata found that Malian schoolwork was overly focused on France, and wondered why this had not changed since Independence. How useful is it, she wondered, for Malians to write sentences about snow? I have often asked myself the same question.

"I was shocked at first that there was only one communal cup at the water fountain—or else we had to drink out of our hands," Aissata said. "Then I realized that, as Americans, we are so spoiled! And this realization rocked my worldview completely. I still feel like I haven't recovered from it. I know lots of people in USA who never question the environment they know. But Mali blew my world apart. I learned *so much*, and I would do it again . . . and I have recommended it to other people. Mali is awesome; but it may lead you to question everything for ever. I loved it in the end, because I loved the simplicity of it. Living in Mali seemed so clear: how to be a good person, how to behave."

Thanks to old-fashioned dictation, Aissata's French improved very rapidly, and she gained confidence. With her American reasoning skills, she began to get good grades. Aissata also took Arabic classes, which actually helped her French more than her Arabic because of the Koranic verses they were reading; but they must have made an impact on her, because Aissata later chose to study Arabic at Georgetown University. Then she studied abroad, and now she teaches the Arabic language in Denver, Colorado.

Both Oumou and Aissata found the constant company of Malians overwhelming. Privacy is an unknown concept in Mali. Aissata shared a bedroom with the three other Daou sisters. If she went into the bedroom to read a book quietly, they would go and get her and bring her back out into the community. "Once I stopped isolating myself, I loved the company. I realize that reading is isolating; books draw you into your own world, and private reading does not fit the collectivist culture of Malian family life. I began to understand why parents in Mali discourage their kids from disappearing into a book and becoming individualistic. If you ask a young Malian what their favorite book is, you will likely receive the astonished response, 'What do you mean? Books are for school.' I would like to study why more people do not read for pleasure, and I would like to research ways to make reading more culturally adapted to African life."

Teaching Timbuktu to Virginia's Teachers with Dana and Lydie

Virginian third, fourth, and sixth graders like to be entertained with colorful stories of lions and hippos, as well as SOL subjects. Their teachers need a deeper background in these subjects, and they also need some good stories to tell. The third-grade SOL emphasizes specific subjects like trade (desert salt was exchanged for the gold brought in Niger River trading canoes, and the gold reached Europe in camel caravans traveling between Timbuktu and the Mediterranean Sea); language (desert salt traders and forest gold merchants did not speak the same language: so students organize silent trading in their classroom, or invent their own new commercial language); economic interdependency (Fulani cattle herders produce milk and meat; Bozo fishermen catch fish, Mandingo hunters catch antelope; Bambara and Sonrai farmers grow rice beside the river; Dogons grow onions, rain-fed millet, and sorghum; and all these people need to eat a balanced diet); and history, which includes Sunjata Keita, the Lion King who founded the Mali Empire in 1235; and his great-nephew Mansa Musa, who crossed the Sahara in 1326 on his return from a famous pilgrimage to Mecca and built the Friday Mosque in Timbuktu out of mud brick. That mosque, *Jingeraiber,* still stands strong today.

After talking to many of Virginia's elementary school teachers, we discovered they wanted "accreditation." If teachers were going to give up their time to learn about Timbuktu, we needed to award them points toward their teacher recertification, which happens every five years.

Teacher-training colleges are not interested in Mali. VCU, JMU, VUU, VSU—these institutions offer credits in pedagogy, English, and math, but not in Timbuktu. We searched long and hard for college credits—and finally we found them, when the University of Richmond created a new teacher licensure program. Dr. Cathy Fisher and her colleagues agreed to endorse an elementary school (ES) teacher class for UR credits. This was an exciting offer, so I designed a curriculum around three weekend workshops held on Friday evenings plus Saturday mornings and afternoons over three months, combining "face time" with "class time." We would present and discuss Mali with teachers, giving them face time with Mali instructors; they would create Mali lesson plans and test them with their students (working in-class time); and they would come back to report and compare their results (more face time).

Lesson plans could concern any aspect of Malian life and teaching: art (fabric designs), math (weighing gold and salt), geography (the Niger River), history (the 1235 founding of Mali by the Lion King), or Islam (the great mosque of Timbuktu built in 1326)—whatever the teachers wanted to teach. Thelma Williams-Tunstall was enthusiastic, and she found a budget that allowed us to offer the first class free to ES teachers in Richmond Public Schools. Dr. Thomas Beatty of Thompson Middle School gave us space in his school library for our workshops and for a Mali exhibit. Our Mali accreditation class was ready to begin.

Later, having perfected the course, we realized that Virginia Friends of Mali can only reach all the teachers in Virginia through an online course. Neither UR nor any other institution has so far been willing to fund the creation of such an online course, and our own volunteer resources are limited. We have made some YouTube teaching videos that teachers can find on our website and our blog, but these do not comprise a course for credits. So our recertification teaching has been so far limited to Greater Richmond and bits of central and coastal Virginia.

The teaching of teachers was great fun! Robin was the main instructor, supported by my VFoM friends Lydie, who is West African, and Dana, who is African American. Surrounded by a spectacular presentation of Malian fabrics, artifacts and books, we presented Malian history, life, and culture, and discussed how to teach these subjects to third graders. Our first class comprised a dozen teachers, all women—unsurprising, since most ES teachers are women. Half were white, and half were black, which allowed us to create hilarious situations and break down barriers people didn't even know were there.

"Come on," I urged the class while we were talking about family hygiene in rural Mali. "It is well known that the Europeans are among the least hygienic cultures in the world. My ancestors actually believed that washing was bad for the skin. Medieval ladies used 'nosegays' or 'tussie-mussies'—bunches of flowers held to the white medieval nose to disguise or cover the filthy body odors of other English people. When the English colonized Virginia, all of them stank." The teachers giggled; then they laughed. "Queen Elisabeth I," I continued, "the Virgin Queen, was famous for washing 'at least once each year, whether she doth need it or not' . . . and she stank as well." Our student teachers kept laughing as my truths struck home.

"You know and I know," I continued, "that black and white body sweat smells different. African and African American people hate the smell of white people. We are actually not different people, but we all know that we look different and smell different. So I smell bad! Tell me, what to African Americans say about the smell of a sweaty man like me?"

After much hesitation, an intelligent teacher called Simone admitted, giggling with embarrassment, "We say that white people smell like wet dogs!"

I laughed delightedly. "That is fine! I can assure you that is far preferable to being told by a Malian that a white man smells like a dead man." More laughter.

"But Africans are very clean," I continued. "Every Malian courtyard seems to contain a baby in a bucket covered with soapsuds and wailing, while women scrub the poor tot until his skin shines. The first thing any Malian adult does in the morning is seize a tube of toothpaste; and those without toothpaste use a 'chewstick' to clean their teeth and gums. On the other hand, I take great care not to get too close to white American mouths, which often smell very bad."

My friend Lydie agreed enthusiastically, "Yes, in our house in the morning, everyone is trying to get into the bathroom to brush their teeth! No one will speak to another member of the family until they have cleaned their teeth."

In the informal atmosphere of this class, we were able to dig deeply into Malian family life, the role of women, and the high status of mothers. Lydie told us how even she, French by nationality but born in Africa, was surprised by the fuss that was made of her when she gave birth to twins. After a few weeks, she had carried her twins to West Africa to present them to her mother and the rest of her family. At the airport in Paris, the African ground staff mobbed her! "Call the captain!" cried an air hostess. "Tell him he will be carrying twins. He will be so happy! This will be a safe flight, blessed by God and protected by angels!"

To her surprise, Lydie was bumped up to first class on the order of the captain, to honor the Mother of Twins. West African mothers, we explained to the astonished Virginian teachers, are like goddesses. This led us into a discussion of the importance of mother's milk—for a mother gives life through birth, and also by feeding her baby. Not only that: if a Malian mother does not have milk, or if she is unwell, and her baby is fed by another woman, this person becomes the child's second mother. In Britain and America, wet nurses used to be paid, not admired. In Mali, children who nurse from the same breast are considered brothers and sisters: the greatest honor you can pay a friend is to call them a "milk-brother" or a "milk-sister" and this relationship involves the same taboos as birth siblings. For example, you cannot marry someone who has been fed from the same breast.

So mother's milk in Mali has the same value as—or even greater value than—paternal sperm. As we know from the Fulani creation myth, Guéno, the all-powerful Creator, fashioned the world from a drop of milk. First, He created the cow; then He created the woman; finally, He added the man.

It was amusing for us trainers, raised in Africa, to see the initial discomfort of these Virginians when discussing what seemed to them to be highly intimate subjects like breastfeeding. "Not in Mali," we assured them. "Malian mothers do not cover their breasts. There is nothing 'sexual' in the African breast, which is a proud symbol of motherhood. Women will cover up from the waist to the ankle, but they will be happily naked on top. In a country as hot as Mali, it makes sense to work without being covered."

I described my first case of "culture shock" in Virginia, when I found myself staring at the back of an elderly African American woman and wondering what was "wrong" with her. She was walking into the supermarket, dressed in a respectable blouse and knee-length skirt. Then I realized what was wrong: I was perfectly used to seeing elderly African women with naked breasts, but I had never before seen an elderly black lady with her legs uncovered. There was nothing wrong with her. But I needed time to adjust to the strange American custom of wearing short skirts.

Dana's story was the best, producing the loudest laughter of all. She described her own mother's visit to her West African village, while Dana was a Peace Corps volunteer. Dana's mother is very well-endowed. As they walked down the village's one street, an elderly African woman approached Dana's mom, shrieking, "Oh, look! You must be such a good mother!" while grabbing her breasts with both hands. Virginian ladies are not used to having their breasts grabbed by anybody, let alone by a complete stranger! But as Dana translated the elderly lady's enthusiasm into amused English, her American mother slowly came to understand that she had received a huge compliment. Big breasts are a proud demonstration of motherhood; and mothers are goddesses in West Africa.

Teletandem Teaching and Richmond-Mali University Spin-Offs

The new University of Ségou was created in 2009 and opened its doors to students in January 2012. A delegation of faculty members from VCU visited Ségou and Bamako in January 2013, at the very moment that jihadist armed forces were massing at Diabaly with the intention of sweeping down to capture Ségou and Bamako, while others at Konna prepared to capture the eastern towns of Mopti and Sevaré. If the French air force had not smashed the jihadist forces on January 11 and sent them fleeing northward into the Sahara Desert, an extremist Salafist army might have seized power—and six thousand foreign hostages, including our VCU delegation. Fortunately, this disaster was avoided. Four thousand French-led counterterrorism troops now garrison Mali and its neighbors, and the UN has a large number of peacekeepers in Mali—twelve thousand at the time of this writing.

The faculty's visit in 2013 was followed by a visit from VCU students in 2014, and as a result, partnerships have begun to emerge. The first educational spin-off has been teletandem teaching: VCU French Professor Kathryn Murphy-Judy's students in Richmond have weekly Skype sessions, conversing with English language students taught by Professor Macki Samaké, rector of the *Université des Lettres et des Sciences Humaines de Bamako* (ULSHB). Teletandem teaching works best as structured conversations between groups of three or four students at each end of the internet connection, developing conversation fluency in the foreign language: thirty minutes in English, followed by thirty minutes in French. One-on-one conversations do not work so well, because these students are not yet fluent. The experience of Africans and Americans meeting every week for discussion has proved immensely enriching in terms of cultural understanding, as well as language fluency for both sides. Here is a wonderful example of "people getting to know each other" in the way that President Eisenhower envisaged when he started the sister city movement.

Meanwhile, anthropology research on AIDS has been progressing between VCU professor Christopher A. Brooks, and Ségou teacher Salim Coumaré: their book *The Most Vulnerable: Women with AIDS and Islam in Mali* was published in early 2017. Medical research on probiotics and AIDS is ongoing, led by VCU medical Professors Daniel Nixon and Saba Masho in Richmond, with Dr. Fanta Diabaté in Mali, in partnership with Dr. Abdoulaye Sanogo at Ségou's main hospital and Dr. Mohamadou Drabo of the medical association WALE. This book is the fruit of ongoing historical research in Ségou, while books by Malian women have been translated by Dr. Patricia Cummins and Dr. Michelle Poulton. A series of African researchers have worked at VCU: the first have been gynecologist Dr. Fanta Diabaté; Kakotan "Bako" Sanogo, a biostatistician who did his master's and MBA at VCU; Ivoirian scientist Jeremie Zoueu, who is researching medicines; and Kalifa Touré, who worked with the VCU School of Business. Our first Malian undergraduate was Ms. Kadiatou Samaké, who graduated in economics in May 2017. Further potential VCU and VFoM teaching and joint research at UniSeg—a university with a practical vocation in agricultural science, engineering, and public health—is being discussed with the newly appointed (as of 2016) rector Professor Souleymane Kouyaté and his team. UniSeg is preparing to play a role in the transformation of agriculture and the optimal use of water during the twenty-first century.

In May 2014, as a follow-up to the 2013 faculty visit, my wife and I supervised a group of six VCU students on a visit to West Africa under a Title VI grant obtained from the US Department of Education by Professor Patricia Cummins. The School of World Studies (SWS) had been slated by VCU's president, Dr. Michael Rao, to make the university more international, and the sister city adventure is a natural partner for SWS. Because of perceived insecurity in Mali, the USG grant trip was rerouted to Abidjan and Yamoussoukro, the commercial and political capitals of Ivory Coast, where VCU's Professor Brahima Koné had excellent contacts.

One of the lessons we learned on this journey was that mixed-gender student groups need mixed-gender leaders, especially when minor health or emotional problems arise. A second lesson was that students must have proper health and accident insurance as part of their university travel; otherwise, experience shows that the professors' credit cards have to pick up the check. Other than that, however, the 2014 visit went perfectly. Everyone got along well, there were no major problems, and the Americans enjoyed their African hosts. We were received by Ivoirian families that were wealthier than most of the people in our group—surprising our American students with an effective demonstration that every country has rich people as well as poor people. VCU students tend to be from families with middle-class incomes at best, and some are the first in their families to attend university. AGITEL-Formation, our Ivoirian exchange institution, is a private engineering and management school for the sons and daughters of wealthy Abidjan families.

L'Institut national polytechnique Félix Houphouët-Boigny (named after the country's first president) in Yamoussoukro, where we stayed for one night, is an equally sophisticated scientific "Ivy League" university campus, enjoying an international reputation. We visited academic classes, the music and art centers, and the nearby beautiful Basilica of Our Lady of Peace, belonging to the Vatican. Filled with African sunlight and sacred African sculptures, this cathedral building was built by the late Félix Houphouët-Boigny in his birth city to match St. Peter's Basilica in Rome—but its dimensions are slightly larger, making it the biggest church in the world.

From Ivory Coast, the six VCU students flew to Bamako at their own expense, purchasing five-hundred-dollar air tickets to visit the ULSHB. Taking a different view from the US State Department, we judged the security risks extremely low in Bamako, Mali's capital city, where I had been working to advise the United Nations peacekeeping mission in Mali on civilian disarmament. As well as sightseeing and academic study, the students were excited to visit MINUSMA headquarters, walking past tanks manned by Pakistani army units wearing UN blue berets, meeting Senegalese and Nepalese peace officials, and getting magnificent views of Bamako from my twelfth-floor office in the Amitié Hotel.

The two great highlights of the students' 2014 West African journey were not academic. In Mali, we spent a delightful evening at the Bamako residence of US ambassador Mary Beth Leonard, where students listened to off-the-record advice about the political situation in West Africa, enjoyed her generous diplomatic hospitality, and heard an impromptu jazz piano recital by Taron Ware, one of the talented

VCU students. In Ivory Coast, we visited the coastal resort and former capital city, Grand Bassam, where we entered the throne room of His Majesty Awoulae Tanoe Amon, king of the N'Zima Kotoko people and a very influential local ruler. During the formal ceremony, the forty-year-old king spoke only in whispers to his counselor, who then gave voice to the king's wishes. His Majesty later abandoned protocol and took questions directly from the American students, whose French skills were becoming increasingly impressive. They were awed by the throne room; by the pomp and circumstance; and perhaps most of all, by the size of the four-liter bottle and the strength of the gin, augmented with chili peppers, with which they had to toast His Majesty. They survived!

The VCU students proved to be very competent in French, and they became adept at public speaking. The ULSHB experience in Bamako added to their academic discoveries at the engineering college AGITEL-Formation in Abidjan and Houphouët-Boigny University in Yamoussoukro, creating a life-changing francophone experience for them all. Some are now teaching French in Virginia's public schools; others are pursuing graduate studies in various fields. Dr. Cummins' Title VI grant has brought immeasurable value to students, and also to the sister city relationship, by funding visits to Mali for VFoM members working with Ségou and by adding a wealth of new activities to VCU and to the Richmond-Ségou partnership.

The spectacular educational visits launched a range of research and commercial spin-offs between Richmond and West Africa. The main sea port for Ségou (and for landlocked Mali) is Abidjan, with which Richmond's river port is now exploring trade opportunities. American academic Dr. Stephen Sacco is now teaching in Yamoussoukro. An African business conference held at VCU in October 2017—led by Professor Van Wood of the VCU School of Business—explored partnerships in solar energy and water management, generic medicines, agribusiness innovations like insect farming, using Malian shea butter for cosmetics, exporting Ségou's colored cotton yarn, and other opportunities for Virginia and for West Africa.[26] The institutional power of VCU has added hugely to the Richmond-Ségou sister city portfolio and increased the range of potentialities for both cities.

Richard Woodward's African Art Collection at the VMFA

Naturally, the Virginia Friends of Mali take our Malian delegations to visit the Virginia Museum of Fine Arts (VMFA), one of the top twelve museums in the US, even when the Malians' first priority is usually to go shopping. While the Black History Museum in Richmond's Jackson Ward is focused mainly on Richmond's African American population since the Civil War, and the Virginia Historical Society presents Virginia's history, the VMFA includes an excellent African gallery with many fine pieces from Mali: Dogon masks, Bambara hunting costumes, protective Senufo initiation statues, Tuareg leatherwork, ancient clay sculptures from Djéné-Djéno in the interior delta of the Niger River. Our Malian visitors take pleasure in seeing their nation and culture well represented in the museum, alongside mysterious religious statues from many Congo cultures, decorated Christian crucifixes from Ethiopia, stunning geometric wall paintings from South Africa, bronze royal heads from Benin, queenly beadwork worn by the Yoruba kings of Nigeria, and two galleries of amazing artifacts from the tombs of ancient Egypt. The exhibit honors African culture and history, just as it honors the life's work of its curator, Richard Woodward.

When Richard Woodward came to Richmond a quarter century ago, the VMFA had no "African" art—Egyptian, yes; but people barely realized in those days that ancient Egypt was a great African empire north of Nubia and Kush. Europeans puzzling as to why the Sphinx at Giza had African features missed the obvious answer: the Sphinx is the portrait of a great African king. That seemed impossible to eighteenth-

---

26 *The Doing Business in Africa Conference brought entrepreneurs and academics to the VCU International Business Forum and the annual bilingual meeting of the Africa Business and Entrepreneurship Research Society (ABERS). A dozen participants from Ségou took part and several, including the UniSeg Rector, chaired ABERS panels.*

and nineteenth-century Eurocentric visitors ignorant of Africa and its history. In those days, no one had discovered what we believe we now know: that humankind evolved in the Great Rift Valley in East Africa. We also know that three hundred thousand years ago, *Homo sapiens* had reached, and were living in, Morocco. The debate continues over how long ago and where and when the first human migrations took place: the recent archeological discovery of an ancient skull in Israel seems to place African outmigration two hundred thousand years ago. In any case, we believe that all humans originally came out of Africa. There were no "Arabs" in Africa at the time of ancient Egypt, although the ancestors of Arabic-speaking people presumably existed in Yemen. We should here tip our hats to the late great African scholar Cheick Antar Diop, who changed our vision of Africa by showing that elements of the coastal Wolof language of Senegal are directly related to the language of ancient Egypt—thus explaining the waves of African herders and hunters and explorers moving westward across the grasslands of the Sahara from the Nile River to the valleys of the Niger, Gambia, and Senegal Rivers in great migrations over thousands of years. Camels first came to North Africa only around the time of Jesus of Nazareth.

These days, the VMFA is in the vanguard of museums that are breaking down those artificial intellectual and geographical boundaries we inherited from our forebears. One of these boundaries concerns the meaning of "art," which the European tradition turned into static objects to be looked at, such as statues, pictures, collages, and wall hangings. But looking is not enough for understanding. Richard Woodward explains that African art always has a context, without which the meaning is lost. Masks are made for performances (his museum shows exciting films of mask dance performances) associated with life-rituals of great importance to their communities. The Dogon *sigui* is a spectacular dance performed every sixty years to honor the ancestors. In Dogon society, mask roles and dance traditions pass from father to son, but few Dogons get to see more than one *sigui* during their lifetime. Other masks are associated with justice, initiation, healing, or agriculture and fertility.

The governor of Ségou, Monsieur Georges Togo, was privileged to be taken into the bowels of the VMFA to see a new Malian gift being preserved: two chiwara masks, complete with straw-and-raffia costumes, had been donated to the VFMA by a medical doctor who worked for many years in the interior delta of the Niger River in central Mali. Chiwara masks are typically brought out—normally in pairs, one male and one female—to dance for agricultural activities; to encourage the farmers in their collective efforts of plowing, sowing, hoeing, and harvesting; and to seek the blessing of *Nga* the Creator for good rains and good crop yields. Dozens of wooden chiwara masks can be found on sale in the markets of Mali, often made for decoration or for tourists. The male chiwara—with its elegant fusion of a lion's mane, ibex horns and the shape of a farmer bending over to hoe his crops—has become one of the symbols of Malian national identity. The male chiwara decorates the letterhead of Virginia Friends of Mali and is also the logo of WARA, the West African Research Association.

What excites Richard Woodward with both the eye of the art historian and the heart of an anthropologist, is that this new gift includes the complete costume of the chiwara pair. "Here we can see what the mask is for," he told me excitedly. "It is not a static wooden artifact to be placed behind a glass window, but a real and living spirit of nature that dances and turns and whirls to the beat of drummers, as the farmers work their fields and the women process out of the village carrying food and water for the farmers to eat during a well-earned rest period. With the raffia skirts flowing down from the wooden masks, attached at they were in the village to form a complete costume, we are able to present the chiwara as it is supposed to exist."

The other boundary that Richard is keen to dissolve—after restoring static "art" pieces to their living tradition and function—is the artificiality of countries and continents. Colonial frontiers established during the 1900s cut across cultures and languages without regard for the local people. After Mali gained independence from France in

1960, some African farmers discovered that their house was now in a different country than their fields. This made little practical difference to the local economy; but in the museum field, categories became unrepresentative of cultural and artistic reality. The medieval Mali Empire, as large as Western Europe, stretched across the artificial frontiers of nine modern nation-states. To say that "this mask comes from Mali" or "from Senegal" has very little meaning if—like the chiwara—the mask is a part of a Manding culture that exists in various forms in Senegal, The Gambia, Guinea, Guinea-Bissau, Mali, Ivory Coast, Burkina Faso, the frontier zones of Mauritania and Niger, and the Manding diaspora now present in northern Ghana, Liberia, and Sierra Leone.

The VMFA's magnificent African gallery attempts to break down the barriers. Malian masks and the robes and attributes of Yoruba royalty share a space with pagan Congo, ancient Egypt, and medieval Christian Ethiopia. The sacred Egyptian ibis is found revived in a majestic and protective Senufo *kalao* bird from the southern Sahel, where the artificial frontiers of Mali, Burkina Faso, Ghana, and Ivory Coast meet: a fusion of the sacred ibis, the maternal pelican, the colorful hornbill with the continuity of ancient Egyptian spirituality. This book is not the place to trace three thousand years of religious traditions, but we should remember that Africans are monotheistic—long before Christianity or Islam existed, Africans worshipped one Supreme Being, while also venerating the spirits of ancestors who act as intermediaries to that Being, who is too powerful to be approached by mere humans.

Barbara Grey and the Virginia Union African Collections

The VUU art museum also has some fine wooden chiwara sculptures called *kankalan* in Senegambia, masks that were and still are danced at times of sowing and harvest, and for communal agriculture days. The chiwara mask is a socializing force, bringing everyone out of their compounds to join in the communal cultivating activities, stimulating the farmers' ardour and increasing the harvest. Often the chiwara calls out the young men to till the fields of an Elder who is unwell; or to harvest the crops of a widow with young children. Acrobatic dancing is performed, the drumming becomes frenetic, the raffia skirts swirl. To make their dancing seem more like that of four-legged bush animals, the young men presenting the masks sometimes hold in their hands wooden canes, and they embellish their dance with metallic bells worn around the ankles. They are allowed to visit all the houses to rouse the lazy and punish those who do not contribute their share to the community.

According to Mali's retired museum curator Abdoullaye Sylla, who visited Richmond for his son's graduation from University of Richmond, the name "chiwara" derives from *chi,* meaning "agriculture," and *wara,* meaning "deer." Other Malinké linguists say that *tji* means "work," and *wara* means "lion." I offer no linguistic opinion, but I will offer an interpretation. The carved wooden male mask has horns and a perforated lion's mane, sometimes with hair and often with an apparent masculine sex, making it an obvious symbol of power and hunting. The horned female carries a fawn on her back, the image of the antelope, of motherhood, and of course, of fertility. Together, the masks, normally a male-female pair, represent rich harvests being drawn from Nature's soil and the generous but dangerous natural world that surrounded early humans.

Fig. 10. *Male chiwara images, ancient and modern. Illustration by T.L. Miles.*

Malians say that the curved shape of traditional chiwara masks illustrates farmers bending over their crops and hoeing the soil with the short-handled *daba*. Malians will tell you that the mask is an antelope spirit which taught men how to plant and harvest. This refers to a complicated and oft-changing Bambara legend involving an antelope that wanted to marry an exceptionally beautiful young girl called Sanoukolonin. Well, I hope they were happy together!

Malians see chiwara as the symbol of God sending down an animal spirit to teach humans the skills of agriculture. I believe that a far deeper signification lies behind the chiwara mask. My research suggests that the traditionally curving horns soaring above the lion's mane represent those of the Abyssinian mountain ibex (*capra walie*), the most agile and most inaccessible of all the mammals in that region of East Africa from which Humanity sprang. Modern sculptors sometimes carve straight horns for aesthetic reasons; but ancient masks more often have the long and very curved horns of *capra walie*. This ibex must have been the ultimate target, the most challenging hunting trophy for early African hunters in the foothills of the Abyssinian (Ethiopian) mountains—just as the lion must have provided the most dangerous of the hunter's tests on the savannah lands. Throughout Africa, lion-hunting stories are told that honor great hunters and challenge the skill and courage of their young would-be emulators. These are the two supreme trophies. The chiwara encapsulates them both. The hunter who could show both an ibex and a lion among his trophies would rise to the summit of the ancient hunters' association.

Yet the Mandé culture says that "chiwara" means "agriculture"? I believe these elements fuse together to show that the chiwara mask is one of the most ancient African masks. Originally a hunters' mask, chiwara masks came to symbolize the transition of human progress from hunting to agriculture, from a nomadic to a sedentary life style. So the chiwara represents the beginning of human settlement, the collective life of a community, and the start of "civilization" as we know it—which began in Africa. Civilized life did not begin in Mesopotamia, nor with the wanderings of the nomadic Old Testament Abraham: farming, community life and human settlements—"civilization"—first developed in Africa, when hunters began to grow crops.

This realization emerged slowly in my consciousness, but it was certainly helped by working with the Virginia Union University (VUU) African collections organized by Mrs. Barbara Grey, VUU alumna and Richmond's most distinguished elementary school teacher. After serving as principal of two Richmond schools and finally retiring from the Fox School in The Fan, Mrs. Grey decided to throw herself during retirement into saving, cataloguing, and enriching the African and African American collections of VUU that she found stacked away and mostly forgotten in cupboards and attics around the university. At the age of ninety, Barbara Grey is still managing her art collection. Her commitment to African art is a gift of dedication to her alma mater.

Having persuaded one of the many VUU presidents to allocate her a small room in the Douglas Wilder Library building, Mrs. Grey cleverly managed to expand her allotted space into a museum hall. Barbara then began inviting student groups from local schools to visit the collections. Members of Virginia Friends of Mali brought our Teaching Timbuktu program into the VUU collections, using as teaching tools all the wonderful Malian artifacts on display. We are able to play riffs on the *balafon*, the traditional wooden xylophone of the Malinké griots, and follow up with CDs of Malian musicians who stimulate students' awareness of their African musical roots and the cultural importance of griots as historians and national memory deposits. We use the lion manes of the VUU chiwara masks to introduce the story of Sunjata Keita, the Lion King. Surrounded by beautiful African sculptures, third graders feel the atmosphere and are able to understand—better than before—the glory and meaning of Virginia's ancient ancestral heritage in Africa.

Barbara Grey herself is generous with lectures about African American art, her special area of expertise. Her personal collection of work art by African Americans, is among the finest in Virginia. Inspired by Barbara's dedication to art and to education, VFoM created an education travel award in her name to send one educator each year to Ségou. We ask educators to pay 60 percent of the cost of the trip to Mali themselves, and we provide the rest, so that teachers can attend Ségou's magical Festival on the Niger River, where they can hear the best music and discover the best West African art and crafts brought together for the festival.

Our main target was intended to be third- and sixth-grade teachers, the people who are teaching about the Mali-Sonrai Empire to their elementary school students; and fourth-grade teachers who focus on America's African heritage. It has turned out to be difficult to find teachers excited enough to want to pay their fare and negotiate their time away from school in early February. Our first Barbara Grey Travel Laureate was an artist and public history teacher named Ana Edwards, a VFoM founder-member who fell in love with Mali. Returning to Richmond, she became president of VFoM. Later she joined the Richmond Sister City Commission. Like Barbara Grey's magnificent contribution to African art in Richmond, the Barbara Grey Travel Award has turned out to be a great investment.

Richmond's Academic Contributions to Ségou

A lot of Richmonders visited Ségou during the early years of the new millennium—and a lot more would have come to the Ségou festival, if two disastrous events had not changed Mali from "fairly safe" to "pretty dangerous." First was NATO's destruction of Libya in 2011, and the murder of President Muammar Gadhafi in November: Libya dissolved into chaotic civil war, Libya's vast stocks of weapons and ammunition flooded Africa, and Malian Tuaregs serving in the Libyan army Southern Brigade returned home with their weapons and vehicles. Second—directly linked to the Libyan disaster—was the coup d'état on March 21, 2012, that ousted Mali's President Touré one month before the scheduled April 29 elections. The presence in North Mali of two armies, the Libyan Tuaregs and the Malian army, had brought tensions and armed confrontations during 2011; but after the coup, Mali's army abandoned Gao, Timbuktu, and Kidal. The undefended North quickly fell into the hands of jihadist groups more or less linked to Al-Qaida, funded by Arab Gulf State extremists and run by armed criminals. The jihadists would have taken over the entire state of Mali, but were stopped by French military action in January 2013. Since then, North Mali, and to a lesser extent much of the country, has been a semi-war zone. There is a government, but not much democratic governance, and Malians are distraught. It is very sad.

Richmonders still visit Ségou, and we feel fine when we are there; but it has been tough to promote Mali to Virginians as a safe place for a cultural holiday. There are great memories of those tours we ran, of the Americans with whom we became friends, and of the many interesting folks we met along the way. One year, for example, Mayor Simaga took our group of visiting VCU faculty for drinks in the riverside villa of his friend Jacky Ickx—the Belgian driver who is married to the fabulous African diva Khadia Nin, Burundi's most famous citizen and one of Africa's greatest singers. From 1967 to 1979, Jacky was world-famous in Formula 1 and then in Indy Car racing. Now he works as an ambassador for Volkswagen. Their house near Ségou is stunningly beautiful, filled with Khadia's flair for design in the furniture carved from hard woods to fit each room and terrace of their elegant villa. Khadia is warm and charming, and her chocolate cake was wonderful.

The sister city partnerships have been rich on both sides of the Atlantic. VFoM are not the only people teaching Virginians about Mali, of course. The VMFA has conducted an important outreach program, which we supported from time to time with Mali teacher workshops, and they have produced some magnificent materials and posters about Mali. The same is true for JMU and their Museum outreach program run by Melanie Mason Brimhall and Dr. Kathryn Monger Stevens. In the area of art, there used to be an active VMFA African and African American art society, which we supported by providing Malian art objects for their fundraising auctions; and our friend Sandra Anderson-Taylor is a regular participant in VFoM meetings. Sandra is an art collector who travels frequently in Africa, having visited twenty-three African countries. Another Richmond art collector is Rick Pilgrim, a member of the Black History Museum who generously lends us magnificent Malian sculptures for VFoM exhibits. On the artisan side, Charlie Brown's store, Urban Traders, sells Malian and other African fabrics and jewelry, and every year he swears he will come with us to Mali . . . one day! We are waiting for you, Charlie!

We have also promoted Malian art and culture through Richmond's Black History Museum, with help from their exhibits coordinator Mary Lauderdale. Ana and Dana organized a day of hands-on activities that taught children about their Malian heritage through a 2010 photo exhibit titled *What is Africa to Me?* This project sought to link the personal experience of visitors (and especially young African Americans) to Mali and to their African identity. A second exhibit in 2011, *Djita: Pearls of Wisdom from a Sister City*, highlighted the story of a seven-year-old Malian girl who was born in Virginia, and who is therefore not unlike the third-grade students who are the targets of the Virginia SOL . . . except that their lives are not quite like Djita's.[27]

Dr. Maureen Elgersman-Lee, a Canadian expert on African American women's history who hosted these exhibits as director of the BHM, is now chair of political science and history at Hampton University, offering a potential new partnership for our Ségou-Richmond adventure. Experience shows that it is individuals who create partnerships: institutions do not seem to collaborate, but people do. So we have a personal partnership with Dr. Bruce Hall at Duke, because of his expertise in Timbuktu manuscripts; with Dr. Delores Koenig at American University, because of her anthropology work at Manantali; with Dr. Bruce Whitehouse at LeHigh, because of his work on Mali's urban trends; with Dr. Mary Jo Arnoldi at the Smithsonian, because she works with Malian artists; and with historian Dr. Willie Hobbs and African Arabic imam and linguist Dr. Shaheed Coovadia—both founding members of the VFoM—at Virginia State University . . . but these are not "institutional" relationships. Even our regular exchanges with the VMFA and VUU African collections owe more to Richard Woodward and Barbara Grey as individuals than they do to the institutions themselves. We have found it difficult to involve Richmond institutions in the sister city process. Is this a weakness in the way that American institutions approach life? In Mali, the first step in a partnership is always a "Letter of Understanding" such as the one VFoM

---

27 *You can view images from VFoM exhibits at http://vafriendsofmali.org/outreach/exhibitions/.*

recently signed in formal ceremonies with the new *Université de Ségou* and with the *Fondation Cheick Mansour Haidara*.

Among Virginia's academic institutions, the College of William & Mary makes a special contribution to historical work on Mali and America, through Dr. Michael Blakey's *Remembering Slavery* project. An archeologist and a world expert on cemeteries, Dr. Blakey is the person of reference for the African burial traditions of early America, and therefore for Richmond's Sacred Ground. He is also one of the experts advising Richmond's "community conversation" around the future of the Shockoe Bottom. William & Mary in Williamsburg, just one hour from Richmond, is Virginia's oldest university, the place where America's earliest presidents, including Jefferson, Monroe, and Madison, learned and taught. It was also, of course, a city of slavery; and it is the place where Dr. Maureen Elgersman-Lee is currently studying African Americans who settled after the Civil War.

One exhibit in particular sticks in my mind, because it proved how unartistic I am—especially compared to Ana. We were preparing to host one of our September 22 parties for Mali's national day with an exhibit in the foyer of the Afrikana Studies Department of VCU, at the kind invitation of Dr. Shawn Utsey. I had carried some of our VFoM materials to the department, placing carpets, hats, embroidered robes and various posters on the walls of the foyer. I was admiring my handiwork when Ana Edwards arrived. "Oh, dear!" she said. "We must change this around." Ana began giving instructions: "We can take that shirt down; let's move the hat nearer to the window; the swords won't look nice up there; we had better place the map on the other wall . . ." Finally, I burst out laughing, as the very last item I had put up so proudly was taken down and moved. After one hour of placements, Ana's exhibit looked wonderful, and I realized that my best efforts had simply created a mess!

Northern Virginia Community College, encouraged by Dean Jimmie R. McClellan, has been a partner of our Malian work through the added value of two professors who have been great friends of Mali. Dr. Laura Franklin is a French professor whose expertise includes distance learning. Laura and Dr. Moustapha Diack of Southern University together run the MERLOT online resource center for language teachers, which has strengthened the VCU "teletandem teaching" experience with Dr. Macki Samaké's students in Mali, led by professors Kathryn Murphy-Judy, Patricia Cummins, and Brahima Koné. Laura Franklin's colleague, Dr. Joseph Windham, who welcomed us to lecture in his classes at NOVA, was a leading scholar of African history and an expert on the exploration of Brazil by the Malian Emperor Abubakr II, known in Mali as Mandé Bakary. Abubakr II was a scientist and an explorer. He handed power to his brother Mansa Musa in order to lead an expeditionary force of two hundred war canoes across the Atlantic Ocean in the year 1312. Many place names and artistic productions attest to the fact that the Malians reached northeast Brazil, and VFoM celebrated the seven hundredth anniversary of his journey with our friend Dr. Cheibane Coulibaly, president of the Mandé Bakary private university in Bamako. We had wanted to put on the play in Richmond about Mandé Bakary, written by Malian author and professor Gaoussou Diawara, who sadly died in 2018; but it proved too complicated to produce an English translation. Indeed, the Brussels editor who published the French version of the play in 1996 could not even find a copy for us!

To our great sadness, Professor Joe Windham passed away on December 7, 2014. One of his students, who had been a discussion leader at VFoM's Women War & Peace Conference at VCU in 2013, spoke at the memorial service of her memories of Joe arranging for her parents to come down on the bus that he drove to our conference. In attendance at the memorial was Dr. Shonette Grant, whose African literature students may join in the Mali-Virginia partnership in the same way that UVA's Drs. Stéphanie Bérard, Kandioura Dramé, and Alison Murray-Levine bring us incidental support through their teaching of African literature and film studies related to Mali and the Caribbean diaspora.

Many of these links came about thanks to the Title VI grant that Professor Cummins and VCU obtained from the US Department of

Education. The VCU French department wanted to ensure that their students learn not just about France and Belgium, but about the whole *Francophonie*: the many countries where French is spoken. West Africa and Mali and Ségou are part of this *Francophonie*. VFoM was not paid to help this project, but we found it very valuable for VCU and for VFoM. The grant proved wonderful for faculty, for students, and for building relations between America and Africa. In the case of VCU's School of World Studies, the grant stimulated partnerships between many different US colleges, and between Virginian and Malian colleges; the grant launched the Mali teletandem teaching and a number of joint research projects in health and anthropology, women's education, business studies, and peace promotion. It led directly to the formation of new Virginian partnerships with Ivory Coast as well as Mali; and it allowed the sister city relationship with Ségou to flourish. In addition, the Title VI partnership between VCU and VFoM allowed faculty and students to visit West Africa, and stimulated the creation of the 2013 Women, War & Peace Conference, which one VCU student told me had been a "life-changing experience."

Another of VFoM's natural academic partners is the Virginia Conference of Social Studies Educators (VCSSE), which brings together every year six hundred or eight hundred social studies and history teachers. This is one educational conference where Malian history is actually on the agenda, through the SOL. Since VFoM was created to support teaching about Mali, we have attended the VCSSE several times—but it costs us a lot of money! We pay for a stand where we exhibit Malian fabrics and other arts to show teachers . . . but our nonprofit association is treated much the same way as commercial publishing houses. What are we selling? Only our love of Mali, and a couple of books that we sell at cost—and most of the potential teacher-clients already have these books. VCSSE allows us to spend a couple of days talking to people we already know. We can give a Mali lecture to a dozen teachers during the conference, but is the impact worth the enormous effort we have to make as volunteers? We appreciate that the conference organizers also put in a lot of effort; but while it is easy for us to drive over for the day when the conference is held in Williamsburg or Richmond, we had to stay overnight in a hotel to support the conferences at Tyson's Corner and Roanoke—money coming out of our own pockets. Recently, they have allowed us to offer information about our free Teaching Timbuktu on their Facebook page, but we still find it is a slightly unequal partnership with VCSSE, with whose members we should be working more closely.

We certainly worked with them, when the Virginia Board of Education wanted to remove social studies and history from the third-grade curriculum. This disgraceful idea was dropped, fortunately, but not before Virginia Friends of Mali had testified in person before the board on the importance for Virginia's schools of maintaining a balanced curriculum that includes geography and history and understanding of where Virginia fits into the overall pattern of world history—which, in the case of third grade and fourth grade and sixth grade, includes the history of Mali and the role that Africans have played in creating and building Virginia.

The First Sister City Projects in Richmond and Ségou

Returning Home to Bamako

7:00 a.m. I am back in Mali. The air is delightfully cool in Bamako's early morning light. I stretch my back, as noises fill the courtyard around me. Ami Coulibaly is lighting the charcoal brazier to make tea and some sorghum porridge. Small children are getting their schoolbags ready. A twelve-year-old maid is noisily sweeping the dust with a broom made of twigs. I have no idea where she comes from, but Ami knows. I must ask Ami if this girl also attends school. The domestic noises tell me it is time to emerge from under my mosquito net.

I wonder why I do not sleep during the afternoon heat, and spend the cool, dark hours awake? That is what I used to do when I worked in Gao and Timbuktu: there, the sun of the Sahara made it too hot to stay in bed by 6:30 a.m., and by 7:00 a.m., it was too hot to stay in the courtyard. In Bamako, the afternoon temperatures seldom rise above 100 (occasionally 110) degrees Fahrenheit. But in Gao, it can reach 120 degrees, and during the very hot season, offices close at noon, for there is no air conditioning in the poor and remote parts of Africa.

Sleep is better in the cool air, and sleep is important for good health—which is why I abandon the house with its sun-warmed cement walls to sleep outside in Africa's cool night air—unless it rains. Then I make a quick retreat indoors with my bedding, and leave the rain washing the sky.

Bamako's air this morning is filled with the dust of the city and the sand of the Sahara. It smells of burning trash, filthy sewers, and fume-belching elderly motor vehicles, enriched by carbon monoxide from one hundred thousand charcoal-and-wood cooking fires. Cool air, but dirty air. Ségou is cleaner. If I could, I would move this house to Ségou.

My cold morning shower is vivifying. Toothpaste makes my dry mouth feel fresh again. Several visiting men are hanging around in the courtyard—"We slept well, the family is well, there is peace only"— and the living room is full of women waking up. One is praying. The young maid is rolling up the sleeping mats and piling them inside Ami's sleeping room. We have visitors because Ami is organizing a wedding.

12:00—midday. I have moved to the house of my friend Hallassy, because my house is filled with women and wedding. I am not even sure whose wedding it is. My courtyard has nowhere left to sit. Every space is filled with amazing embroidered costumes containing flabby, bulging women. Seated on crowded mats, cutting meat and onions, and gossiping, the women eat and cook, laugh and shout, listen to the praise singers and throw them coins. Later, as the sun cools and the drums begin to beat, the women will dance. Weddings in Mali are for women.

Hallassy Sidibé is a geographer and academic who has been my "milk brother" for three decades. We lounge on the carpet in his quiet house, reclining against leather cushions from Timbuktu, and sip the ritual three small glasses of tea that Malians have adopted from the desert people. The first is bitter as life; the second, as more water is added, and some sugar, is smooth like the love of a woman; the third— by now there is more sugar than tea—is sweet as death: for where life is harsh in the desert, the inevitability of death can seem more like a well-earned holiday than a loss of pleasure. Hallassy's wife Bana brings us grilled chicken and salad, telling us we are a useless pair of nobodies and she needs to find some new, better husbands. We laugh, and eat. Then we stretch out on the carpet, and snooze.

7:00 p.m. I cannot come home until nightfall, because my court-yard is filled with women eating and dancing. When I do get home, the courtyard looks like a bomb site and the fizzy drinks have all been drunk. I recuperate in my comfortable wooden deck chair. I distribute balloons to my Malian "grandchildren," who amuse me with their giggles. Several have come from neighboring houses. Others belong to Ami Coulibaly and her children; others are her nephews and nieces; and four of them are children of my adopted son Kalifa Touré, who teaches economics and finance in one of the universities and has become a key logistical organizer for Virginia Friends of Mali.

8:00 p.m. Edoir arrives. He is Ami's son and is studying at the University of Bamako to become a customs officer, although mostly he plays soccer. I promised all of Ami's children that I would educate them, and Edoir is the fourth. Is he the last? Each of the first three has already had two of Ami's grandchildren, so I doubt it.

Edoir was named after my son Edward when the latter was fifteen. Edward was very pleased to have a baby as namesake—or homonyme in French, which is often shortened by Malians to homo. (The natural Malian sentence "You are my homo" therefore causes some confusion among Americans!) Technically, Edoir should have been "Edouard," in accordance with the typical French spelling; but when Ed's father went to declare the baby at the local mayor's office, a Malian official who had never heard such a strange name wrote "Edoir" on the birth certificate.

Ed looks good this evening: instead of the usual T-shirt, he is wear-ing the three-piece blue embroidered *grand boubou* I gave him after Bana provided my new gray robes (glistening embroidery on magnif-icent shining robes, for $600). Weddings demand fancy clothes, and Edoir likes his new outfit.

9:00 p.m. The house is quiet, and the crowds are gone. Ami has prepared some of my favorite *lenburuji* drink, made from fresh ginger root, sugar, and squeezed lemons. With a hammer, she breaks some splinters from a block of ice and throws them into my metal goblet. I stretch out and sigh with pleasure. She has some millet porridge, *degeh,* that will fill up the corners of my stomach before sleep comes to me where I lie under my mango tree, protected by my mosquito net. Lovely Mali—a land of warm friendships, warm air, and simple pleasures.

Virginian and Malian Musicians Play at the Ségou Festival

It was at the Richmond Public Library's Mali exhibit that the Virginia Friends of Mali first met Heather Maxwell, in October 2005. She had been a Peace Corps volunteer in Minianka country, near Mali's border with Burkina Faso, and her passion was Malian music. Not just Malian music: Heather was a professional African musician, already well-known in Ghana and in America, leading her own group, *Afrika Soul.* She taught ethnomusicology at the University of Virginia after her Indiana PhD thesis on Malian music, and we traveled from Richmond as a group to hear one of her concerts in Charlottesville. We loved the fusion of Mali, Ivory Coast, and Ghana rhythms with her childhood training in Michigan gospel music. Her rendition of *"Pata Pata,"* perhaps the most famous modern song to come out of Africa, is as good as the original version sung by Miriam Makeba. When Ambassador Diop decided to bring Mali's prime minister to Richmond, and the City of Richmond agreed to fund a reception for the Mali delegation, I called Heather, and she agreed to play for us.

At the end of his VCU speech, Allan Levenberg and I took the PM and his senior officials, the ambassador and a couple of ministers, to a salon in the Richmond Public Library for a few minutes' private rest and refreshment. Then we hitched up our embroidered robes—because you do not want to trip on the stairs while wearing six *pagnes,* the equivalent of eighteen yards of embroidered damask fabric—and descended three flights of stairs into the basement reception area. At the far end of the hall on stage, Heather Maxwell was singing a traditional Bambara song and playing the *kamalen ngoni,* often called the hunter's harp. When Prime Minister Ousmane Issoufi Maiga entered the hall, *Afrika Soul* stopped playing. Everyone paused. And then Heather began a new song, a famous Sonrai praise tune from Gao,

Maiga's hometown. I was escorting the PM, and I can bear witness that he almost wept from emotion as he walked to the front of the hall through a crowd of four hundred people, accompanied by the Sonrai music of his homeland.

Since then, we have heard Heather play at the Ségou festival, watched her travel to Mali in 2011 on a Fulbright scholarship, and seen her join Voice of America as host and producer of the worldwide radio-and-TV program *Music Time in Africa*. Other fine American musicians have supported the Ségou-Mali partnership: Corey Harris, Seth Swingle, Chuck Kerwath, and Julie Moore immediately spring to mind, as well as our local DC griot Cheick Hamala Diabaté. Each of them enriches the life of Americans and West Africans through their concerts and creativity.

We meet lots of African musicians at the Ségou festival. Vieux Farka Touré is the talented musical son of my old and much-missed friend Ali, who lies buried in his hometown of Niafunké. Everyone should listen to Ali Farka play the traditional tune *"Debe"* with Toumani Diabaté.[28] Toumani, whom I have known since he was a boy, is a master of the *kora*. After *"Debe"*—an ancient tune that was played at the court of Sunjata Keita—you should hear Toumani and Ali play together on the magical Grammy-winning CD In the Heart of the Moon.[29]

The famous group *Ngoni Ba* is led by Bassekou Kouyaté and his diva wife Ami Sacko, both from Ségou. We have hosted both Vieux Farka Touré and *Ngoni Ba* at the Richmond Folk Festival, heard their music in Ségou and visited their homes. It was when Vieux came to play in Richmond, that I first met Corey Harris, a blues and reggae musician who collaborated with Ali Farka Touré on his blues-fusion album *Mississippi to Mali*. I found Corey speaking French with Haoua Cheick Traoré in her Mali boutique at the Richmond Folk Festival.

---

28 See *https://www.youtube.com/watch?v=pJUE03aeaQ4 to listen to Debe.*
29 See *https://www.youtube.com/watch?v=NpWUcI7bGmY* to listen to In the Heart of the Moon.

Impressive skills! Originally from Denver, Corey and his wife Ife now live in Richmond. The first thing I noticed was their hair, mounted under elegant turbans; then their eyes and their intelligence. In 2007 Harris was awarded a Macarthur Foundation "genius grant" and he continues to travel to West Africa, exploring the roots of the African American experience. It is sweet to hear Corey and Ali Farka play *Catfish Blues*, singing in Sonrai, in English, and talking philosophy: although the ocean may separate us, says Ali, Americans and Africans are still the same people. Ali tells Corey he is home, at the source of his inspiration and his wisdom.[30]

Corey Harris often plays with our talented local griot Cheick Hamala Diabaté, based in Northern Virginia, who is often the musical star of our Mali events. When we organized a Peace Conference on Mali and Liberia is 2013, Diabaté came to Richmond to play for peace. At the Richmond Folk Festival, Cheick Hamala rocks the casbah! It takes him just ninety seconds to have five hundred people up and dancing to his Mali guitar rhythms, or to his *ngoni*. You can hear a musical fusion with Corey Harris on Cheick Hamala's *Ake Doni Doni*, "take it slow."[31]

One of Cheick Hamala's most brilliant students is Seth Swingle from Charlottesville, a talented banjo musician who also wanted to learn the banjo's ancestral *ngoni* instrument. Seth has played with Cheick Hamala at the Kennedy Center. Then one day, as I was sitting with friends in Bamako drinking tea, half-watching a concert on television, I saw that *Ngoni Ba* was playing in the vast concert hall of the *Palais de la Culture Hampaté Ba*, beside the Niger River. Suddenly Bassekou Kouyaté was introducing this young white musical genius Seth—Waraden Diabaté by his Malian moniker—sitting center stage wearing shiny green damask fabric, and playing the *ngoni* in front of three thousand Malians. He had been studying with Bassekou in Ségou, and had been sleeping on the couch in our Ségou lodgings during the festival. Seth had to make our coffee, because he was the youngest in

30 https://www.youtube.com/watch?v=uahUgXnhcUk
31 https://www.youtube.com/watch?v=A_g7ilQYdO0

the group (the rest of us were VCU faculty members). Seth is a Fulbright music scholar whose Bambara-speaking father Craig (Waraba Doumbia in Mali, meaning "lion") was once a Peace Corps volunteer in a village near Ségou. Craig is a carpenter, like plenty of people called Doumbia, but his son quite naturally adopted the great musical name Waraden Diabaté. His first name, Waraden, means "lion cub."

All these gifted American musicians participate in Ségou cultural life and follow the traditions of the Mandé, seeking out the deepest roots of American music. Meanwhile, Julie Moore, a classical cellist, has been bringing the music of the Mandé to the Charleston Jazz Initiative in the Carolinas and to her music school, *Cradle of Jazz*: notably the Malian/Wasulu female vocalist, percussionist, and *kamelen ngoni* player Kokanko Sata Doumbia, and Dogon scholar Assigué Dolo, with whom Julie is also studying musical roots and traditions.

In Richmond, the members of VFoM have welcomed Kokanko and Julie to play several concerts. Julie and I have presented papers together to the African Studies Association on the role of music and civil society in building peace. Praise singers the griots may be; but they are much more than musicians: they are also diplomats and mediators. Does music in Mali have more meaning for the people and their culture than music in America? Is music the lifeblood of Malian culture? That would be a great subject for a master's thesis.

Mayor Brahima Thiero and Hala's Ashes

Shortly before leaving America to visit Ségou, I received a phone call from Dennis Brennan, an old friend who had been my boss twelve years before, when he was the director of USAID in Bamako. "Did you know Hala Pietkiewicz?" Dennis asked me.

I told him I remembered her name from my time in Mali with USAID. "Well, let me tell you about Hala," Dennis continued. "She became a very close friend of my late wife Barbara, whom you and Michelle knew well. Hala was a lady of about seventy, originally a Polish refugee who became an American sculptor and artist. On reaching retirement age, Hala decided to become a Peace Corps volunteer.

She worked in the region of Mali's Manantali hydroelectric dam, helping villagers to resettle after their farms and villages had been flooded by the new lake. You were working mainly in North Mali, so you may not have come across her work, although you might have met her in USAID or even at my house. Anyhow, I shall come to the point: Hala has died and she has been cremated. One of her daughters called me and asked if I had anyone I could trust to scatter half of Hala's ashes in the Niger River. The other half will be scattered in Texas, where she lived and died."

I said I would be honored to scatter Hala's ashes over the surface of the *Ba Djoli Ba*, the Great Lifeblood Artery of Mali. The ashes arrived in a packet through the mail, and they traveled to Mali in my suitcase. In Ségou, I purchased a small box fashioned from a gourd and poured the ashes out of their plastic bag and into the gourd. And it was with this small gourd that I set off across the river with the mayor of Ségou, Brahima Thiero; his brother, Karamogo Thiero, head of the fishermen's cooperative; Cheikh Kalil Doumbia, a marabout; and Laji Nentao, a griot; Bandjougou Danté, a journalist who had come to record the event; and a couple members of the Richmond delegation, Allan Levenberg and Carol Zuckert, who had kindly volunteered to come with me.

We stepped into the canoe as it lay on the sandy shore beside where the donkeys come down to drink, and pushed off from the riverbank at 7:00 a.m., carrying Hala's ashes. The traditional leaders of Ségou, the Nentao and Thiero clans, had taken the whole event in stride, and made it work wonderfully well. Karamogo Thiero had organized the ceremony. As the chief of the fishermen of Ségou, he had arranged for a fisherman named Sidiki Diakité to pole us out slowly into the river, while Laji Nentao sang Islamic prayers in a melodic voice.

Names like Nentao and Thiero belong to the ancient Somono fishing people, who founded Ségou and many other communities along the banks of the Niger long before recorded time. Karamogo's ancestors may have been fishing here for four thousand years or more, and Laji's ancestors may have sung beside them—just as Laji was doing now, weaving a haunting eulogy in praise of Hala, of her Creator, and for all those whom He protects in life and after death.

Once we reached the center of the river, we stopped. Above the waters of the Niger, we stood in the canoe with palms raised while the *marabout* Cheikh Kalil Doumbia read from the Holy Koran in classical Arabic. Then I read a brief funeral oration in French on behalf of Virginia Friends of Mali and in the name of Hala's family and friends, commending the spirit and soul of Hala to eternal peace with God. Allan Levenberg and Carol Zuckert took photographs, while Danté sat spellbound. He said he was spooked because Malians bury their dead, and he had never heard of cremation. The idea of scattering ashes in an intimate, commemorative event left him speechless.

Finally, as the mayor of Ségou and I scattered Hala's ashes across the surface of the Eternal River, Carol Zuckert sang the *Kaddish,* the Jewish prayer for the dead. In this way did four monotheistic religions—ancestral African, Muslim, Christian, and Jewish—combine to produce a single magnificent, simple ceremony to honor the life and love of Hala Pietkiewicz: former Peace Corps volunteer, friend, and permanent admirer of the people of Mali. Thus did we invoke for Hala the protection of the Creator—Nga, Allah, Dieu, Jehovah.

It was an ethereal moment. The beauty of the Jewish lament, the cool breeze over the river, the stillness of the waters, the ashes gently falling from one white hand and one black hand, the feeling of blessing, quiet, and peace—all of this represented Hala's true homecoming to the land of her friends, and of all our ancestors. Hala was smiling down upon us in that moment, and we could feel her pleasure. Her smile completed our own moment of joy, calmness, and peace.

Thank you, Hala. God keep you safe!

Letter from Ewa, Hala's Daughter:

Hello Dear Robin:

I just cannot get over how appropriate this ceremony was for Hala, and you had not even met Hala.
We read your account, and we cried tears of emotion.
When we came to America instead of moving to Aus-
tralia, grandma was here but mainly we came here
because of the American ideals "liberty, freedom for
all." And when living in Glen Ridge, NJ, (a rather
lily-white community where everyone had an ancestor who "came over on the Mayflower"), Hala was
shocked to learn of the difficulty a black family had
trying to move in the "neighborhood." It is at that
time that she joined the NAACP and started getting involved with racial equality issues. Fania Davis
(sister of Angela Davis) lived with us for 2 years in an
exchange student program run by the Quakers, which
enabled black students from the South to find a better
education up North. Fania ended up being the vale-
dictorian speaker at high school graduation. We have
many other such stories. Hala was quite the freedom
fighter, with a huge humanitarian spirit. How very
special she was, and she was loved.

Veronika and I planted a harvest-moon colored
hibiscus around noon, which was the time Hala died
and also the time she was born, in the garden at the
hospice where they have a labyrinth and walking
garden. It was a bit overcast at time of digging the
hole and placing her ashes under the plant. We didn't
realize at the time we picked the spot for the plant that
it faces the Catholic church and every day at noon the
church bells ring (surprising us when we finished the

planting). We felt peaceful and happy with our little memorial to her. About an hour later it downpoured, watering in the plant, and then the sun came back out with many glorious clouds. The rest of Hala's ashes were released from a glider above Texas. The Hospice, the Air of Texas, the Waters of Mali: perfect!

Much love and gratitude,
Ewa and Veronika

Fig. 11. Hala's ashes drift across the surface of the Niger River. Photo: Allan Levenberg, VFoM.

Richmond Volunteers Trying to Make a Difference in Ségou

VFoM's first contribution to Malian health and hygiene was providing clean water to Sokoura elementary school—thanks to the initiative of a brilliant young lady called Lakshmi, who spent six months teaching and working with a Malian NGO during 2007. Lakshmi—as her name suggests—has an Indian Brahmin father, while her mother is a white English doctor. Lakshmi is now a doctor herself; but after leaving high school and before going to university, she wanted to learn to speak fluent French . . . but not in France. And so, Lakshmi came to Mali to work as a volunteer in a local NGO called SOS-Sahel.

To be sure she would be protected and cared for, Lakshmi was adopted by the family of one of the NGO managers, a forester named Monsieur Mamadou Diakité whom I have known for twenty years. I remember how nervous Lakshmi was the first night in her new family; but also how excited she was! I spent that evening with Monsieur Diakité, while Lakshmi ate dinner with his daughters. "I was able to talk to them quite well in French, and they understood what I said," Lakshmi told me happily. "Their accent was strange at first, but even that was getting better by the end of the meal."

Lakshmi proved an asset for SOS-Sahel. She taught English to the NGO staff, fixed their computers, and taught them to master Excel and other software. Lakshmi also loved the elementary school where her house-mother Madame Noëlle Diakité was a teacher. I presume Madame Diakité was born around Christmas, and while her husband is Muslim, she is Christian—but no one in Mali worries about such details. Lakshmi helped with teaching and sports at Sokoura elementary school. She realized that water was a problem. So Lakshmi decided to raise money using her parents' connections to provide a school water storage facility, providing the children with clean water for washing and drinking.

Lakshmi took me on an exploration of water equipment suppliers in Bamako. She compared the prices of metal water towers, and large, heavy-duty plastic water containers—the sort of equipment that Oxfam or the UN's High Commissioner for Refugees install to ensure safe and clean water supplies in refugee camps. Lakshmi prepared her budget, and sent off letters asking her parents to arrange a program of fundraising presentations to medical and other generous donors when she returned home. The money was duly raised, and sent to Mali where (to my relief—I did not have time to handle it) SOS-Sahel and the Diakité family organized the purchasing and installation of the Sokoura school water system. Which is still going strong!

While Lakshmi was settling in for her six-month stint with SOS-Sahel, James was being installed on the roof of Ségou's Allaire High School. It was Mayor Thiero who asked us to support the Allaire, maybe because, as I discovered later, his own children were studying there. There was an empty room on the flat roof. Maybe it had been built for a security guard? The head teacher, Monsieur Sidibé, had the room cleaned out, and wired with electric light for his native English-speaking volunteer teacher. James—who is also now a doctor—was Lakshmi's boyfriend, and he had followed her to Mali on the clear understanding that they would be doing different jobs in different places. James could only stay for six weeks, because he had an orchestra tour lined up for later in the summer. Six weeks is too short for working with a rural development program, but it can be useful for teaching English. James was a precious teaching resource for Allaire's English department, and a great language-immersion opportunity for the students.

Monsieur Sidibé already had experience of volunteer teachers. He knew the value of conversation with a native English-language speaker, not least for his own teachers. In any event, the people who benefited most from James were the half-dozen smart seniors who adopted him as their friend. James ate every day with one of these Malian families, chatting with students of his own age who later obtained very good English grades in their baccalaureate school-leaving certificate. James told me very proudly one day, that he was asked to fill in for a teacher who was sick, and he handled a two-hour English class just fine. Sadly, it was the English teachers who profited the least. Many Malian men feel they would lose face by learning from a "mere boy." This might seem absurd—why would anyone feel ashamed of speaking less well than a native English speaker? Traditional teachers believe in teaching grammar; perhaps this allows them to conceal the limits of their English conversation skills.

We see a wealth of opportunities for professional volunteers to work with Ségou. (Managing teenage volunteers is more complicated.) Commercial initiatives are being explored concerning solar energy, manufacturing medicines, and transforming Malian shea butter for cosmetics. Richmond has experience to share about drainage and flood control and riverbank erosion, derived from the flood and water management of the James River and the Chesapeake watershed. Ségou, on the Niger, and Richmond, on the James, have different and yet similar problems related to water management, flooding, water pollution, and the supply of drinking water. Some Ségoviens see an urgent need to improve Niger River ecology and water management. Mamou Daffé, chair of the local economic development council CPEL (*Conseil pour la Promotion de l'Economie locale*) has created an *Observatoire du Fleuve Niger* to study water usage, riverbank maintenance, cleanliness, pollution, and hygiene.

Public health issues offer partnership opportunities to both cities. VFoM has provided latrines and clinics, as we shall see below. The mayor of Ségou asked us in 2007 to help with waste disposal, taking us around the empty municipal garage he had inherited. Richmond City has no trucks to donate: the city hires all its equipment. After much searching, we found a Richmond company, Eubank Trucks, that was willing to help clear Ségou's trash. The owner and the general manager, Lance Eubank and Larry White, agreed to supply seven-thousand-dollar secondhand ten-ton trucks and front-loaders, as well as plenty of spare parts. The trucks were rusty from the distribution of salt and sand, but rust does not spread in Mali, one of the world's driest countries. Nevertheless, Mayor Simaga was not impressed with this offer, so Ségou's piles of trash continued to grow.

Richmond can also learn from Ségou. While Richmond's AIDS awareness campaigns could illuminate Ségou, the simple organization and cheap medical services offered by Ségou's community-owned heath centers would astonish Richmonders. The world-famous Bamako Initiative for the cheap supply of essential basic medicines, supported by the World Health Organization, focuses resources on a limited number of inexpensive generics—unknown to Virginian doctors dominated by Big Pharma.

Health in West Africa starts with the distribution of mosquito
nets to fight malaria, and intensive AIDS education programs to protect mothers and children: preventive public health. At the other end
of the medical scale, Richmond's world-class hospital systems include
VCU's Medical College of Virginia, Henrico Doctors, St Mary's,
Retreat, and Bon Secours. A joint research project on AIDS has begun
between VCU's Aids Clinic and Ségou's Hôpital Niankoro Fomba,
which has ambitions to become a teaching hospital. Our VFoM mothers, knowledgeable about West African family life, are keen to improve
mother-and-child health and early childhood education in Ségou. It
is useful to remember that most young mothers are still teenagers . . .
and that is true even in Richmond.

Another creative initiative brought Dr. Shawn Utsey, head of VCU
Afrikana Studies, to Ségou to make a film by and about adolescents.
Shawn's project, Peep This, had done similar work with young Richmonders, encouraging young urban boys to express their frustrations
and their creative skills through a medium they like. (Films are better
than books, which resemble schoolwork.) The result was exciting for
the dozen young girls and boys who participated in Ségou. The sister
city commission selected participants from among the top students
in certain high school classes, creating a small, elite group. Dr. Utsey
found that his best Richmond filmmakers were also among the top
students. Movers and shakers are usually dynamic students. Reaching
into the lethargic lower ranks is not easy.

As their theme for the Festival of the Niger River, the Ségou adolescents chose *bogolan mud cloth,* which was naturally abundant in
the artisan stalls, as it is a specialty of the region. They interviewed
sellers and buyers; they took their movie cameras and overhead micro-
phones into the *bogolan* workshops to see and hear how mud cloth is
dyed with leaves; they filmed the cloth being stained and decorated
with fermented black river mud that reacts chemically with the dye.
Finally, the young people struck lucky when they happened to meet
the former minister of culture and Mali's most famous film director,
Cheikh Oumar Sissoko, coming out of a meeting. With elegant flu-

ency, Monsieur Sissoko agreed to be interviewed, and his positioning of *bogolan* in the history and culture of Mali provided the perfect context within which Dr. Utsey was able to frame the story. The result was a charming short film that we were able to distribute on DVD, and that we projected onto a screen the following year at Mamou Daffé's Centre Koré in Ségou, to the delight of the student filmmakers and their families. After the screening, however, we were left with the same feeling we'd had in Richmond: What next? Should we put the film on television? Will these students ever have a chance to repeat and develop their film experience? Will other adolescents be able to try filming? Or will this be a one-off, a chance encounter between twelve young Ségoviens and one VCU professor?

Richmond's department of education identifies clear links between education, health, and economic poverty—an idea from which Ségou could benefit, if both sets of city officials spent time together. We have introduced many Richmond officials working in education, drainage, road maintenance, traffic management, health, water management, and solar energy to Ségou's mayor and his delegations. I remember translating for one very interesting discussion between, among others, Viktoria Badger, the Richmond urban planner; Travis Bridewell, the city engineer; and Chris Beschler, the public works guru, in the elegant surroundings of Richmond's Main Street Station. We discussed transport and water management experiences, and later we even found some bilingual Canadian materials on the internet to help the Ségou officials follow up issues that I had been translating during our meeting. But we cannot make the technical partnerships work for them. Officials need to explore partnership opportunities in their technical sectors. The French-English language barrier adds an easy excuse to the general tendency toward lethargy.

It should be easier to work with schools, but unfortunately, it has not proved so. Not all Malian children attend formal schools, which are less prevalent in Mali than in Virginia. One year, the VFoM initiated an exchange of artwork and photos between schools; we brought paintings and photos from six elementary schools in Mali back to Virginia and shared them with six Richmond teachers who had worked with us on Teaching Timbuktu. We did not receive even one photo in return. Not a single Richmond school responded to the Malian initiative. Sister Cities International's annual art competition has had a few entrants from Malian lycée students, but not every year. When they respond, VFoM awards prizes and certificates to the best entrants from Ségou.

One of our favorite Malian women is singer and songwriter Rokia Traoré, an inspiration for young Malian women. Her song "Sabali," available on YouTube, features a slideshow of Malian girls. Her songs, and those of Fatoumata Diawara, have inspired us to support young women as a sister city priority.[32] After several years of reflection and experimentation, we believe that girls' education offers the best opportunity for the Ségou-Richmond partnership to have an educational impact. Through a focus on supporting girls' education both in and outside of school, the sister city partnership can make a real difference in both cities. As our Malian friends like to tell us, "If you educate a boy, you create a man. When you educate a girl, you build a nation."

The Bill & Melinda Gates Foundation: Fighting Poverty in Africa

In 2008, Sister Cities International (SCI), which is based in Washington, DC, negotiated an exciting project with the Bill & Melinda Gates Foundation called the African Urban Poverty Alleviation Project (AUPAP). This was a building project run by engineers, with the goal of improving community hygiene.

Many parts of Ségou lack proper health and sanitation facilities, which leads to disease and environmental degradation; so we were understandably thrilled to undertake such a project. Filled with enthusiasm, we started work on our hygiene strategy in the spring of 2009, before the sister city agreement with Ségou had even been signed—Richmond being bogged down for more than a year with the minutiae of appointing its new sister city commissioners—even

---

32 Hear Rokia at *https://www.youtube.com/watch?v=92ahok3oy6Q*; listen to Fatoumata at *https://www.youtube.com/watch?v=DaZT3I3Zd1Q.*

though we could not be awarded the any money until after the signing ceremony that made us official sister cities.. Long before the official signing ceremony in October 2009, we had named Allan Levenberg the Richmond project manager for AUPAP, and Madani Sissoko took on the same role in Ségou. At that time, Michelle had just retired from CFI. With twenty years of field experience and time enough to make the trip, she volunteered to travel to Ségou to work with Ségou's sister city commission to identify priority activities.

While in Ségou, Michelle visited the local kindergarten, a community health center, and a marketplace. She returned to Richmond with a proposal to build a maternity clinic and marketplace latrines. This proposal included preliminary designs, estimated costs, and an evaluation plan for a new maternity unit, a laboratory for medical analyses, and three blocks of latrines. The evaluation plan in particular was critical to our receipt of a grant, for the Gates Foundation was determined we should produce numbers, although some of us remain skeptical about the utility—or even the feasibility—of counting the numbers of people using a school, a clinic, or public toilets.

A love of data can be very misleading, as I have found while working for USAID and evaluating projects for the European Union. "People use statistics like a drunk uses a lamp post: for support rather than illumination," say the Irish; and how right they are! If you measure the wrong things, you get the wrong results. An obsession with numbers in education, for example, produces lists of classrooms; records the number of desks, chairs, and books purchased; and counts the children sitting on these chairs—but it tells us nothing about the quality of the education being provided. Are the children reading the books? Are they understanding them? Or are the books locked away in a library so that the children will not make them dirty?

I have seen elementary schools in Bamako where 120 children are chanting their letters in the same classroom—and learning almost nothing. A class of twenty children is better than a class of 120; yet USAID and the EU follow the same maddening logic of celebrating the larger number simply because it is bigger. But a class of 120 is not six times better; it is probably ten times worse. Projects should be evaluated by their impacts, good and bad, on health or education after several years, not by counting numbers every time someone goes to the toilet.

How many years is several years? Well, it depends. Donors like to talk about the "project cycle," the duration of which usually corresponds to however much time is left before the answer to the question: "When is the donor's next accounting deadline?" That is a complete misuse of the concept of a "project cycle." Accountants should not determine development strategies—and when they do, the results are calamitous. Even a third grader can work out that it does not take the same amount of time to build a bridge as to build the education of a child. For a bridge, two or three years may be fine; but the project cycle of a child's education is twelve years. For community and agricultural development, a cycle may last fifteen to twenty-five years. That is a more reasonable project cycle for social change—which happened, as Malian cotton farmer Monsieur Traoré explained when he came to visit Ten Thousand Villages in Richmond, after his generation of twenty-year-olds had mastered their new skills in functional literacy and accounting and were able to take control of their village development association when they reached the age of thirty-five or forty. By contrast, three-year projects are all too often a waste of taxpayers' money; USAID and EU, please note!

SCI headquarters loved our enthusiasm for AUPAP, and I hid my doubts about the value of Gates' insistence on an evaluation plan. AUPAP managers were also impressed with Richmond's proactive attitude, with our experience with Africa, and with the efficiency of our partners in Ségou. We were lucky to have Madani Sissoko, for he is the sort of man who sees a pothole in his driveway one morning, and has resurfaced the whole road by nightfall.

The engineers were also very concerned with "risk"—a theoretical insurance concept in American public works projects that, when imposed here, proved extremely counterproductive to the microtask of building rural latrines. Risk is usually assessed at 10 or 15 percent of the cost of a project—but for a block of latrines costing only $25,000, closely supervised by two sister city commissions, how much "risk" can there really be? In reality, the financial risk here was less than the cost of the bank guarantee the engineers wanted—a concept unknown to the small contractors in rural Mali whose total capital assets may amount to one old vehicle and a wheelbarrow. Most latrine builders in Mali have no cash reserves and no bank account—although we insisted they open an account for the AUPAP project.

The engineers wanted to advance just 10 percent of the total budget—but that meant that our latrines simply could not be built. Cement, steel rods, doors and windows, plumbing, and other supplies, all imported into Mali from Europe via the Ivory Coast, had to be prefunded, and they represented 80 percent of the project cost. We finally persuaded the engineers to change their cash-flow rules, and the AUPAP team based in Accra, Ghana agreed to advance 60 percent of the cost to build the latrines. But it had taken so long to negotiate this arrangement that the rainy season had arrived, and construction had to stop. We lost a whole building season—a cost that the engineers had not, apparently, considered when engaging in risk management.

The volunteers in Ségou were disheartened, but after the rainy season ended, they threw themselves into the project once more. With the funding provided by the Gates Foundation, we built blocks of latrines and handwashing facilities for *Les Poupons* Kindergarten, the Médine Community Health Center, and the Water Tower Public Market. The market is in a busy part of the city: as many as one thousand people each day use the sanitation facilities, and this of course improves hygiene. I was worried about the management of the public latrines, but it turned out to be the most successful of the three projects because the Market Management Committee decided to charge a tiny fee, which they used to pay an elderly watchman. Clients at the public market received water in a kettle from this official watchman; plastic kettles, found in every Malian bathroom, are used for washing the feet before prayers, and for more intimate washing after defecation. This fusion of the spiritual with the defecatory that has produced our happy outcome under the supervision of the elderly cleaner, who alone manipulated the equipment; and as a result, unlike the facilities at the school and the clinic, which soon had broken faucets, the marketplace equipment lasted much better. During the inauguration ceremony, we awarded this market latrine supervisor a standing ovation for his achievement and left him beaming, holding a welcome banknote in his hand.

The Médine Community Health Center was renovated using the rest of the AUPAP money. An extension was constructed with laboratory space, a second labor ward, a pharmacy, and consulting rooms; and the waiting area in the main building was renovated, increasing access to health care services for twenty-eight thousand people in Ségou. Because the Gates grant included money for travel, Ana, Dana, and Michelle all visited from Richmond to encourage the project team and report on their progress.

We had carefully managed the budget so that $4,000 would be left over to equip the laboratory, but we were never able to get that money from the Gates engineers in Accra. The Accra team consisted of a Briton, a Serb, and an American, and none of them had any prior experience in Africa. During their visits, their aloofness went down badly with the Malians; instead of spending some evenings socializing with the Malian team, they preferred to retire to their hotel to drink beer—a choice that showed insensitivity to the fact that they were guests in a Muslim country.

In early 2012, a large Richmond delegation, including Michelle, Allan, and US ambassador Mary Beth Leonard, visited Ségou to attend the Ségou festival. Since the AUPAP project was still short $4,000, Michelle invited our visiting American friends to donate money to help equip the laboratory. We all contributed, and came up with $3,500. Michelle and Dr. Patricia Cummins, who had just become the RSCC president, presented this money to Ségou's sister city commission, and Madani Sissoko arranged the purchasing of the equipment. When I visited the laboratory in February 2018, Dr. Basile Diarra enthused about how much money the health center had saved by no longer needing to pay for external analyses that he was now able to carry out himself with his own simple laboratory equipment.

Despite delays and difficulties, our project was a huge success. The inauguration ceremony for our AUPAP clinic, laboratory, and latrines took place on Saturday, February 18, 2012, with the minister for local government, Mr. David Sacko, officiating in the presence of the US ambassador to Mali, Ms. Mary Beth Leonard; and Richmond's third sister city commission president, Dr. Patricia Cummins—who had succeeded Ms. My Lan Tran (the first) and Ms. Susan Nolan (the second; Richmond has been lucky to have three strong women leading its sister city commission, just as VFoM is led by strong mothers). Ségou's Mayor Ousmane Simaga and sister city commission president Madani Sissoko were still in office, and we all celebrated the new latrines by dancing wildly on the market square with Ségou's women, whirling to the rhythm of Ségou's drummers. This happy event took place just one month before the March 21 military coup d'état in Mali—an event that would set our sister city programs back by three years, and set Mali back ten years; but that is another story.[33]

Later, we would bring other health projects to support Ségou. Gates was our first supporter, but Project C.U.R.E. in Denver, Colorado and Supplies Over Seas in Louisville, Kentucky were the next. With their help, the partnership of VFoM and the Fondation Cheick Mansour Haidara (FCMH, founded by Ségou's newly elected parliamentarian Abdoul Galil Haidara and his wife Djeneb Diarra) was able to supply more than one million dollars in medical equipment to Ségou's hospitals and community health centers. This would not have happened without Sister City International's network of contacts, further support from rotary clubs in Mali and America, and the Orange Foundation (the telephone company), as well as private donors who provided funding for the transportation of containers

---

33 *That story is told in another book I coauthored with Rafaella Greco Tonegutti: The Limits of Democracy and the Postcolonial Nation State: Mali's Democratic Experiment Falters, While Jihad and Terrorism Grow in the Sahara. Lewiston, NY & Lampeter, UK: Mellen Press, 2016.*

filled with equipment and supplies. In addition, we were able to partner with the medical charity *Physicians for Peace* in Norfolk, Virginia,
who donated equipment for a blood bank to Dr. Abdoulaye Sanogo's
Hôpital Niankoro Fomba, the main hospital in Ségou. In 2018, we
were able to verify that the blood bank is also working, although the
initial stock of chemical reagents has been exhausted, and the hospital
must now find money to purchase additional supplies.

Through AUPAP, the sister city relationship was strengthened,
and friendships were deepened. All of Ségou saw that partnering with
Richmond could be useful, and so did our French friends in Ségou's
sister city of Angoulême. This was a Gates Foundation success story,
and we are grateful to our friends at SCI, and to Bill Gates and his wife
Melinda, for their generosity and vision. The project had excellent
impact, and Gates should be very satisfied with this experiment.

During the project, Allan Levenberg and Madani Sissoko traveled
together to Kenya for AUPAP training, and they enjoyed working as
joint project managers and bonding on a personal level. "I enjoyed the
relaxed nonwork interactions with our Ségou colleagues, seeing them
with their families, cele-
brations, soccer matches,
and eating with one
another," Mr. Levenberg
told SCI's author of their
2011 book on AUPAP's
projects.[34]

Madani Sissoko
agreed: "Love of family

*Fig. 12. Allan Levenberg, Robin
Poulton, and Patricia Cummins at
a ceremony to celebrate the opening
of a new latrine in Ségou. Photo:
VFoM.*

34 *The book can be found at http://www.fwsistercities.org/wp-content/uploads/2011/10/
AUPAP-Book.pdf.*

and community transcends boundaries, and we are not the only ones with good ideas. I learned and put to use some great lessons in Ségou." That is the atmosphere of mutual trust and friendship in which any project proceeds best.

Lessons Learned about Water and Plumbing

We were very struck by the success of the market latrines. I had been fearful that public latrines would be difficult to keep clean—but I was wrong. On the contrary, the market latrines were the best managed and the best kept, and doubtless also the most used, although unfortunately, real data on their use are not available.

Our binary world is divided between men and women, urban and rural, rich and poor—and also between washers and wipers, perhaps representing the divide between ecologists and consumerists. More than seven billion rolls of toilet paper are sold yearly in the United States alone. The average American uses fifty pounds of tissue paper per year, which is 50 percent more than the average of other Western countries or Japan. The average Malian uses none. Global toilet paper production consumes twenty-seven thousand trees daily. Malians have few trees, so they are wise to wash. If Indians, Pakistanis, and Bangladeshis all started to use toilet paper, there would be no more forests in Asia. Mali is a part of the ecological washing world, but Malians like to be discreet about it. The Tuareg and Fulani cultures are so private about bodily functions that they like to pretend they don't even happen!

It is difficult to persuade people to effect cultural change. My own father was a public health doctor working for the United Nations in West Africa during the 1950s and 1960s, when colonial governments imposed the legal obligation on all families to dig a latrine with walls and a roof. The problem confronting my father and his African medical colleagues was how to convince people to use the latrine they had dug. Malian elders feel embarrassed and even humiliated to be seen by their children or grandchildren entering the family toilet. During the accreditation training for Teaching Timbuktu, we described to amazed

American teachers how common it is to see elderly Malians disappearing off into the "bush" with a kettle in their right hand and a bar of soap in their left. This desire for discretion means that, unfortunately, they often leave their defecation in the open or under a tree, where flies can feast and then spread infections. People who use latrines improve hygiene.

The Watertower Market latrines built by the AUPAP project used a design known in the hygiene business as "pour-flush latrines," which feature a squatting pan of porcelain, plastic, fiberglass, or cement set into a concrete platform. After use, a bucket of water is used to flush away the human deposit; two or three liters is usually sufficient. Each pan is equipped with a water seal (siphon) that prevents odors and flies from coming back up the pipe. This system is widely used in Latin America and especially the Middle East, where washing, not wiping, is the norm. It does require quite a lot of water, and some scrubbing to keep the pan clean.

Opposite the AUPAP latrine block in Ségou is a second set of Watertower Market public latrines built with the support of Angoulême, Ségou's French sister city, not wanting to be outdone by Richmond. These are dry longdrop latrines built over a pit, and they require no flushing. There needs to be an air pipe that takes odors from the pit up into the air above nose height! Flies and roaches are able to enter and exit, unless a cover is placed over the aperture: this can be as simple as a metal pot cover with a handle for lifting. Cleaning the toilet area is only necessary when a client misses the hole! Getting the right aperture size and shape is important, but fairly simple.

I offer no opinion as the merits of each latrine block. Both the Ségou and the Angoulême models have improved convenience and hygiene. But I do know that the urinals Richmond included in the latrine design for the health clinic have never been used. Malian men who prefer to hide in the trees rather than use a latrine are not going to allow themselves to be seen urinating "in public." Instead, they use the longdrop or the pour-flush facilities with doors.

Next time we build a latrine in Ségou, we hope to test out composting latrines. This will mean investigating the cultural obstacles to using the clean and nourishing compost product to enrich Ségou's vegetable and fruit production. We will try to keep clear of faucets and pipes in future, because of their cost, poor durability, and the problems of maintenance.

The Watertower Market kettle system has worked better than the handwashing water systems at the clinic and kindergarten, where there is no full-time watchman to protect the poor-quality Chinese-made plumbing. Our Ségou business friend Nouhoum Simaga, who runs the Colibris ("hummingbird") Hotel in Bamako, explained the problem: public facilities with high customer usage require high-resistance plumbing fixtures that cannot be purchased in the markets of Ségou and Bamako. The Chinese make four grades of plumbing equipment, Nouhoum told me: American household quality; American hotel quality (far more robust); African hotel quality (less robust); and African household quality, which is cheap and of poor quality. We needed the strong stuff—but the Malian AUPAP builders could not buy it in Mali. In place of the "home domestic quality" faucets we installed, we would need the sort of strong and resistant plumbing fixtures found in US schools and hotels and restaurants, where hundreds of different hands turn them on and off every week. I have concluded that the plastic kettle in Mali is a better solution than running water and faucets in a place where the plumbing equipment is not up to the job.

When I worked for the NGO ActionAid during the 1980s, we solved the plumbing problem in rural African schools. We developed and promoted an appropriate technology for keeping the hands of small children clean, called the leaky tin. Method: take an empty can that previously held two or four liters of food oil, and fill it with water. Hang it from a tree in the schoolyard. Make a tiny hole in one corner, so that a thin trickle of clean water will dribble down from the tin, and line up the children in single file. With one liter of water, a whole class of small children can wash their hands and improve their cleanliness. If possible, ensure that a small channel carries the used water from handwashing into the roots of a fruit tree, or into the school's vegetable garden.

This may sound overly simple, and—to Americans or to Africans who have attended American universities—even primitive, but in a land that is hot and dry, where water has to be dragged up by hand from a deep well, clean water is precious and needs to be used with maximum economy. The Bill & Melinda Gates Foundation would probably agree with using very small amounts of clean water for handwashing. Recycling this precious liquid into a tree's roots or into the irrigation system for a vegetable garden also serves to teach several different lessons to school children, and establishes good practices for their future household management of water.

Africa Is Developing; Poverty Is Down; Women Are Rising

After a nomadic lifetime of working in West Africa, I feel as much at home in Mali as I do anywhere else. While poverty, political instability and the apparent failure of secular democracy cause frustrations for many Malians, it is also true that most (or at least many) Malians are probably better off than ever before.

I first came to Mali in 1980, to work in Gao, Kidal and Timbuktu during a period of extreme drought. There had been almost no rain for seven years, and food was desperately short. The nomads' herds of sheep and goats and cattle had died from hunger, and the Sahel's last surviving herd of giraffes was about to die of thirst as their last waterhole went dry. Mali was run by a corrupt military dictatorship. Life was tough. In May 1981, in the hot drylands of North Mali where I saw and felt the temperature reach a record 125 degrees Fahrenheit, people thought their world was about to end. It remains tough to live in North Mali, where the Sahara Desert has been drying out for three thousand years. Ségou is also having a rough time: natural resources are diminished for all Sahelians, the population has grown, and Bamako centralizes financial resources.

But overall, Africans, including Malians, are economically and socially better off than they were half a century ago. Urban poverty is a new phenomenon, but the family of Ami Coulibaly, whose children were born in our household, is an example of the advantages of rural outmigration. Of course, no single example can ever be "typical," but Ami's elder brother makes a living by selling shoes near Bamako railway station, and her sister is an artisan—although she would be dead from pneumonia if Ami had not brought her to our house in 1989 for penicillin injections that were not available in the village. Ami herself sells wood and iced drinks in the market. Because she lives in our house in Bamako, she also pays no rent. And she has a mobile phone. Ami has gone up in the world.

Ami's late husband came to Bamako from a village in Sikasso and transitioned from being our watchman-cum-gardener, a job that he did very well, to selling cigarettes—which he did very badly. He smoked all his profits, giving away free cigarettes to his friends in exchange for a short-term increase in his social status, and gradually spiraled downhill into petty crime, poverty, and drugs. Having left the village where he tilled the soil, he had come to think of gardening as a retrograde rural task; whereas selling cigarettes seemed like urban social promotion. He was wrong, but I failed to convince him of that. Together, we must have planted more than one thousand fruit trees in rural school gardens. Thanks to the Malian school system and our family's support, his and Ami's four children are urban success stories: the daughters are both in business, the elder son is a carpenter, and the younger son will soon work for the customs department. Two of the four attended university in Bamako.

Malnutrition is still widespread in Mali, but nowadays people seldom die of hunger. In 2016, New York Times columnist Nicholas Kristof wrote that life for the world's poor has become better over the past few decades. Only 1 percent of Americans realize that extreme poverty in our world has fallen by half over the past twenty years:

The number of people living in extreme poverty ($1.90 per person per day) has tumbled by half in two decades, and the number of small children dying has dropped by a similar proportion—that's six million lives a year saved by vaccines, breast-feeding promotion, pneumonia medicine and diarrhea treatments! Historians may conclude that the most important thing going on in the world in the early 21st century was a stunning decline in human suffering.[35]

Among other triumphs, Kristof cites the victory over the affliction of river blindness, which was once very prevalent in Mali. The leadership of former President Jimmy Carter and the World Health Organization (WHO), remarkable field work by NGOs such as Sightsavers, and pharmaceutical donations from Merck have made river blindness fairly rare. When in 1988 I visited the remote village in rural Koulikoro where Ami Coulibaly was born, I found myself eating with the men of Ami's family, half of whom were blind. In this village, blindness was destiny. Men used to marry as young as possible, in order to have children who would be able to guide their blind father around the fields.

But such a future is no longer inevitable in Koulikoro, where the distribution of Vitamin A capsules costing two cents a dose has also helped to reduce blindness. Now, with people like Ami sending money back to the village, life in rural Koulikoro is better than before.

Jimmy Carter also led the fight against Guinea worm, a debilitating and painful parasite that develops inside the body and then exits through the skin. This is the affliction described in the Old Testament as "a plague of fiery serpents," and some say it is also the symbol of the WHO and of the medical profession: that snake you see winding around a medical spatula is actually a Guinea worm. Once the eggs have hatched inside the host's body, the only way to get rid of the worm is to catch the head with a split matchstick when it first protrudes from the leg, and slowly draw out the full six or nine inches of worm over a period of two or three weeks, winding it very gently around the matchstick. If the worm breaks, its back end will remain inside, and the leg will develop a painful ulcer. Victims may not be

---

35 *It is also possible, of course, that historians will conclude that health improvements caused a demographic explosion that destroyed social cohesion and caused wars across Africa and—perhaps—Europe. Time will tell. http://www.nytimes.com/2016/09/22/opinion/the-best-news-you-dontknow.html?em_pos=small&emc=edit_ty_20160922&nl=opiniontoday&nl_art=4&nlid=35302644&ref=headline&te=1&_r=0.*

able to walk, nor harvest their fields. Most Malians now know that filtering drinking water through a muslin cloth will remove the eggs, so that the cycle of reproduction is broken. With so many Malians no longer blind or crippled, and with so many mobile telephones allowing people to communicate easily, their lives have greatly improved.

The World Bank claims that 85 percent of adults worldwide are now literate, but I am skeptical: Mali and its Sahel neighbors are among the poorest countries in the world, and they are bound to be under the average. UNICEF, an organization far more useful and far less extravagant than the WB, offers a figure of 33 percent for Malian adult literacy, with 67 percent of children enrolled in school overall, and for girls, less than 50 percent. I am disappointed with Malian education standards, but Nicholas Kristof is optimistic about global development progress overall: "As girls are educated and contraception becomes available, birth rates tumble—just as they did in the West." I know that is true, and so perhaps we may allow ourselves to be optimistic as well.

This sympathy for the arguments of Kristof does not negate those advanced about rising wealth and income inequalities in America, and in the world. Jason Hickel, a PhD anthropologist from UVA, one hour from Richmond, now carries out research at the London School of Economics Inequalities Institute (the name itself is significant). In his 2017 book *The Divide: A Brief Guide to Global Inequality and Its Solutions*, Hickel argues:

"We have been told that development is working: that the global South is catching up to the North, that poverty has been cut in half over the past thirty years, and will be eradicated by 2030. It's a comforting tale, and one that is endorsed by the world's most powerful governments and corporations. But is it true? Since 1960, the income gap between the North and South has roughly tripled in size. Today 4.3 billion people, 60 percent of the world's population, live on less than five dollars per day. Some 1 billion live on less than $1 a day. The richest eight people now control the same amount of wealth as the poorest half of the world combined. Poor countries are poor because they are integrated into the global economic system on unequal terms. Aid only works to hide the deep patterns of wealth extraction that cause poverty and inequality in the first place. *The Divide* tracks the evolution of this system, from the expeditions of Christopher Columbus in the 1490s to the international debt regime, which has allowed a handful of rich countries to effectively control economic policies in the rest of the world."

The data and my professional experience confirm Hickel's thesis, but sister city partnerships promote a different, more equal relationship, and we of Richmond and Ségou are certainly trying to create new equalities. Not every progressive idea works; not every technology is transferable. When Allan, Madani, and Nouhoum Simaga attended the AUPAP training session in Nairobi, Kenya, they came back with an exciting idea for rural ambulances. Without ambulances, how do villagers living far from Ségou take their sick people to the city hospital? The answer is that they manage as best they can, with available donkey carts or private motor vehicles. In some countries, Allan told us, motorbikes with adapted sidecars are used as ambulances. We kicked around this idea for many months, and discussed with Michelle her experiences with Save the Children and ChildFund across ten countries in West Africa. The ambulance idea is attractive, but putting it into practice raises a host of questions: supposing we were able to supply a motorbike with adapted sidecar, who would run it? Who would "own" it? Who would fuel it? When the time came for a sick person or a pregnant mother to be carried to Ségou, who would provide the gasoline? If this is the only motorbike in the village, the village men will use it for everything. Ambulance duties will be the last of their concerns. Our pregnant mother may be faced with a broken-down motorbike, or with an ambulance for which she and her family cannot afford the fuel. An ambulance only for people who can afford to buy fuel? Faced with so many potential obstacles, the ambulance idea went no further. Donkeys do not feed on expensive imported gasoline. The "appropriate technology" in rural Ségou may still be the donkey cart, improved with a mattress to make the pregnant lady's journey more comfortable.

One of the most exciting developments in Mali has been the rise of civil society. The sister city experience allows us to participate in this adventure: for while the mayor of Ségou is a part of the country's administration (despite the fact that he is elected), the sister city commission and its Ségou regional economic partner CPEL (Conseil pour la Promotion de l'Economie locale) open the door for many other Malian citizens to partner with Richmond in starting new, nongovernment initiatives: in music and culture, new research and economic enterprise projects, environmental and educational activities, news media and sources of information, shea butter production and cotton exports, and so on. Civil society organizations (CSOs) are important for good governance, and they help keep governments on the straight and narrow. USAID has done a lot of good work to promote civil society, local media, and good governance in Mali.

Sister Cities International is an international CSO, like the Red Cross, Oxfam, Save the Children, ChildFund International, Greenpeace, Pugwash, Amnesty, the World Wildlife Fund, International PEN, Africa Studies Association (ASA), and so many thousands of others. Civil society is composed of voluntary interest groups that want to get something specific done. My definition is "citizens who form themselves into associations to promote an interest which does not include seeking or exercising power." The sister city partnership strengthens these groups and associations—which include journalists and the media—and helps to provide alternative Malian voices, ideas, and "countervailing powers" to curb the excesses of administrators, improve the economy, and lead to better performance by the justice system.

Political parties and churches and mosques occupy their own spaces, exercising political or spiritual power. Civil society, as expressed in parent-teacher associations, interfaith councils, unions and cooperatives, women's groups, press associations, and the media, has become one of five pillars of the modern West African state (including Mali):

executive government, civil society, the legislature, security forces, and the judiciary.

Civil society is especially important for giving a voice to women. We started this book by wondering how we might be able to increase women's participation in economic development, in community leadership, and in the sister city partnership. In the short period since Malians regained the right of association, after the 1991 revolution that ended twenty-three years of military rule, the country has seen the emergence of hundreds of associations including strong women's groups. Numerous women's NGOs work in education, economic cooperatives, health and family planning groups, and the increasingly wide network of mutualist community health centers are groups we have managed to reach through the AUPAP project.

With our Ségou CSO partner, *Fondation Cheick Mansour Haidara*, we are trying to strengthen girls' education in schools, and through early childhood learning with young mothers. Mutual credit-savings banks reach deep into rural communities where most women have never had the opportunity to save, borrow, or learn to read. At the national level in Mali, the CAFO (*Coordination des Associations Féminines)* has a high profile, and yet the struggle to find ways for women to influence policy in government ministries and private sector institutions dominated by men is permanent. The obstacles are similar in America, where women have fought to progress in a culture riven with inequality and even misogyny. Through the sister city program, we seek to bring more opportunities to women, developing civil society mechanisms that will help Richmond, as well as Ségou, to grow a new generation of women leaders.

2008- 2009

New Ségou Visits Richmond

Fig. 13. The Reconciliation Statue in Richmond, one of three fifteen-foot, half-ton bronze sculptures created by Liverpool artist Stephen Broadbent. A statue stands at each of three important points of the triangular slave trade: Liverpool, UK; Benin, West Africa; and Richmond, Virginia. Photo: VFoM.

Ségou Visitors at the Folk Festival and at the Cemetery

The tradition of annual visits from Ségou began at the Richmond Folk Festival of 2006. Our first visitor was Ségou festival organizer Mamou Daffé. After visiting Richmond, he traveled on to Mexico City to establish a network of music festivals. It must be said that the company Venture Richmond, the very successful organizer of the Richmond Folk Festival, has thus far shown little interest in the Mali connection—despite the best efforts of Allan, who was one of their volunteer hosts for ten years; despite the support of Haoua Cheick, who ran a Malian craft stall at the Richmond festival for several years; and despite encouragement from staff at the National Council for the Traditional Arts (NCTA), who had helped launch the Richmond Folk Festival in 2005 and ran it for three years before handing it over to Venture Richmond, and who would love to see the development of a joint Richmond-Ségou sister festival relationship.

In 2007, Mamou brought along his festival manager Mohamed Doumbia and his school friend Ousmane Simaga. "Oussou" was vice president of the Ségou Chamber of Commerce, and he would soon become the next mayor of Ségou. They stayed in the houses of VFoM members, and we fed them. When we went to Ségou, they hosted us and fed us. For the first three years, our priority was enjoying the music, organizing "shake-hand" sessions with city councilors and community leaders, building friendships so that Ségou and Richmonders would get to know each other—this was also the period when we were still trying to get Richmond's new sister city commission created. Mamou gave us a huge platform in Ségou. Allan and I became familiar sights at the Ségou festival, two gray men with white beards stalking around wearing beautifully embroidered *grands boubous*. In Richmond, we organized house parties. Mamou and Oussou met Richmond city council members in receptions when Allan arranged invitations. We visited Richmond institutions like the Ẹlẹgba Folklore Society, "Richmond's cultural ambassador"; and the William Byrd Community Center, as well as Richmond's many museums. Ousmane attended city council meetings, and meetings of the Richmond Slave Trail Commission. Our Malian friends spoke to students in high school, middle school, elementary school and university classrooms. People got used to seeing Virginia Friends of Mali turning up, accompanied by gorgeously dressed Malians!

Each October, our amiable Malian guests would speak French with undergraduate language students; present Timbuktu to third graders; and on several occasions they ran political discussion panels at the Maggie Walker Governor's School, for the region's gifted high school students specialized in governance and international studies. In 2014, Maggie Walker was ranked by *Newsweek/The Daily Beast* as the twelfth-best public high school in the nation. How do journalists arrive at such rankings? But they do, and so we report them even when we doubt their utility. We also tried—so far unsuccessfully—to raise support from the two Richmond enterprises that make a lot of money in Mali. Mali's most-smoked brand of cigarettes is Marlboro, made by

Philip Morris (Altria); Mali's most popular mayonnaise is BAMA, sold by the C.F. Sauer company, makers of Duke's Mayonnaise. The only support we have received so far from these massive corporations has been an invitation for the mayor of Ségou and his delegation to eat cake and ice cream in the garden of the Sauer factory on Broad Street on the occasion of the company's 150th anniversary.

The most moving event we remember from these early visits was walking Richmond's Slave Trail. Ousmane Simaga, the new mayor of Ségou, was making his first "official" visit, and he came with a municipal delegation. For most of the delegation, this was their first visit to the US. Some West Africans take a superior view of the African American experience, seeing their American sisters and brothers as exiles from the motherland who know little about Africa's ancient history and culture. There was no such feeling on this occasion, as we retraced the steps of those early African immigrants to Virginia. We imagined ourselves in the bare feet of those sad captives who landed in chains on the Manchester side of the James River, who trudged through the dead of night toward prison cells in the slave markets of "Shockoe Bottom," situated at the place where the Shockoe stream fed into the Turning Basin of Richmond's eighteenth-century river port.

Our Malian guests gazed in silence at Richmond's Reconciliation Statue, newly unveiled in 2007 to remember the thousands of men and women from the lands of the Mali Empire and other Africans who arrived here in chains to build the wealth of Virginia: 2007 marked the four hundredth anniversary of the founding of Jamestown in 1607. During the 1600s and 1700s, and indeed until 1776, there were no "Americans" in Richmond—only Europeans, Virginians, Africans, and some repressed Native American tribes. In the early period, most black Virginians arrived from the West African coast, passing through slave markets on the Isle of Gorée opposite Senegal's capital city of Dakar, or on James Island in the Gambia River—the place whence came Kunta Kinteh, the hero of *Roots*, the film and book by Alex Haley. After the American Civil War ended in 1865, hundreds of liberated African Americans came to Richmond and camped there under the protection of the Union army. Their camp covered the area more or less where the Maggie Walker Governor's School and Virginia Union University now stand; and these freed African Americans named their camp *Gorée*.

Our Malian friends stood silently as Ana Edwards, chairwoman of the Sacred Ground Historical Reclamation Project, told the story of Lumpkin's Jail. She explained that, because of its brutality, this area of slave jails was known to eighteenth-century Africans as "The Devil's Half-Acre." Almost every trader and artisan living here, black or white, was connected in some way to the economy of slavery. Over time, Richmond became the second-biggest slave market in the US, after New Orleans.

From Lumpkin's jail, we walked under shabby railway trestles and across Broad Street to the place where a dozen leaders of the slave rebellion of 1800 were hanged. Thanks to Ana Edwards and her organization's campaign to reconsecrate this sacred ground, an historical marker now stands on Broad Street at 15th as a memorial of the rebellion and the "Negro Burial Ground." At his trial, one of the men facing conviction for his role in the rebellion declared, "I have nothing more to offer than what General Washington would have had to offer, had he been taken by the British and put to trial by them. I have adventured my life in endeavoring to obtain the liberty of my countrymen, and am a willing sacrifice in their cause.

Gabriel was a skilled blacksmith and a natural leader. He expected "the poor white people"—together with the Quakers, Methodists, and Frenchmen living in Richmond—to support his takeover of the city; these were the white people most supportive of liberty. The rebels intended to demand their freedom, and marched with a banner stating "Death or Liberty." Their assault, planned for August 30, 1800, was frustrated by a torrential rainstorm that suddenly made the streams around Richmond impassable. An African might easily interpret such a storm as a negative sign from God . . . and one slave betrayed the plan. The white authorities called out the militia, and the rebellion was brutally suppressed.

The faces of the Malian delegation were moving to watch, as Ana recounted the story of Gabriel. With tears in their eyes, they gazed at the cemetery of their ancestors. It was an asphalt parking lot, then being used by staff of VCU's Medical College of Virginia. Africans revere their ancestors. Just as Virginians worship the memory of George Washington and Thomas Jefferson (both slave owners), every Malian venerates the memory of his or her father, mother, grandparents, and great-grandparents. White families bury their dead and move on. For many other cultures, the Ancestors remain a permanent presence. My friend Toumani Diabate, the famous Malian *griot* and master of the *kora,* the West African classical harp, can recite the names of his illustrious musical forebears for seventy-two generations. Our Malian guests stared at the asphalt and wondered, "Do Americans have no culture? Are Americans devoid of spirituality? How could Americans show such disrespect for the African Ancestors, that they allowed motor vehicles to drive across their graves and cars to be parked over their tombs?"

Ana Edwards' successful international campaign helped to transform Richmond's African Burial Ground into a grassy field. Among many letters of protest that were written in objection to the cemetery parking lot, one came from the mayor of Ségou to his counterpart in Richmond. Mali's Prime Minister Ousmane Issoufi Maiga, who carried the original sister city invitation from Ségou, wrote on the same subject to Dr. Michael Rao, the president of Virginia Commonwealth University, and to Governor Mark Warner of Virginia, with whom he had already raised the subject verbally during his visit on November 5, 2005. In May 2011, with labor donated by three Richmond contractors, the asphalt was finally removed and replaced with 3.1 acres of grass sown over the graves of the ancestors. Many other graves must have disappeared long ago beneath railway workings and highway construction. The full extent of the Richmond African Burial Ground may never be known. For the part that we can identify, a first stage of reclamation and respect has finally been achieved.

Much to our surprise, during our next visit to Ségou, we were presented with a different Sacred Ground. Opposite Ségou's city hall, in the middle of the old French colonial administrative district filled with powerful buildings featuring columns and balconies, lies a patch of grass upon which nothing will ever be constructed. It is a reminder of 1890, when French military officers occupied Ségou. Upon entering the city, they summoned the heads of the city's leading families to a meeting, lined them up, and shot them. Forty heads of family lie in a common grave under that patch of grass, opposite the Ségou city hall. The site needs no commemorative plaque. Every Ségovien knows it. The cemeteries of Richmond and of Ségou are both the subject of intense debates, but the underlying question is identical in both cases: after such brutality, how best can we—their descendants—protect their resting place and honor our ancestors' memories?

Fig. 14. Dieyah Rasheed, a long-time member of the Defenders; Mayor Ousmane Simaga; parliamentarian Abdoul Galil Haidara; and author Robin Poulton hold torches for Gabriel at the annual commemoration of the 1800 hanging of rebel slave leaders at Richmond's African Burial Ground. October 10, 2014. Photo: John Moser; VFoM; and Richmond Defenders for Freedom, Justice, and Equality.

The future of Richmond's Sacred Ground is intimately linked to the future of the Shockoe Bottom historical area as a whole. A community conversation has been started, as part of a campaign to protect the memories of early Richmond. Against the wishes of certain white property developers who want to make a quick million bucks from commercial development using public subsidies, the majority black population of Richmond supports creating some form of historical park. This concept is articulated by academic historians and anthropologists and encouraged by the US National Park Service network, which already runs several African cemeteries and museums in New York and elsewhere. Local activists—many of whom may be descendants of people who were sold in Shockoe Bottom—are determined to keep alive the memory of the slave trade and its victims.

The Future of Richmond's Past: A Letter from the Mayor of Ségou

After the transatlantic slave trade was declared illegal in 1807, Virginia began to export slaves. In the three decades leading up to the Civil War, between 300,000 and 350,000 human beings were sold and sent from Virginia to newly opened plantations in the Deep South. By 1860, there were about four million black people in the United States, the vast majority of whom were held in slavery in the South. Just do the math, and you'll discover that a majority of African-descended people in North America today can probably assume some ancestral link with Shockoe Bottom. As much as anywhere else on the continent, this surely is the birthplace of black America—making the African Burial Ground of Richmond a place of special importance to the whole of the American nation.

The importance of Richmond in America's history was highlighted by the 150th anniversary in April 2015 of the end of the Civil War in 1865, and the end of slavery. A committee was created to plan events, chaired by UR president Ed Ayers. Sacred Ground chair and Virginia Friends of Mali president Ana Edwards was a member of this committee, which took the name "The Future of Richmond's Past." That surely is what the Shockoe Bottom debate is all about.

While Mayor Jones and his staff remained quite remote from the RSCC, the mayor of Ségou has taken a great interest in Richmond and its politics. So when Mayor Jones announced that he wanted to build a baseball stadium in Shockoe Bottom, in the middle of the historic slave trading area, Ségou's sister city team were extremely invested. They were curious to see a lot of Richmonders—including the Friends of Mali—in energized opposition. They were personally and emotionally concerned by the future of the African Burial Ground. They knew that VFoM members had picketed the cemetery parking lot, trying to persuade VCU staff to refuse to park their cars on the Sacred Ground, asking bus drivers to stop outside the cemetery area to force their passengers to walk to their vehicles. Many also wrote to the authorities and signed petitions urging VCU and the City of Richmond to show respect for the African Ancestors.

The baseball park posed even bigger challenges than a parking lot. Commercial developments and parking spaces for eight thousand baseball supporters would obliterate the whole of the Shockoe Bottom historical area—which was probably the intention of the promoters. When the identities of some potential investors became known, including some previously convicted of financial crimes, the African American population of Richmond launched a campaign to stop the construction of the baseball stadium.

Of course, no one is against sports, which are equally important in Malian society as they are in American communities. Both the Flying Squirrels and the Richmond Kickers, the city's baseball professional baseball and soccer teams, attract a lot of interest from Ségou. Malians adore soccer, and Ségou's semiprofessional first-division teams, *Office du Niger* and *Association Sportive Biton*, would both love to play a series against the Richmond Kickers. Other Ségou teams that are now beating the *AS Biton* might claim the same rights. Ségoviens play basketball and admire the achievements of the VCU Rams and the UR Spiders, and tall young Malian basketball stars have occasionally received sports scholarships to both schools. We have tried to interest both VCU and UR coaches in working with Ségou basketball clubs; it would be a great experience for both sides, and maybe it will happen one day.

One man who was upset at the idea of building a ballpark in Shockoe Bottom was Ousmane Simaga, the mayor of Ségou, whose tears had so moved us at the cemetery. Oussou reveres his ancestors. He is a proud descendant of the warrior horsemen who conquered Ségou two centuries ago with the army of El Haj Oumar Tall. The Simaga family made a living from the crafting of horse saddles and harnesses and boots for El Haj Oumar, and later for the French army. From the business of leather and horses, they moved into trucks and buses and pharmacies, becoming one of the leading business families of Ségou.

The commonality of brutality surrounding the stories of the Ségou cemetery and the Richmond cemetery has brought members of the sister city commissions of our two cities closer together. When he heard that the African Burial Ground was no longer a parking lot, Mayor Simaga was delighted. When he heard that Mayor Jones was promoting the building of a baseball stadium in Shockoe Bottom, on the site where tens of thousands of Africans and their descendants—including possibly ancestors of Mayor Jones himself—were sold as slaves, Mayor Simaga was deeply shocked. After hearing the story, and after attending the October 10, 2013 commemoration of the hanging of the black freedom fighter Gabriel, Oussou wrote the following letter to Dwight Jones.

Letter to the Mayor of Richmond

October 2013

Dear Mayor Jones and my Municipal Brother,

I greet you from Ségou, capital city of the Bambara peoples, homeland of many of the ancestors of the people of Richmond. Quite apart from the agreement that you and I signed together in September 2009, linking our municipalities as Sister Cities, it is the blood ties of Africa that really bind us.

I am sure you are aware, my Brother, of the importance of African family ties and the role of the

African Mother. I am sure that the importance of your Mother in your African American family—which is also an African family—matches the strength of my own Mother. I am sure that your love for her equals the love and reverence I have for my own Mother. We are from the same Motherland, and it is this that truly binds Ségou to Richmond.

I wish to tell you, my Brother Mayor, about the strongest and most emotional moment of all my five visits to Richmond. This occurred when we walked along what you in Richmond call your Slave Trail. We passed the landing place of our African ancestors (yours and mine) across the river, we stood and admired the Reconciliation Statue, we stopped at Lumpkin's Jail and the 'Devil's Half Acre,' and finally we reached the African burial ground, which was—in those days—still covered with the vehicles of ignorant drivers desecrating the sacred ground where Malians lie buried. I do not exaggerate when I tell you, my Brother, that we had tears in our eyes at that place.

We were told of the struggle to reclaim the Sacred Ground—and we learned that Mali's prime minister, Mr. Ousmane Issoufi Maiga had asked Governor Mark Warner when he visited Richmond on November 5th 2005, to save the African cemetery and to have the ground re-consecrated. Later the land became VCU's and the same prime minister wrote to President Rao of VCU. When I visited Richmond for the third time, I was told that the City of Richmond obtained ownership, and grass has now replaced the parking lot. My heart rejoiced when I saw the grass. I was told that a "community conversation" had begun about the future of the African cemetery.

Now when I came to Richmond this year to attend the September 2013 Women, War & Peace Conference at VCU, I learned of plans to build a baseball stadium in the very area that has seen so much African suffering. My Brother Mayor, this is the moment when your Sister City would like to offer a modest contribution to the "community conversation"—since we in Ségou feel almost a part of the Richmond community.

I have seen your baseball stadium: it is opposite the Greyhound bus station where I arrived for the conference last month. It looks a fine position to me. Why would you not renovate the existing stadium? Of course, I know nothing of baseball and nothing about building stadiums. But I do know about the Sacred Ground. This area will become a source of fame and income for Richmond, if you turn the whole district called "Shockoe Bottom" into a memorial to the Africans who suffered and died in that place. I beg you not to desecrate the Sacred Ground of our ancestors—your ancestors, Mr. Mayor, and mine.

I send you my deepest respects and my warm fraternal greetings etc.,

Ousmane Simaga
Mayor of Ségou

Tales of Troublesome Statues: Ségou's Approach to History's Cruelties

Mayor Ousmane Simaga took office in 2007. A businessman with interests in transport and hotels, he was vice president of the Ségou Chamber of Commerce and a city councilor. Although his party did not win the highest number of seats on city council, he succeeded in putting together a coalition of smaller parties and independents that voted Simaga into power.

Ousmane Simaga comes from a powerful Ségou family. His uncle had been mayor. His family helped El Haj Oumar Tall's Toucouleur army conquer Ségou on March 10, 1861, creating a short-lived Islamic empire. El Haj Oumar died in 1864 in the cliffs of Bandiagara, probably in an explosion of his own secret munitions store, leaving his son Ahmadou as king of Ségou. But not for long—on April 6, 1890, the French colonel Louis Archinard entered Ségou. He took just two years to dismantle the Toucouleur Empire, orchestrating a new reign of terror. During his conquest of the region, Archinard ordered the execution of male Toucouleurs and organized the pillaging of the countryside, both to feed his troops and to reward his Bambara allies, to whom he also gave Toucouleur captives as slaves. To ensure the submission of the population of Ségou, he assassinated the city's Elders.[36]

When Emmanuel Macron stated during the French presidential campaign in January 2017 that "French colonial history contains crimes against humanity," he was thinking mainly of the brutal Algerian war of independence. However, President Macron was also accurately describing the crime of slavery and the many rapes and massacres that took place during the brutal French conquest of West and North Africa, including Ségou.

In the basement of the town hall, Ousmane Simaga discovered a statue of Archinard that had once stood in Ségou's central square. It had been removed after Independence, for reasons one may easily appreciate. After discussions with the governor of Ségou Region, Abou Sow, the controversial decision was made in 2009 to reerect the statue of the Butcher of Ségou on a plinth beside the Niger River. To Malian critics who asked whether any French city would ever erect a statue of Hitler, Abou Sow responded in his speech, "The Statue of Archinard restores the reality of history. No one should seek to remove a page of history. History should remain as it is, and not as some people would like it to have been."

Abou Sow's logic aligns with the philosophy of Mali's first elected president Dr Alpha Oumar Konaré, an historian whose "history park"

36 *The story is told in French government archives at https://lsg.hypotheses.org/267, and also SHD, 15H36, Correspondance d'Archinard, 6 janvier 1891, Nioro, Commandant supérieur à lieutenant Hardiviller.*

created in 1994 on Koulouba Hill in Bamako presents all the main European as well as African figures of Mali's history. Plenty were brutal, black and white both. If we accept Abou Sow's argument, why did he not build a statue in Ségou to honor the Elders whom Archinard assassinated, before resurrecting a public symbol of French repression and colonial conquest? A copy of the Bamako Hunters' Monument would be perfect, standing proud as it does in front of the Russian embassy in the Niarela district of Bamako. Ségou needs statues of other historical heroes as well. Rather than disagreeable military rulers like the Coulibaly and Diarra kings, we would welcome a celebration of the mythical heroine Nyéléni, the "perfect Ségou woman" who encompassed all the virtues of a daughter and a mother. Rather than monuments to famous individuals, which cause jealousies, Ségou might create statues that celebrate the achievements of famous groups: Ségou's hunters, footballers, musicians, or women's agricultural cooperatives.

This story resonates in Richmond, where the city's Monument Avenue lionizes individual Confederate generals who fought to retain slavery. Robert E. Lee, supreme commander of the Confederate army, dominates the Avenue alongside J.E.B. Stuart, commander of the cavalry; Stonewall Jackson, commander of the infantry; and Jefferson Davis, president of the Confederacy. Each is a fine sculpture, but why do we celebrate their actions and symbolism? Farther west along the Avenue stands the statue of Arthur Ashe, world tennis champion and Richmond's greatest sporting son; but a single, isolated monument to one famous African American civilian cannot balance the sinister array of Confederate statues.

Should they be removed? Confederate statues were pulled down during 2017 in New Orleans, Raleigh, Orlando, Tampa, St. Louis, and Baltimore. Richmond's history is even more intimately tied to the Confederacy, and we believe these statues should be removed from their dominant position on the city's central avenue to the civil war museum beside the James River. Removing Confederate statues will not change history; it will make new history. In Charlottesville, one hundred miles west, a bitter dispute over the proposed removal of a statue of Robert E. Lee (at an estimated cost of $300,000) divided the city and provoked pro-fascist demonstrations on August 12, 2017. A white supremacist drove his car into a crowd of pedestrians, killing thirty-two-year-old Heather Heyer and injuring nineteen other people. The old and bad vibes of violent Southern American history once again invaded our modern life, symbolic of a new era of angry deafness in America to the views of other people. It reminds us of the refusal in Southern Mali to hear the fears, and recognize the violence, of North Mali's experiences.

To build a new understanding about Mali's or Virginia's history, we must build truth, as well as reconciliation and consensus. We must accept historical reality, and learn the lessons of violence, of racism and slavery. If Governor Abou Sow and President A.O. Konaré are right about the pages of history, then what conversations could Ségou and Richmond exchange about moving forward? Removing the four main statues from Monument Avenue will cost several million dollars. But this will be money well spent, if it allows Richmonders to rethink the lessons of history—even though former governor and mayor Douglas Wilder believes it would be better spent on improving Richmond's failing schools. Let us not forget that removing the statues will also be a form of education.

There are more than seven hundred Confederate monuments in thirty US states, and they will not all be removed to museums. Richmond alone has another fifteen or twenty Confederate memorials scattered around the city. Nor should we forget that the US is covered with statues of slave owners, including Washington, Jefferson, Madison, and Monroe. Of the eight US presidents born in Virginia, seven owned slaves. We are not going to remove them all. But Richmond will only be able to reinterpret its history of slavery and oppression after we retire to historical museums the monuments that were erected to rehabilitate the image of the slavery-defending Confederacy, and to reimpose the cultural principle of white supremacy after Reconstruction was dismantled and Jim Crow established. That was the worst post-slavery period for black people in US history. Richmond's mayor, Levar Stoney, rightly described the Confederate statues on Monument Avenue as "Equal parts myth and deception . . . a false narrative etched in stone and bronze more than one hundred years ago—not only to lionize the architects and defenders of slavery, but to perpetuate the tyranny and terror of Jim Crow and reassert a new era of white supremacy." There are no easy answers, but we still need to find some. Richmond would be foolish to deny the reality of history and its importance in the present.

Why does Monument Avenue not celebrate famous artists, scientists, and even (a daring suggestion!) women? Virginians are overly obsessed with military uniforms (not just Confederate uniforms). Poor, lonely Arthur Ashe needs some nonmilitary company. The most obvious gap in Virginia's statuary is the absence of women, including women who worked for the Union side of the Civil War. Instead of seeking to deny the military history of Richmond's past—using the Abou Sow test—Richmond's city fathers and mothers might try to complete the historical record.

There are some obvious candidates. Among Richmond's Civil War women, the top candidates might be Elizabeth Van Lew and Mary Bowser, spies who together provided immense amounts of information to the Unionist army. Mary Elizabeth Richards Bowser was a free black woman believed to have been hired as a servant—on the advice of Elizabeth Van Lew—by Mrs. Varina Davis, wife of the president of the Confederacy. Bowser would have been able to spy from inside the "White House" of the Confederacy, even reading documents on Jefferson Davis' desk, passing her information via Van Lew to the Union army.[37]

Elizabeth Van Lew herself came from a Philadelphia Quaker family. Her father owned slaves, but when he died in 1843 she and her mother freed all their slaves. Thereafter they purchased families of slaves who were at risk of being split up, and freed them. A giant statue

---

37 *See Lois Leveen's June 21, 2012 New York Times article "A Black Spy in the Confederate White House," as well as her novel* The Secrets of Mary Bowser, published by *Harper Collins.*

of Bowser and Van Lew, American women heroes, one black and the other white, would challenge the racist militarism inherent in Richmond's otherwise beautiful Monument Avenue. Harriet Tubman and Sojourner Truth were famous antislavery women heroes, even though they—like Rosa Parks, who would also be a good subject—were not Virginians.

Local statue candidates might be two famous women leaders of the Powhatan Confederacy, Oppussoquionuske (died 1610) and Pocahontas (also named Matoaka, Princess Matoika, and Rebecca Rolfe; died 1617); Angela from Angola, the first African woman to arrive in Virginia in 1619; Gabriel, the slave who led the 1800 rebellion for freedom and against slavery in Richmond; civil rights lawyers Sam Tucker (1913–1990), Spottswood William Robinson, III (1916–1998) and Oliver Hill (1907–2007); and Congressman John Mercer Langston (1829–1897) an abolitionist lawyer who was the first dean of the law school at Howard University and the first president of what is now Virginia State University, an historically black college in Petersburg, near Richmond.

In 2019, Virginia will celebrate the four hundredth anniversary of the arrival of its first Africans (twenty Angolans, who had been seized from a Dutch slaving ship and who were deposited at Jamestown Settlement). A new statue is planned, an $800,000 twelve-foot-high bronze monument to be erected on Brown's Island in the James River, not far from the existing statue of a magnificent African boatman rowing in Richmond's nineteenth-century Turning Basin. The new—and somewhat controversial—statue will feature a slave being magically levitated out of his shackles in an abnormal, catatonic state. Beside him, a female figure cradling a baby in one arm will hold a document showing the date of Abraham Lincoln's 1863 declaration of freedom for slaves, also commemorating the 150th anniversary of the Emancipation Proclamation. The base of the statue will feature profiles of ten distinguished activists from Richmond's pre-war and postslavery history. It is a classic example of American administrative process. Years of wrangling in committees, and arguments about the ownership of pieces of land, has finally produced a statue that leaves the central problem untouched: that Richmond's Monument Avenue is dominated by men wearing the uniforms of the Confederate Army. A leader with political vision would have placed the new statue on Monument Avenue, close to Robert E. Lee. Richmond's Monument Avenue needs a dozen statues celebrating civilian women and men who symbolize the complete history of Richmond and the happy city that its citizens want it to become.

Statues of artists and musicians, scientists and writers (especially women) would bring complexity and truth to Richmond's history by creating rich new pages about the city's story. A statue of Richmond's Maggie Walker (1864–1934), the first woman in America to head a bank, was erected in 2017 on Broad Street, not far from her home in Richmond's Jackson Ward, which is a National Parks museum. In the same district is another African American statue honoring "Bojangles" —Richmond's world-famous film actor and tap dancer Bill Robinson (1878–1949), which honors his work for poor Richmonders during the depression of the 1920s. At the very intersection where his statue stands, Mr. Robinson paid for the installation of a traffic signal to prevent repeated deaths and injury from automobile accidents—because Richmond's white city council refused to cover the expense. However, a statue of a tap dancer—even the world's most famous tap dancer—is no answer to the political legacy of slavery and violence that still dominates Monument Avenue.

Vieux Farka Touré Opens the Ségou and Richmond Folk Festivals

The greatest guitarist of them all was Ali Farka Touré, who, partnering with the American Ry Cooder, was the first African to win a Grammy Award—in 1994, for their album *Talking Timbuktu*. My USAID colleague Carol Hart—who became a founding member of VFoM—threw a celebratory party that evening in Bamako in Ali's honor, after the American ambassador had presented the award, and Ali became our friend. I attended many of his Malian and American concerts—including his last concert in 2003, when he traveled to

Washington, DC at the personal request of Mali's president to play at the official opening of the Mali Folklife Festival on the National Mall. That evening, as Ali played his guitar, I was the first fan in Malian dress who danced onto the stage to place a one-hundred-dollar bill on Ali's sweating forehead, following Malian tradition. Ali laughed with pleasure and played me an extra riff on his guitar. "*Tu es si beau!*" I told him: "How beautiful you are!" And he was!

In early March 2006, I visited Ali on his deathbed in Lafiabougou, a district of Bamako. There, his son Vieux told me that they hoped to take him home the following week. They did, but he was in his coffin. The international press said he had died of bone cancer. How boring! Most Malians believe Ali was poisoned by aristocratic politicians in his home town of Niafunké, angry that he had been elected mayor. How exciting!

The following year, in October 2007, Vieux opened the Richmond Folk Festival with Ali's musicians. In February 2008, we heard him in Ségou. His music was a tribute to Ali, as much as a demonstration of the skills of Vieux himself. In those days, he mostly played Ali's tunes. These days, Vieux Farka Touré has found his own musical idiom. Now he is famous for his own music. Perhaps a sapling cannot flourish in the shade of a great oak tree. But the oak tree has passed on, and the sapling has become a fully grown tree.

On that 2007 occasion, Allan Levenberg was the festival's official host for the Malian group. Did they need anything? One of the musicians needed a pair of shoes; on their nonstop tour of American festivals, his shoes had broken. I dived into my shoe box and found a pair of slip-on shoes. I took them to the back of the stage and waved at Vieux, who recognized me from my visit to his father six months earlier. The shoes fitted well enough, and life went on. The next day I went with Allan to Richmond's Hilton Hotel, where the bands were all staying. Someone very kindly gave me a food ticket so I could lunch (or was it breakfast?) with the band. It was self-service. The musicians were all eating chicken.

Vieux was a marvel at the Richmond Folk Festival. Like every Malian group since then, his music provided the gig that got the audience most excited. Vieux Farka Touré had three thousand Richmonders dancing and screaming for joy. Well done, Vieux! Since then, I have heard him play in Georgetown, and in Mali. The Richmond Folk Festival has also heard Bassékou Kouyaté with his amazing Ngoni Ba from Ségou, Abdoulaye "Djoss" Diabaté from New York, and Cheick Hamala Diabaté from Washington, DC, whom I hear at many Richmond festivals. Cheick Hamala opened the 2018 Ségou festival. Every time, the Malian bands send the audience wild with joy and dancing. Richmond's festival needs Malian musicians. Malian music rocks!

DEATH OF A MUSICAL LEGEND
Ali Farka's life was remarkable—from poverty to fame
By Robin Poulton; published in the Richmond Defender in 2006.

In 2006, Ali Farka Touré and Toumani Diabaté have just won a Grammy for their 2005 release *In the Heart of the Moon*. If you haven't heard this wonderful music, BUY IT NOW! The Sahelian rhythms of Timbuktu are blended through Ali's magical guitar, with the forest beat of the traditional 21-stringed *kora* played by Toumani. (In Casamance—southern Senegal—you can also find *koras* with twenty-four, twenty-five, or twenty-six strings.) *In the Heart of the Moon* you will hear West Africa's music as traditional, and also as new and renewed. This is Ali Farka Touré's musical epitaph, his last gift to us.

Toumani Diabaté's father, the late Sidiki Diabaté, came from a family of Mandinka musicians who migrated from the Manding heartlands to the coastal valley of the Gambia River. Kunta Kinteh in *Roots* was born there, and so was Sidiki Diabaté. As a young man, Sidiki returned to newly independent Mali to become the country's greatest *kora* player—

but he himself admitted that his son Toumani had surpassed him. *In the Heart of the Moon* you may hear two of Africa's greatest instrumentalists creating their own fusion of World African Music. Their music sings through my bloodstream and touches my soul.

Ali came from the northern end of Mali—in the desert fringes near Timbuktu. Born in modest circumstances in Niafunké nearly seventy years ago, he was apprenticed to a fisherman. Speaking all the languages of North Mali, the young Ali was brilliant, but he never attended school. He never was very strong on reading and writing. His strength lay in his music and his personality. Ali Farka fought his way up from the remoteness of a desert village near Timbuktu, to the center of the world stage.

American commentators called Ali "the inventor of African Desert Blues," but he always refused this description of his music. Ali repeated constantly that he was not playing "The Blues"—he was playing the music of his culture in North Mali. When he heard Ry Cooder and other American guitarists, there was a mutual learning experience. With Ry Cooder, Ali made the 1994 album *Talking Timbuktu* that won him his first Grammy Award. As the first African to win a Grammy, Ali Farka became West Africa's most internationally acclaimed musician. But listen to Ali's music: you can feel the movement of the camels plodding across the desert sands. The music of Timbuktu gave birth to American Blues. Like reggae and jazz and pop and hip-hop and rap and soul and gospel music, the dominant influence for American Blues music came from West Africa. We can be proud of the glorious legacy of Africa's Empires and its ancient civilizations that created the music we hear through the fingers of Ali Farka Touré.

Que la terre lui soit legere (as we say in Mali): may the weight of the desert sands lie lightly upon him. What a great man! We shall miss him. Listen to his music, and join me in thanking God for the life and music of Ali Farka Touré.

Virginia Friends of Mali held a commemoration of Ali Farka Touré on Thursday, April 27, 2006 at Mamusu's African Restaurant, 200 East Main Street. It was a lovely evening. We ate African food, and heard Ali and Toumani *In the Heart of the Moon*.

How Film Festivals Have Brought Africa to Richmond

The best way to understand Africa is to see Africa. While the Richmond Folk Festival brings a wide and wonderful variety of world and African music to Virginia, films bring us Africa alive. Twenty-five years ago, Dr. Peter Kirkpatrick of VCU and his wife Françoise, who teaches French at the University of Richmond, started an annual French film festival, now the most important in the western hemisphere. The university's French Film Festival (FFF) presents three days of nonstop viewing at the end of March every year, set in the magical nineteenth-century surroundings of Richmond's Byrd Theatre. The frescoes and gilt of the Byrd have been preserved by some miracle from demolition. When American businessmen and politicians talk about "redevelopment" they actually mean "destruction" of historic buildings and their replacement with concrete boxes that bring profits to builders and bankers. Or parking spaces! To replace beautiful nineteenth-century buildings with asphalt car parks is vandalism. Ségou and Richmond share a common problem of cultural vandalism: ugly, gray, cement blocks replace beautiful, elegant buildings. Richmond's historic buildings are built in stone or red brick; Ségou's are built of mud brick covered with red plaster. They are elegant, redolent of history and culture—which cement most definitely is not.

Perhaps inspired by the Kirkpatricks, a group of UR faculty under the leadership of Professor Louis Tremaine, who taught African literature and international studies, decided in 2002 to devote a weekend to the screening of African films for the public. That was the birth of UR's African Film Weekend. The project was driven by a desire to challenge stereotypical descriptions of Africa and Africans propagated in the West by powerful institutions like Hollywood; and secondly, to give African filmmakers the opportunity to describe Africa in her own images, speaking her own voice. The most important Malian screening has been Adberrahmane Sissako's *Timbuktu*. Mr. Sissako had just spent six months in residence at UVA, the University of Virginia in Charlottesville where there is an important department of film studies one hour west of Richmond. Born in Mauritania and raised in Mali, Sissako studied in Moscow before settling in France in the early 1990s. He now travels the world directing and screening his films— and accepting awards for his work.

Timbuktu shows the drama of *jihadi* rule after the Mali military coup d'état of 2012, and the destruction of Sufi tombs in Timbuktu. This vandalism gave rise to the first condemnation by the International Criminal Court for destruction of a world heritage monument. The film was selected to compete for the Palme d'Or at the 2014 Cannes Film Festival and for a British BAFTA, and was one of five 2015 US Academy Award nominees for Best Foreign Language Film. *Timbuktu* collected seven coveted César Awards in France, including Best Film, Best Director and Best Original Screenplay, and won Best Film at the eleventh African Movie Academy Awards, held in South Africa.

Four years earlier, Sissako had presented his 2006 film *Bamako* at the French Film Festival. Set in Mali's capital city, Sissako's film pillories the "New World Order" by putting the International Monetary Fund, the World Bank, and the Western banking system on trial. The banks are accused of destroying Africa's economy, deliberately condemning poor countries to permanent debt. Mali's public debt is equivalent to 36.3 percent of its GDP,[38] which is colossal for a country with so few resources.

The *Bamako* plot is fairly thin, but the subject matter is heavy. A cabaret singer, Mélé (played by actress Aissa Maiga), comes home after a degrading night of work to find her Bamako compound transformed into a tribunal. Her sister (played by Djénéba Koné) is one of the witnesses appealing for justice, alongside peasant farmers and Malian economists. The most delightful aspect of the film is that life continues in the family compound while the trial proceeds: children come home from school and kick up dust in the yard; women pound millet in the background, peel onions, and prepare lunch while the judges— real Malian magistrates dressed in their official garb of black gowns and white bowties—sit on wooden chairs behind a kitchen table and hear the plaintiffs. You can feel the dust on your skin. You can almost smell the cooking, in this familiar domestic environment where the witnesses sit at children's school desks and neighbors come and go and gossip as if the film set was not there. Sissako's scenario provides an eloquent contrast between the poverty of West Africa and the obscene concentration of wealth accumulated by the less than 0.01 percent of the population that runs banks, hedge funds, and weapon and oil companies.

For those of us who work in African rural development and humanitarian relief, the story strikes home. The 1960s brought great political change to African countries like Mali, but political independence brought no economic independence. Ségou's farmers still send most of their cotton to French textile mills. The prices of cotton, coffee, cocoa, and other crops are fixed by Westerners living far away from where they are grown. African farmers grow and export groundnuts to feed industrially raised French pigs while their own children suffer from protein deficiency. Every African country is burdened with debt.

The World Bank should not pretend it is solving poverty if its main purpose is to gain interest from loans. In 2004, our skepticism

---

38 *See http://www.heritage.org/index/country/mali.*

about the WB was confirmed by American economist John Perkins' book *Confessions of an Economic Hit Man,* in which he describes how he designed projects that put countries into debt, deliberately creating dependency on Western banks and governments. Debt service enriches banks and starves Africans. After more than seventy weeks on the *New York Times* bestseller list, Perkins' book was translated into thirty-two languages and it is now used in many college and university programs. But the immoral debt crisis continues.

Most years at the FFF, the Kirkpatricks present a French-language film about Africa. The 2009 festival presented Serge Le Péron's *J'ai vu tuer Ben Barka* (2005), a film about the 1965 assassination in a Paris street of the Moroccan opposition activist Mehdi Ben Barka. Stylistically a French *film noir* thriller, it addresses the clumsy cover-up by President de Gaulle's policemen of an unexplained political murder. The previous year, the festival presented Dyana Gaye's short 2006 Senegalese film *Deweneti* ("Merry Christmas" or "Happy Holidays" in the Wollof language), which examines the West African problem of young Muslim beggars. This medieval custom is supposed to inspire humility in each *talib* (Koranic student), a form of education for parents who cannot afford—or do not agree with—the official, government and secular, French-language school system.

Koranic education is often pathetic. The *talibs* (the Arabic plural would be *taliban*) are exploited as child workers begging food and money to feed their barely literate marabout—a religious title most of my educated Malian friends translate as "charlatan," showing how little respect they have for the system. When I am in a rural town, I often pay a local restaurant to feed one decent meal to all the *talibs* who are hanging around begging me for money. That way I know they eat the food, rather than their charlatan.

Close to eighty feature films have been screened during UR's African Film Weekends. The organizer, Professor Kapanga Kasongo (who helped write this section), has shown plenty from North Africa (Mohamed Mouftakir's *Pégase*, Morocco, 2010; Ben Hania's Le Challat de Tunis, Tunisia, 2014), and from the Caribbean (Deslauriers'

Aliker and *Beguine*; and 2010 was devoted entirely to Haiti). Yet most of the UR films are from sub-Saharan Africa. What is the part of Mali in this celebration of African cinema, culture and art?

After *Timbuktu*, the next UR screening was *Morbayassa* in 2016. This film by the late Cheick Fantamady Camara featured Fatoumata Diawara, the Malian singer and actress, in the lead role of Bella, a cabaret singer who wants to find a daughter she had given up for adoption to a Parisian couple. Fatoumata Diawara's connection with Richmond materialized in person—*en chair et en os*—when she performed live in the UR's Camp Concert Hall on February 15, 2014: a fabulous "Night of Mali Music" that also featured Ségou's famous group Bassekou Kouyate & Ngoni Ba. Fatou Diawara—described in the fliers as having "packed a lifetime experience into her thirty-three years"—was so impressive that she has become VFoM's favorite singer. Her concert was also tied in with UR courses concurrently running during that spring semester. Blending Wassalou traditions from southern Mali with international influences, Diawara has reached the stratosphere of "world music stardom": she has performed and recorded with Oumou Sangaré, AfroCubism, Dee Dee Bridgewater, and the *Orchestre Poly-Rythmo de Cotonou*.

Besides fictional works, the UR festival also screens short films and documentaries related to the environment and the relevance of Africa in the unfolding world tragedy of climate change. Mali was referenced in the 2012 Cameroonian film *Land Rush*, directed by Osvalde Lawat and Hugo Berkeley, which showed the difficulties that African farmers encounter to remain afloat against the overarching arrival of agro-industrialist businesses, some of which these days carry China's footprints. We discover once again—as we did when Oxfam brought Monsieur Traoré in 2003 to visit Ten Thousand Villages—that the fate of Malian cotton growers is inextricably linked to powerful financial interests against the backdrop of intense international competition. The lives of Richmond's public audiences have been much enriched through VCU and UR African film and music experiences. Since

2005, Africa and Mali have increasingly become part and parcel of artistic celebrations in Richmond.

Bed Fetishes, Lodging, Food, and Malaria Pills Build Friendships

Oussou, the mayor of Ségou; and Mamou, the Ségou festival director, both own hotels in Ségou, which gives them an edge over the rest of us when it comes to finding bedrooms for visitors. As a general rule, if we visit Ségou, we pay for our accommodation with a US government education grant or money from Gates Foundation; otherwise, we expect free beds, and we provide similar hospitality for the Malians in Richmond. Hospitality comes from kind Richmonders.

The great advantage of homestays, apart from not having to pay hotel costs, is that they build friendships. Hospitality is an important part of Mali's social capital, and is often linked to trade relationships and to longtime links between families through their grandfathers. A lot of Richmond citizens have been generous with their hospitality, and a number of friendships have developed. When Yah Traoré came to Richmond, he stayed with Su Boer, a RSCC commissioner who teaches German at VCU and in Chesterfield County high schools. Yah is the director of budget for the region of Ségou, and one Malian visitor who speaks good English. The following year, when Yah came to the US on a private visit to his daughter studying in Massachusetts, he made a special trip to Richmond to visit Su—demonstrating a Malian form of respect that deepens friendships. Richmond also benefitted from the link with Yah, when one year later Su agreed to join the Richmond Sister City Commission. I personally have been lucky since Su has several times invited me to eat at her house . . . and Yah provides generous hospitality for Richmonders in Ségou.

There is a Malian proverb that states, "It is better to change cities, than to change lodgings." This shows how a sacred bond develops between people who offer and accept hospitality. Called *jatiguiya,* this hospitality is linked to trading relationships and to African concepts of trust, for if you stay in another man's house and eat the food prepared by the women of that family, then you are placing your life in their hands. Staying with people creates links of mutual respect. To change houses would be disrespectful, and would disrupt trade.

In the same spirit, a Malian would never say "Your food is delicious," because that might imply that he is surprised his host (or hostess) is a good cook—or that he is not poisoning his guest! Instead, a Malian is likely to praise the food to someone else, who will pass on the message. If you give a gift to a Malian, he will thank you by showing it proudly to his or her neighbor; this honors you, and the neighbor will thank you for your generosity to their friend. Americans are direct (sometimes too direct); Malians are indirect, but no less polite or grateful.

Not every Richmonder can visit Mali, so giving hospitality is a valuable way of participating in the sister city relationship. On the other hand, things can go wrong—sometimes because the host speaks no French and the Malians speak no English. When Oussou Simaga stayed with Carol Warner, we made sure that his cousin Nouhoum was there as well: Nouhoum studied IT in Pennsylvania and therefore speaks good English. Carol had two spare bedrooms, so the arrangement seemed perfect. The fact that the lock on the bathroom door did not work seemed a minor matter—after all, Carol lives alone, and so she never locks the door. Carol explained that her guests should not try to lock the door. Oussou forgot, locked the door . . . and could not escape! After a lot of banging, a great deal of laughter, and the fetching of tools and ladders and whatnot, Nouhoum succeeded in releasing the mayor of Ségou from his unexpected prison cell. In the meantime—and fortunately—Carol was able to use the other bathroom downstairs. We are still laughing, and often tease Oussou about his imprisonment.

So good humor is an important part of a successful sister city relationship. On the other hand, mutual tolerance is also needed. Malians are much more relaxed about accommodation than Americans will ever be. Americans and Europeans have a bedroom fetish, which is not true in West Africa. It is difficult to imagine a circumstance in which an American would show a stranger into his or her bedroom (well, the imagining is not that difficult, but the circumstance would be exceptional). The famous lexicographer Samuel Johnson (1709–1784) translated a French poem that illustrates the point about our fetishism:

In bed we laugh, in bed we cry,
And born in bed, in bed we die;
The near approach a bed may show
Of human bliss to human woe.

People in Mali may or may not die in bed, but they tend to sleep wherever there is a space to sleep; and they will probably have sex wherever and whenever it is convenient, unlike the rigidly Protestant traditions of America that limit sex to bedrooms (and then, only in the dark). As the Welsh writer Bernard Shaw observed, the reason for the popularity of marriage in buttoned-up western Protestant society is that "it combines maximum temptation with maximum opportunity."

The idea of rigid sexual taboos may surprise younger, liberated readers who have benefited from the relaxed mores that followed the sexual revolution of the 1960s and the invention of the birth pill, but traditional Western culture is highly repressed. In America, as in Britain, sex was a taboo subject from the Victorian age until very recently, although pre-Reformation mores were far more relaxed.

In this spirit of relaxed Malian attitudes to sleeping spaces, I have a mattress in my Richmond sitting room on which many Malians have slept, though I probably would not offer it to someone as senior as the mayor, or the governor of Ségou Region. In October 2012, I received the head of the national electricity company in Ségou, who has a very senior position. I cannot remember whether Monsieur Hamma Ag Mohamed was originally supposed to stay with me; but when I collected him from the airport, he arrived with a suitcase and an attack of malaria saying, "I must see a doctor, and get some malaria medicine."

I laughed. "Probably no doctor in Richmond has ever seen malaria, and the nearest medicine is probably in Washington, DC. However, I am an experienced African traveler, and I always keep malaria medicine in my house." Hamma swallowed some malaria pills from my cupboard, and slept in my bed for the next twenty-four hours. Not wanting to disturb his malaria cure, I slept on the mattress in my sitting-room. The next day he was fine, and we have been firm friends ever since.

The following year Hamma received the whole Richmond delegation in his house in Ségou, where his wife issued the threat: "In my house, you will eat until you sleep!" Hamma and his wife come from Timbuktu, where the cooks are famously excellent and the portions are famously huge. We were served large quantities of salads; then succulent roast chicken; next came steaming grilled lamb; and finally—the killer dish—*wijila* bread dumplings in a rich sauce flavored with the twelve Moroccan spices of Timbuktu. The rich flavor of the *wijila* sauce whirled around our heads and through our nostrils. Even though my belly was full, I could feel my digestive juices running in anticipation of the taste of those spices in Timbuktu's richest dish. That evening in Ségou, we ate until we could no longer sleep, and Hamma's household was honored by the amounts we consumed! Hamma Ag Mohamed has since been promoted to run the electricity of Bamako, Mali's capital city—making him one of the country's top engineers— and I seldom visit Mali without spending an evening, or a night, in the company of Hamma and his delightful family and meeting interesting people.

While our first host was Mamou Daffé, our chief Ségou hosts have been the family of Madani Sissoko, the SCC president from 2009 to 2016, who runs a martial arts club *dojo* and various carpentry-related businesses. The large Sissoko clan descends from blacksmiths, and they sprawl across several large compounds occupied by his father (a distinguished Elder whom we visited in 2006, now deceased) and a couple of his father's wives, as well as married brothers and nephews and nieces galore. Hospitality here is not a mattress on the floor, but a private room with a mosquito net; it is the children who get to sleep on the floor, when they move out of their room to accommodate guests.

Madani's wife Fati is a smiling, cuddly mother figure who has become a sister to Ana Edwards (called Ana Tall when she is in Ségou) and our other Richmond Mothers. Fati runs Chez Mamy, a restaurant attached to their home, where we sometimes eat. It is named for her eldest daughter, who is sweet-natured and vivacious and dreams of becoming an English-language journalist; hence she is studying in Ghana. On one occasion, Yah Traoré, Ségou's director of budget, generously hosted the whole Richmond-Ségou delegation of twenty hungry people at Mamy's Restaurant. That evening during dinner, Mamy whispered into my ear, "I need to speak with you privately." She must have been about thirteen at the time. Somewhat bemused, I followed her into the yard and took my place in a chair under the stars. Mamy pulled a stool up beside me, took out her notebook, and announced: "I have to interview an uncle for my school project, and you are the uncle I have chosen." Whew! That was a relief: I was not needed to preside over the confessions of a confused adolescent, but simply to answer a list of questions about where I had been and what I had seen during the past fifty years of my existence. I was Mamy's first assay into journalism.

Fig. 15. Gifts: A small donation of balls and shirts from the Richmond Kickers to Ségou's youth soccer team. From the left: Shawn Utsey (VCU professor), Madani Sissoko (president of the Ségou Sister City Commission), Allan Levenberg (VFoM treasurer and Richmond Sister City commissioner), Kalifa Touré (VFoM's Bamako representative), and Oumou Koné, a.k.a. Michelle Poulton (VFoM). Madani and Allan were the two AUPAP project managers. Photo: VFoM.

Press Release: Richmond to Sister City with Segou MALI

VIRGINIA FRIENDS OF MALI
LES AMIS DU MALI EN VIRGINIE—Richmond, Virginia
virginiafriendsofmali@gmail.com
FOR IMMEDIATE RELEASE: 8 OCTOBER 2009

Richmond to become Sister City with Segou MALI

Mayor Ousmane Simaga of Ségou MALI travels to Richmond to meet Mayor Dwight C. Jones and sign the agreement that will make Ségou Richmond's seventh sister city.

Richmond, VA, October 8, 2009—Through the efforts of locally based Virginia Friends of Mali (VFoM) and Richmond's Sister City Commission, on June 3, 2009 Richmond City Council passed a resolution patroned by 1st District councilman Bruce Tyler to pursue an official sister city relationship with Ségou. In his letter of introduction to Mayor Simaga, Mayor Jones stated, "Our cities have many things in common, from our identity as capital cities, to the rivers that flow through our vast landscape, and the history and culture that make us educational and recreational destinations." On Tuesday, October 13, 2009, the two Mayors will meet in person for the first time to sign the Sister City Agreement and enjoy a few moments to get acquainted.

Mr. Ousmane Simaga, Mayor of Ségou, second largest city in the West African nation of Mali, will visit Richmond from Friday, Oct. 9—Tuesday, Oct. 13. In his letter of response, Mayor Simaga stated "the strength of this long-term association rests in the hands of our citizen volunteers and participants," and described the formation of a *Comité de Jumelage* to work with Richmond's Sister City Commission, the Virginia Friends of Mali and other "citizens interested in promoting understanding and helping to fight poverty in our two communities." Visiting with Mr. Simaga will be Mr. Mohamed Doumbia, Assistant Director of the Festival on the Niger and representative of the Ségou Economic Development Council as well as Mr. Kalifa Ahmadou Toure, Mali-based representative of the VFoM. Oregon-based Malian social entrepreneur Ms. Haoua Cheikh Seip is also in town to run the VFoM booth at the Richmond Folk Festival's Marketplace.

The delegation's itinerary includes visits to the Richmond Folk Festival, to Southside Child Development Center in Richmond's Manchester neighborhood, to the 3rd grade students of Southampton Elementary School, to VCU's Department of African American Studies, to the Afrikana student organization of VCU, to the Black History Museum and Cultural Center, to Richmond's October City Council meeting, and a private reception hosted by Dr. Robin Edward Poulton, president of Virginia Friends of Mali.

Mr. Simaga will also take a walking tour of Shockoe Bottom and attend a program honoring the memory of Africans from the Mali region who may be buried in the Burial Ground for Negroes, the "Sacred Ground." Past visits to Richmond from Malian dignitaries have included Ambassador Abdoulaye Diop in 2005, 2006 and 2008 and Prime Minister Ousmane Issoufi Maiga in 2005. Discussions have taken place with civic, social and educational leaders in Richmond and many Richmonders have visited Mali.

Mr. Mamou Daffé, President of the Festival on the Niger (www.festivalsegou.org/new) and of the Ségou Economic Development Council, first raised the idea of programmatic collaborations with National Folk Festival director Julia Olin during a visit to Richmond in 2006. As Mr. Daffé's emissary, Mr. Doumbia's focus will be to further explore ideas of partnerships or exchanges between the two festivals. The Ségou festival's website states that the 6th Festival on the Niger runs from February 1–7, 2009 in Ségou offering a unique spectacle of "music and dance from the region, as well as well-known West-African artists, who will play on the banks of the river Niger. The Festival on the Niger offers an interdisciplinary and inter-cultural meeting, bringing together people from Ségou, Malians and foreigners from all over the world, sharing the same wish: to discover the other and to learn from our differences."

To commemorate the new "twinning" of the two cities, Richmond will be the city of honor during Ségou's 2010 *Festival sur le Niger* and a delegation from Richmond will attend.

Virginia Friends of Mali is a 501(c)(3) organization that creates and promotes educational and cultural pathways to understanding and cooperation between the peoples of the African nation of Mali and the State of Virginia, USA.

Learn more at www.vafriendsofmali.org.

Sister City Signing Ceremony in Richmond, October 13, 2009

Back in 2005, when we received Mayor Thiero's letter inviting Richmond to become a sister city of Ségou, Richmond had no sister city commission. The old one was dead. By 2007, however, we had established a new RSCC, and the process of responding to the mayor's invitation began.

In Mali, such an effort might take a week or two. In America, it takes a year or two; but finally, the first official meeting between our two mayors was scheduled. It would be a signing ceremony, arranged to coincide with the Ségou delegation's October 2009 visit to the Richmond Folk Festival. Protocol was set: first, we would meet Mayor Dwight C. Jones in his private conference room. There would be a short get-to-know-you discussion; then we would move to the main city hall conference room, where documents would be signed, hands would be shaken, and photographs would be taken; finally, drinks would be served. It seemed simple enough.

Ségou's delegation naturally included the acting Malian ambassador, H.E. Muhamed Ouzouma Maiga, who wanted to witness this major event for Malian diplomacy. His three vehicles brought Malian advisors, journalists, and cameramen. Mali's national TV station wanted pictures! The mayor of Ségou's delegation included both his own Malian people and the RSCC chair and members, as well as the VFoM executive committee. I served as translator. We were more than twenty people hanging around the elevators outside the Mayor Jones' office when his head of protocol opened the door and screeched, "I can only take ten people!" She then read out the names of the Ségou delegation. The RSCC chair was not on her list. She even tried to refuse entry to the Malian ambassador—his name was not on her list either.

To save everyone further embarrassment, I took control as politely as I could and ushered the ambassador and his photographer, Mayor Simaga, the presidents of the Richmond and Ségou sister city commissions, the assistant director of the Ségou festival, and some VFoM executive committee members into the room. We took our seats around the table and waited.

After three minutes, Mayor Jones entered with his chief of staff, Suzette Denslow—a smart lady with whom we had had preparatory discussions. We all shook hands. Jones took his seat at the head of the table, beside Mayor Simaga. Then he turned to the translator and asked, "So these people come from Mali? Is that in Africa?"—to his eternal shame!

We made small talk around the table, and Ambassador Maiga led the conversation in English since he was the most senior person in the room. After ten minutes, we moved to the main conference room, where city council members were waiting for us: notably Kathy Graziano, chair of the city council; and Bruce Tyler, who was then the councilman in liaison with, and *ex officio* member of, the RSCC. Sam Patterson, the personal assistant to the city council for handling sister city affairs, presented the documents. Pens were produced, signatures were appended, hands were shaken, papers were exchanged, speeches were made, and photos were taken. As the mayor of Ségou stated in his speech, the dream of forming a sister city partnership had been realized, and we knew that a new, long, and exciting journey was beginning.

Fig. 16. Mayor Dwight C. Jones of Richmond and Mayor Ousmane Simaga of Ségou exchange signed papers under the guidance of Ana Edwards, vice president (soon to become president) of VFoM. Behind are Ambassador Maiga, Council Chair Kathy Graziano, and Councilman Bruce Tyler. Photo: Allan Levenberg, VFoM.

Mayor Ousmane Simaga: Ending a Dream and Starting a Journey

Mayor of Ségou's Speech in Richmond - October 13, 2009

Monsieur le Maire de Richmond: Honorable Dwight C. Jones,

Madame la Présidente du Richmond City Council: Madame Kathy Graziano,

Monsieur le Conseiller municipal chargé des Jumelages: Councilman Bruce Tyler,

Madame la Présidente de la Sister City Commission de Richmond: Madame My Lan Tran,

Excellency the Ambassador of Mali in Washington, DC: Monsieur Ouzouma Maiga,

Monsieur le Président of Virginia Friends of Mali: Dr. Robin Poulton-Tall,

Honorable invitees, all Virginia Friends of Mali, Ladies and Gentlemen:

This is the end of a dream, and the beginning of a journey!

We have traveled from Ségou to begin with you, and with all the citizens of Richmond, a partnership that will be a journey in geography and in friendship. The friendship part has already begun, thanks to the generosity and warmth with which we have been received in every corner of Richmond: in your schools, in your homes and your administrative buildings.

I believe that this spirit of cooperation will allow us to weave a fabric of friendship and solidarity between the two cities of agro-industrial Richmond and agricultural Ségou. We are complementary in many ways, and this will help us find mutual benefits in the fields of music and culture, education and health, in commerce and in small business creation.

The economic aspect is important, for our Sister City relationship should contribute, above all, to improving the conditions of our inhabitants and fighting poverty in our two cities. This can be done through investment, by creating jobs, and with exciting new activities that generate revenues for our young people.

Our youth need employment, but they also need activities that are fun and that bring new skills. We dream of building—with our American partners—a center for sports, crafts and culture for the youth of Ségou: a center to be called the RICHMOND HOUSE. In Africa I am afraid that we have no tradition of baseball or American football, but our young people love table tennis, and the game you call "soccer"—the Richmond Kickers will be very welcome when they visit Ségou!

And our young people love basketball, a game that was invented in America. In fact, last year, the star attacking player of the Spiders—the University of Richmond basketball team—was a young Malian called Oumar Sylla. We hope very much that the basketball players of Richmond will come to Ségou to play some games, and also to train our young people.

Our Richmond-Ségou partnership should also focus on creating sustainable development that offers new perspectives to our young people through the optimal management of water and energy resources.

Our entrepreneurs should work together in both Richmond and Ségou. I hope we will be able to encourage initiatives in solar energy, improved drinking water supply, and projects for health and sanitation in both cities. We exist as cities only because of the two great rivers that bring us water. Water is both a blessing, and a risk to the health of our populations. In Mali, extensive irrigation of rice and sugar removes water from the Niger River. We have created a River Observatory, and we hope to benefit from your extensive experience in managing the James River and the Chesapeake Bay.

That is just a small sample of the future opportunities I see emerging through the partnership between Richmond and Ségou. Immediately we can bring you our music and our culture: in fact, last year, the Malian singer-guitarist Vieux Farka Touré opened the Richmond Folk Festival.

We can also bring to Richmond our ideas and our experience . . . and our African history, which is also your history. Our two cities are linked through our common African ancestors, by those Malian men and women who helped to build Virginia after 1620. That gives us four hundred years of shared history. I believe that our common experience offers a solid foundation upon which we can build a new future together.

May God Almighty bless our endeavors!

I thank you all.
Ousmane Simaga
Mayor of Ségou

The Richmond and Ségou Sister City Commissions

Ségou's Festival of the Niger River and the Richmond Folk Festival on the James River have been two of the focal points of our early sister city adventure; but what of the commissions that coordinate sister cities? How do they work, and how important are they?

When we attended our first Ségou festival, there was no commission in Richmond. We had dinner with Ségou's sister city commission, which was an association of artisans. I recall meeting carpenter; a trader; and a mechanic who ran a motor workshop, all named Traoré.

During the dinner, Mayor Ibrahima Thiero made it clear that he thought the Traoré artisans were excluding other citizens, and that he felt that relations with Angoulême—at the time, Ségou's only sister city—were unsatisfactory. Amid mutterings about a lack of transparency, we gathered that the relationship with Angoulême had been more or less dead—or at least sleeping—until Richmond arrived. Not to be outdone by America, the French leaders of Angoulême quickly revitalized their actions, and we have since become good friends.

Thiero and his successor, Mayor Ousmane Simaga, dissolved the Traoré committee and announced that the Sister City Commission henceforward would be composed of elected members of the Ségou council. This arrangement would not work in Richmond, where the city council has only nine members. Ségou has thirty-two, and about a third of them sat on Simaga's sister city commission (*comité de jumelage*), one of the more prestigious subgroups of the municipal council. Though dominated by men, it included some women councilors, which we think is a good thing; only three or four Ségou women have visited Richmond in the past ten years. On the other hand, more thirty of the forty-plus Richmonders in our delegations to Ségou have been women—students, musicians, artists, teachers, and people who just wanted to visit Mali and the Ségou festival.

After the municipal elections of November 2016, Mayor Simaga was replaced by Monsieur Nouhoum Diarra, the leader of one branch of the Malian president's party, RPM, *Rassemblement pour le peuple,* in Ségou. Political parties in Mali are more geared to personalities than to policies, and splits are endemic. Mayor Diarra appointed his fifth deputy mayor, Madame Sacko Djélika Haïdara, a teacher, to be in charge of maintaining the sister city relationship with Richmond, and a small commission of six elected councilors was named under the chairmanship of Monsieur Dramane Traoré, an accountant. The mayor and his colleagues are committed to opening the sister city to members of Ségou's civil society, by creating a broader "committee" that will include more women, media specialists, teachers, artisans and business people. Among their early initiatives, they intend to encourage English teachers in high schools and the university to create a Richmond Club that will be able to take more advantage of the fact that Virginians speak English.

Madani Sissoko was the commission president under Mayor Simaga, and proved to be an effective and dynamic partner for both Angoulême and Richmond. No longer an elected councilor, Sissoko remains active as an advisor to the new municipal team. Instead, he is treasurer of the Angoulême citizens group, as well as the Ségou project manager for VFoM. In a sense, he has switched sides from Ségou to its partner cities.

Compared to Ségou's, Richmond's sister city commission has a much lower profile in a city led by very wealthy but inward-looking corporate interests. Since we recreated the RSCC after 2005, the city council has raised the grant from $2,000 per year to $9,000 per year. Unlike his predecessor, Douglas Wilder, Mayor Dwight Jones showed little interest in things international. Support from city council members has been as effusive, as the mayor was elusive. Whenever a Malian delegation has visited the city council chamber, Kathy Graziani, Ellen Robinson, Bruce Tyler, Cynthia Newbille and other council members have left their seats, coming down to the floor of the chamber to greet the mayor of Ségou, chat, and take photographs. After the elections of 2016, we have no reason to doubt that the warmth and hospitality displayed by the city council will continue. The new councilman serving on the RSCC is the Honorable Andreas Addison, and his regular visits to the RSCC monthly meetings are greatly appreciated. With a view to building more international trade, Andreas is interested in bringing new sister city partners to Richmond, starting with Latin America.

What the RSCC has not yet worked out is a mechanism by which news on how Ségou and the other sister city relationships are progressing can be sent to the city council and multiple city institutions. Richmond maintains the following sister city relationships:

Richmond upon Thames, England (Europe)
Saitama City, Japan (Asia)
Windhoek, Namibia (Africa)

Zhengzhou, China (Asia)

Ségou, Republic of Mali (Africa)

Ségou, supported by the Virginia Friends of Mali team, has the most varied range of activities. The two Richmonds have regular exchanges at the commission level, but there has been little citizen involvement. The idea of exchanging cricket teams has not yet taken hold; yet Richmond's Asian community is enthusiastic for cricket, which used to be played throughout the US until Slazenger made a commercial fortune by promoting baseball as "the American game." The relationship with Saitama City is dynamic, thanks to the RSCC's Catherine Nexsen, who coordinates youth exchanges and baseball matches involving Richmond high schools. The Japanese are Richmond's most active participants in the annual international youth art exhibition organized by SCI. (Our Ségou high schools participate episodically.) Zhengzhou is developing commercial ties: Diane Greer of the RSCC runs the Richmond branch of the Chinese Friendship Society with support from the Chinese embassy. Although the Namibian ambassador recently visited Richmond, and despite the enthusiasm of German teacher Su Boer and the Namibian honorary consul Larry Morgan, Windhoek has struggled to establish active links with regular activities. Other sister city relationships are dormant. President Eisenhower created the concept of sister cities to promote citizen diplomacy; to develop a good relationship, each city needs an active citizen group to maintain links and create activities in the way that VFoM is doing.

On its website, the RSCC describes itself as having been "an early champion of international relations" as early as the 1930s. Indeed, the RSCC ought to be the focal point for an outward-looking and international Richmond. The first three presidents of the new RSCC have all been dynamic women with strong international connections: My Lan Tran from Virginia's Asian Chamber of Commerce; Susan Nolan, a management consultant for the airline industry; and Patricia Cummins, a professor of French, Francophonie, and world studies. But the commission as a whole needs more institutional roots in order to establish a coherent Richmond identity that prompts investment from corporations, educational establishments, and local associations.

While Richmond's commission has a rotating six-year membership of thirteen individuals with few institutional roots, Ségou suffers from the opposite problem: their commission of elected councilors has trouble involving the citizenry, especially women, in sister city activities. In both cities, the mechanism for popular participation is fluctuating. Greater and more regular involvement of schools and universities seems to be one good route, but that will happen only if teachers in Ségou and in Richmond understand the potential of the partnership. Greater regular support is needed from chambers of commerce in both cities, whose entrepreneurs might see value in promoting, for example, water treatment and solar power; sporting exchanges (soccer and basketball) would bring benefits to both sides of the Atlantic; and Richmond's cultural institutions (dance, music, museums) should see value in their city looking outward toward the rest of the world. As Mayor Simaga said, we are at the beginning of a journey.

Richmond and Ségou: Similarities and Differences

While the table at the end of this section shows that our sister cities have many aspects in common, our approaches to the sister city idea have been rather different. The mayor of Ségou is heavily invested in the relationship: This initiative was Ségou's, and the original invitation letter to Richmond was signed by Mayor Thiero in 2005—and Ségou's sister city commission is composed of elected councilors. The mayors of Richmond, on the other hand, have remained rather distant from the process that is entirely citizen-run. The RSCC is composed of volunteers and one elected city councilor (in 2018 this is Councilman Andreas Addison). The difference is partly due to the differences between our two cultures, and partly a matter of politics: Richmond is an inward-looking city where the city council and mayor run separate—even rival—operations, while Ségou's mayor runs his city council and gains prestige and political capital from his city's links with America. Richmond is a far richer city than Ségou, just as Virginia is a far wealthier state than Mali, which is also landlocked; and so there is less for its government to gain. Mayor Levar Stoney has already shown a lot more interest in Africa than his predecessors.

Expectations of mutual hospitality also differ between Virginians and Malians, with community links and traditions of hospitality running far deeper in Ségou than in Richmond. Hospitality is a Malian tradition, passed down from grandfather to grandson: if your grandfather always stayed with the Konaré family in Bamako, then that is where you will also stay when visiting Bamako. Americans, on the other hand, have a far greater tendency to stay in hotels when they venture to other cities, even when visiting friends. As a result, the Ségou City Council has far more facilities for hosting Richmond delegations than do the Virginia Friends of Mali or the RSCC in Richmond. Ségoviens often keep in touch with their Richmond hosts via phone calls and even visits—which is not generally true of Americans who have been hosted by Malians. President Eisenhower's idea for sister cities was based on his desire to create new international friendships, but the friendships we have developed in Ségou seem broader, deeper, and more positive than the friendships that visiting Ségoviens have established with the Richmonders who have hosted them. It is a matter of culture.

As an anthropologist, I have noticed that in Virginia, the most expensive part of most homes is the heavy front door, which is often equipped with multiple locks and chains and even a spyhole. This speaks to a well-established American culture of suspicion, fear of "the other," and doubt concerning the objectives of any stranger—who may be a thief or an armed aggressor. The US creation myth evokes a Wild West that was conquered and defended by violence.

In contrast, Malian houses certainly have no spyholes. Most have no doors, although the relatively new, modern urban environment in Bamako and even Ségou has paved the way for the construction of some houses that do have front doors. Still, most rural Malian homes are open. The traditional compound or yard seldom has a gate—and if does, it is closed only at night, to keep the animals inside and protected from marauding hyenas or lions hoping to grab a goat for supper. Bambara compounds often have low mud walls and an entrance lobby where the head of household meets his guests and checks who is coming in and out of the dwelling, but few Malians think of the stranger as a potential aggressor, although the jihadist menace that has been active in the region since 2012 may be changing this north of Ségou.

The creation myth in Malian villages concerns a famous founder who cleared the bush, grew crops, and gained prestige by offering land to newcomers who were welcomed and whose presence made his village more important. The Other is traditionally a welcome addition to the Malian community, an ally who increases production and provides protection. Therefore, a respectable head of household ensures that there is always spare food available in case of an unexpected visitor. At lunchtime in Mali, the kitchen will often set aside a portion for this express purpose. Although eighteenth-century Virginians may have done the same, this is no longer a tradition in Richmond, where people are more likely to arrange to meet friends in a restaurant than to invite them into their houses.

It would be great if Richmond had a city guesthouse, but this is not the case. Neither the Richmond City Council nor the mayor's office has ever become involved in hosting our out-of-town guests. In support of their sister city, many individual Richmonders have generously offered lodging and taxi services to our Malian guests over the past ten years—long may that continue! When we run out of options, we have to pay for hotel accommodation, although we did draw the line at funding hotel rooms for the governor of Kayes Region, who turned up unexpectedly one year as a tourist, coming along "for the ride" because his friend, the governor of Ségou, was visiting Richmond. Governors from other regions are not involved in the sister city partnership, and we do not feel bound to pay for them. Even the regional governor of Ségou is not, strictly speaking, part of the "city." But when we take the Ségou delegation of twelve visitors to lunch during the Doing Business in Africa Conference, for example, we have to pay for all of them. We cannot tell the governor that he and his head of protocol are excluded! So a commitment to a successful sister city arrangement comes with personal financial implications.

Ségou's tradition of hospitality, on the other hand, seems boundless. When we visit Ségou, the city council, patron of the Ségou Sister City Commission, takes on the task of lodging and feeding us. During the Ségou festival, they feed hundreds of musicians and other guests. Malians arrange hospitality in a relaxed, communal fashion. And so, if we were to compare the two cities, we must conclude that Richmond clearly has a lot more money, while Ségou has a far richer culture of hospitality and humanity.

The Richmond and Ségou city commonalities

Commonality	Richmond, VA, U.S.A.	Ségou, Mali
Historic Capital cities	Historical capital city of the State of Virginia since 18th century	Historical capital city in 18th and 19th centuries of the Ségou Kingdom
Political Organization—Country	Multi-Party Democracy with directly elected President and Congress; and a directly elected Governor of Virginia	Multi-Party Democracy, Univer. Suffrage with directly elected President and Assembly; and a government-nominated regional Governor of Ségou
Municipal Organization	City Council elected with two political party labels, headed by a President; and a mayor directly elected by universal suffrage	City Council elected by the citizens, with 5-6 political party labels; the Council elects its may who chairs the Council
Number of elected council members	9, none of whom is mayor	32, one of whom is mayor
Elections Nov2016	New mayor Levar Stoney	New mayor Nouhoum Diarra
Economic Organization	Greater Richmond Partnership	Ségou Region Economic Development Council (CPEL)
Primary Language	English	French and Bambara
Port city	Richmond on the James River	Ségou on the Niger River
Music Festivals, both founded 2004	Richmond Folk Festival succeeded the National Folk Festival	Ségou Music Festival of the Nig 14th edition in 2018
Common musical roots	4 Malian bands have played the Richmond Festival	3 Virginian bands have played th Ségou Festival
Center of Tourism	Civil War Battlefields, Capital of Confederacy, Black History, Lumpkin's Jail and Shockoe Bottom memorial sites	Festival on the Niger River: Pottery, Masks, Fabrics, Dance, Music; Sikoro and other historic village Colonial Architecture
Important Nearby Tourist Sites	Jamestown, Yorktown, Williamsburg University of Virginia, Monticello, Mount Vernon. Washington D.C.	Djenné Mosque: the world's larg adobe building. Dogon cliffs. Timbuktu university and mosqu Trading port of Mopti. Bamako
Center of History & Culture	First US colony Jamestown 1607, first landings of Africans 1619; Richmond capital of Virginia which was home to 8 US presidents	Historic Bambara Kingdom, Dynasties of Coulibaly & Diarr Kingdom of Amadou Tall (Fula French Colonial Period 1880–1
Common History of Slavery	1600s and 1700s many Virginian slaves came from the Empire of Mali through Goree Island, Senegal or James Island (River Gambia)	Mali also had slavery. Some Malians in 1600s and early 170 must have sold slaves to the slav traders, who carried them to the coast and across the Ocean

Racism and brutality	Richmond and New Orleans had the largest slave markets in North America: oppression of black African by a White society	Monzon Diarra kept albino slaves in a hole beneath his throne, and sacrificed one from time to time: oppression of white skins by a Black King
Historic Cemetery heritage and debate	Richmond's "Negro Burial Ground" and the whole history of Slavery in Shockoe Bottom is an issue of hot debate and division between Black and White. How should slavery be remembered? Should there be a museum and memorial park?	Ségou's Family Heads were slaughtered by French colonel Archinard in 1890. Their commo grave remains untouched opposite City Hall, a symbol of White brutality and a source of debate: should a monument be built on that space in remembrance?
Cult of great heroes	Lee, Stuart and Jackson Arthur Ashe and Gabriel	Sunjata Keita and Mansa Musa Keita Biton Coulibaly and Monzon Diarra
History of famous women	Maggie Walker; Mary Bowser and Elizabeth van Lew	Sunjata Keita's mother Sogolon; Nyéléni, the mythical perfect woman
History of great explorers	Columbus sailed to Haiti 1492 William Byrd 1747 Lewis & Clark 1806	Abukari sailed to Brazil 1312 Mungo Park, the first European t see the Niger, reached Ségou 179
Common African Heritage	Music—5 String Banjo Southern Food (African + French) House and Family Structure	Music—*Akonting* dili bo 5-string *Ngoni* Malian and French Food House & Family Structure
Both cities have very religiou societies, strongly divided by their faiths. Most people are tolerant, but some are not.	Many churches and many different denominations in Richmond. Catholic cathedral. Presbyterian seminary. Baptist churches, mosques and synagogues. Christianity is the dominant faith, with multiple Christian religions; Center for Interfaith Reconciliation offsets some very illiberal colleges	Head of Tijania (Sufi) and an important Bozo Marabout (Teacher) are in Ségou. Islam is th dominant religion. Catholic Bishop is in Ségou. Many small Protestant groups are out in the villages. Is the Great Fetish still extant and active in Ségou, city of 4444 acaci + 1? In Mali, "to breathe is to pray"
Both Cities have fine women leaders, fighting for space in a male-dominated society	Delores McQuinn, Cynthia Newbille, Ellen Robinson, Kathy Graziano, Anne Holton, Ana Edwards, Dana Wiggins, Lydie Alapini Sakponou, Omilade Janine Bell, Patricia Cummins, Susan Nolan, My Lan Tran, Pattie Parks	Singers Babani Koné, Awa Sako. City leaders Fabété Tall Diao, Am Gao, Djélika Haidara, Alimata Ali Sacko, Djénéb Diarra. Social leaders: Djénéba Cissé Thiero, Awa Diarra, Ina Daffé, Fanta Diabaté, Bana Diabaté Sidibé, Safiatou Coulibaly,
Center of agriculture, light industry and commerce	Light Manufacturing; C.F. Sauer	Comatex: Textile Manufacturer Other cotton manufacturers

	is big exporter to West Africa of BAMA mayonnaise; Altria's Marlborough cigarettes are the biggest seller in Ségou (tobacco); BioPark with multiple Medical & Tech Research companies	*Bogolan*—traditional dye works Ségou Lait: major dairy products; Niger River Fishing; Office du Niger (irrigated sugar, cotton, cereals, rice); shea butter; cattle: milk, hides & meat
Sports	Triple AAA Flying Foxes baseball team; Richmond Kickers soccer team VCU Rams and UR Spiders are strong basketball teams	Ségou Football Team (soccer) called 'Biton' after the founding king (1743). Amateur soccer leagues, all ages. Basketball popular but under-developed
Active, dynamic urban civil society	Hundereds of associations work in Greater Richmond.	There is an office coordinating th 90 + NGOs in Ségou.
Media Outlets Newspaper Radio Television	The Times-Dispatch, Free Press, Richmond Defender, Style Weekly, Richmond Magazine NPR: WRIR, WCVE, Richmond Independent Radio WRVA, PBS and National TV	The Segovien and Balanzan newspapers Radio Sikoro National TV from Bamako Mali has more than 200 local rad stations covering most of the country Many national papers in Bamako
City Population	250,000	120,000
Regional Population	1,250,000	1,750,000
Median Income	$35,000 per year	$1,600 is an estimated average Skilled Worker = $3,000/year (e
Education	Richmond has many high schools and several universities, public as wel as private	Ségou has 8 high schools and a n Ségou university focused on technical agriculture and public health
Poverty Rate	22 - 40 %	Unknown (estimate of 40-50%)
Poverty	Poverty has varying cultural interpretations. Money is not the best measure. Medical coverage may be better in Ségou than in Richmond because of the community health centers: or not, depending on one's interpretation. Many old people are very lonely in Richmond, but non is lonely in Ségou where family and community are strong. Education equally terrible for the poor families of both cities. In Richmond, obes = poor ... but not in Ségou	
	The Mayors of both cities have stated that fighting urban poverty is their primary objective, but much more remains to be done	
	Richmond has a large debt economy with usurers extorting high rates of interest, creating stress	Ségou is only partly a cash economy, much is subsistence; de is widespread and most people subsist on weekly credit

Pride	In Richmond in seems to be only middle-class families who exhibit pride; the poor are neglected and the neglect themselves. Money seems to be the main yardstick by which people judge and are judged	In Ségou even poor families are proud of their name and of the achievements of their ancestors: about which the *griots* remind the at every social event. Money is less important than you name your reputation and your childen

Conclusion
Ana Is the Spirit of the Niger River

"We are ready for your speech, Macky Tall."

I was sitting next to Ana, listening to Mamou Daffé orchestrate the closing ceremonies of the 2010 Ségou Music Festival, when a young man murmured this message in my ear. Speech? What speech? No one had asked me for a speech! But all you can do in such circumstances is follow along cheerfully and find out what is going to happen.

I pulled Ana's sleeve and warned her we must go onstage. Ana told the rest of the delegation to follow. *Thank goodness,* I thought to myself, *I am wearing a magnificent new* grand boubou *made by Bana Sidibé, so that I shall look sufficiently elegant to impress Ségou's massed citizens.* In Mali—like the Oscar awards ceremony in Hollywood—dress is an important part of culture.

Ana and the rest of the Richmond delegation followed me down from the VIP seating and along the concrete dock toward the river. Five minutes later, we found ourselves on the main stage, facing eight thousand people lining the banks of the Niger, waiting for the next installment. That next installment was us!

The master of ceremonies was announcing that an award would now be made to the sister city delegation from Richmond. I asked Daffé, who was standing on the stage beside me, "What is this all about?"

"I find it is better never to warn people in advance." He smiled. "Spontaneity makes for better speeches."

Mamou Daffé took the microphone and informed the assembled crowd that Richmond was the sister city of Ségou, and that we were to be awarded the Spirit of the Niger River trophy for cultural achievement (even though, so far, we had done nothing!) and international cooperation. The Sister City Agreement had only just been formalized, but that didn't worry Daffé, who had decreed that Richmond was the Official Visitor for this year's event. He held up the wooden carving of a mermaid. Eight thousand music lovers cheered across the water.

"So we award this trophy 'the Spirit of the Niger River,' to Virginia Friends of Mali—our friends from Richmond, Ségou's sister city."

Okay, thank you, Mamou—and now I had to think of something intelligent to say. Should I speak in French? or in Bambara? I grinned at Ana, and she smiled back at me. Allan had decided he would miss the festival's closing ceremony, but together with Michelle and Shawn, we made a reasonable delegation and occupied a fair slice of the huge stage.

I stepped up to the microphone and waved in my right hand our wooden mermaid. On the base of the wooden effigy were engraved the words "Spirit of the Niger River."

"*Hallo,* Ségou! *Aw ni ché! Aw ka kéné wa?*" I cried.[39] A roar from the riverbank was my reward.

"Thank you for this beautiful carving! This is the Spirit of the Niger River, the *Ba Djoli Ba;* and the Spirit of Ségou. We will take the spirit of your wonderful city back to Richmond, your sister city. May our spirits be joined to become One Spirit!"

I stepped back from the microphone. That was enough, I thought. Plenty for an impromptu speech. Then, to my surprise and delight, Ana stepped forward. She was dressed in a magnificent red Malian gown. At that time, Ana was already the president of Virginia Friends of Mali. Soon she would be living in Ségou for two months as artist-in-residence, painting for the next festival's art exhibition and working in the riverside studio of the renowned Malian sculptor Amaghiré

---

39 *"Hallo, how are you all?"*

Dolo, whose work with sculptured tree branches I had already seen in an exhibition in France fifteen years earlier.

Ana is beautiful. She radiates joy and confidence, her hair surrounds her face like a halo, and she has a personality that can charm eight thousand people. Did she, I wondered, need me to translate? Not at all!

Ana stepped forward and made her speech in French: "*Bonjour, Ségou! Merci! Je vous aime!*" What a woman! What courage and assurance! I handed Ana the statue of the mermaid, and she raised above her head the female Spirit of the River—often called in the *krio* languages "Mamy Wata," who is the Mother of the Waters, the Source of Fertility. The woman holds the woman. The Art Mother from Richmond waves the Earth and Water Mother of Ségou's wealth, and in happiness she laughs. Eight thousand Ségoviens laugh with her.

"Thank you, Ségou. We love you! And thank you for this gift, for the Spirit of the Niger. We will treasure it, and we will carry it safely back to your sister city, to Richmond."

Perfect. Our two cities are in harmony. Ana has honored both Ségou and the efforts of her high school French teacher. Balance has been achieved: the black and the white, the African and the American, the male and the female, the beast and the beauty. . . . This is what sister cities are meant to be. This is "citizen diplomacy" at its perfect best. We are in symbiosis.

Everything You Need to Know to Travel to Ségou

This is the advice that the Virginia Friends of Mali gives to Richmond travelers headed to Ségou for the first time.

Hospitality

Every society has codes of behavior, which often vary greatly between cultures. For example, in Mali, if a Malian woman offers to cook for a man, she may be offering marriage or something similar—so acceptance of food can have strong implications (though not if the mayor of Ségou is inviting you to taste his wife's cooking!). When a West African accepts food from another person, it implies that he trusts his host with his life, since a host could so easily put poison in the food. So a guest honors a host by accepting his hospitality, as much as the host honors a guest with an invitation. Such an idea would probably not enter into the head of an American.

If you wish to honor a Malian, therefore, you will visit him at home. From this reasoning, it follows naturally that Africans seldom issue formal invitations to their homes. On the contrary, an African may honor you by coming to eat in your house, showing how much he trusts you to give him good food. If you wait for an invitation, you may wait forever. Eating alone is seen as standoffish; inviting African colleagues to a restaurant can provide an elegant compromise. In this case, a modestly priced restaurant serving African food is best, and the Americans must pay. Remember that the US is the richest country in the world; even someone of modest means in America will be far wealthier than the people who will be using the health centers that the Virginia Friends of Mali have built in Ségou.

When I worked for USAID, I witnessed many misunderstandings caused by Americans. For example, our Malian colleagues felt insulted when they were encouraged to "bring a plate" to an American party. The idea of "bringing a plate" is unfamiliar to Malians. If they honor you by coming to eat in your house, they do not expect to have to bring their own food.

Conversely, if you honor your African friends by visiting their house and accepting their food, do not compliment the cook: this may give the impression that you are surprised their food is so good. Americans tend to overdo compliments; Africans will probably err in the other direction. Thanking the cook is always acceptable, while criticizing or leaving food on your plate is not. Sniffing food in Mali suggests that you are suspicious about what has been served, rather than that you are enjoying the aroma of the flavors, so this should be avoided as well.

Bringing presents for the host's family can be appreciated. Giving presents to children is always acceptable—especially and preferably useful things, like school supplies. You can only give money politely if you insist that it is for the children or specifically to buy something for the baby of a new mother, in which case it is known as "soap money."

Drinking and Dehydration

In Mali, you should *seek the shade*. The country is hot, and sunstroke is unpleasant. Mali also tends to be very, very dry. Because it is so hot and dry, dehydration is the biggest health risk. The more you are in the sun, the more you may burn and the more you will dehydrate. If you feel thirsty, you are already dehydrated. Try to drink a lot of water—at least one mouthful of water every fifteen minutes throughout the day. You will not sweat, so you will not realize how much moisture is being sucked out of your body by the dry heat.

Bottled water is best for visitors, and any foreigner should drink at least three liters per day—the equivalent of about two large bottles of water. Water is better than beer. If you are fed up with water, drink hot tea—made with boiled water and nonfattening—or cola, said to be good for the digestion and upset stomachs, as is pastis, an anise-flavored French *apéritif* diluted with water. Keep in mind that as coffee and tea are diuretic, they encourage water loss, so bottled water (or oranges!) is a better choice.

In African countries where beer is drunk, the quantities consumed are enormous. An American beer drinker will probably find himself rapidly outdrunk and outspent. This may cause problems for an American who thinks he will just offer everybody "a drink"—for if you say so in front of Rwandans or Cameroonians or Zambians, you will need to budget for a full crate of drinks for each person! But this is not the case in Mali, where, as in most Muslim countries, few people drink alcohol. In fact, beer-drinking in Mali can be a way to offend people without really trying. Even going off for one beer can appear offensive—indeed, during the AUPAP project in Ségou, our Malian hosts found the foreign engineers' frequent beer-drinking culturally insensitive, and therefore extremely rude.

Insects and Illnesses

Before your trip, you will need to get a few vaccinations—yellow fever, tetanus, meningitis, and polio vaccines are essential. You'll also need to bring malaria medicine and obtain MEDEVAC insurance, in case you become seriously ill or injured and need to be flown home. You may already be covered by your existing health insurance or vehicle insurance, or by your posh credit card (provided you use it to purchase the air ticket) or another insurance. You can obtain special travel insurance through your travel agent, or from SOS International.

There is no reason why anyone should fall sick if they respect simple rules of common sense. If you are going to arrive in a different climate and different time zone after a long journey, it is sensible to plan a period for rest and relaxation. Try not to be too ambitious for the first couple of days. In fact, stopping off for a weekend in Paris before continuing to Mali is a good way to ease jet lag and break up the journey.

Malian food is good and healthy, but you should avoid uncooked food like raw salads, which can carry germs and give you parasites. While eating yoghurt is fine, consuming unboiled milk is dangerous due to the risk of contracting TB and brucellosis, which you definitely want to avoid.

Malaria is endemic in Mali. It is carried by the female anopheles mosquito, which mostly appears at night. Therefore sleeping under a mosquito net at night is highly recommended; you will avoid bites and the unpleasant whine of mosquitoes in your ears.

The use of mosquito repellent is good, particularly in the evening, when the mosquitoes like to bite. We use a natural, citronella-based essence, which is effective and smells nice. Many Malian gardens feature citronella plants, which discourage the mozzies. Citronella-based infusions may also be drunk, and have an agreeable taste. Clothing may also dissuade mosquitoes: wearing long sleeves, long skirts, or trousers, as well as a double layer of socks in the evenings and a light scarf around your neck, are all good anti-mozzie techniques.

You can also avoid contracting malaria by using preventative prophylactic drugs. Thanks to strong marketing from the pharmaceutical industry, doctors in each country tend to recommend the medicine they know—which is not necessarily the best. I disapprove of American doctors who prescribe an antibiotic as malaria prophylaxis: they should do more study to find better options. Avoid Mefloquine, a very strong medicine with nasty side effects. Many specialists recommend PALUDRINE (proguanil, made in the UK by ICI): one pill per day, to be taken for the duration of your stay in Africa, and for three weeks after your return.

When you arrive in Mali, VFoM strongly recommend that you buy and carry with you an artemisinin- or quinine-based malaria treatment to use if you do get any sort of fever after you return. There are some effective Chinese treatments, but you will not find them in American pharmacies. A single malaria treatment costs about nine dollars in Mali.

The biggest danger for American travelers to Africa is your own US doctor when you return. It is overwhelmingly likely that your physician will never have seen African malaria, and may not recognize it if you present with symptoms of malaria fever when you get home. On returning from Mali, you should treat *any* and *every* fever as if it is malaria. If your US physician says it's not malaria, you should assume that he is wrong!

Clothing

To protect against the sun, you should wear long sleeves and a sun hat, and bring good-quality sunglasses that offer UV protection. We recommend everyone wear a broad-brimmed hat (you can buy one in Mali for five dollars): a baseball cap protects the nose, but it does not protect the ears or neck.

In order to feel comfortable and look respectable, men and women alike can wear loose cotton pants with a tunic or shirt that covers the buttocks. Women may prefer a flowing skirt—or better still, a simple, loose-fitting cotton dress without elastic, which can cause irritation around the waist. In lieu of long sleeves, women can also wear a cotton scarf or shawl over their shoulders. In general, clothes should be loose for comfort, made of natural fibers such as cotton or linen, and generous enough to conceal the curves of the body. If you have nice curves, it is polite to hide them in Mali.

Please, no shorts! No one in Mali wears shorts except when playing soccer, and Malians dislike those Americans who walk around wearing what Malians think of as underclothes.

No blue jeans! Ladies especially, and gentlemen too, please leave your blue jeans at home! Denim chafes, and it is very difficult to squat behind a desert shrub in blue jeans, which are not comfortable in the heat and are culturally unsuitable for women. Instead, choose loose cotton pants. Dresses are even better. Wear a dress over loose pants, and you will look perfect.

Malian dust is red, and the sun is hot. This means that white clothes do not remain white for very long, and blue shirts immediately show sweat marks. Because white becomes stained so quickly, choose beige, brown or bright-colored cotton clothes. Cotton is cool and easy to wash. Washing dries in less than two hours, so you can take just a very few comfortable clothes—or you can buy great Malian cotton outfits cheaply in the market, or have a tailor sew them for you within a few hours. Malians admire the beauty of fine cloth; they wear bright colors and flowing clothes. In Mali, good clothes, fine fabrics, and bright colors are important status symbols.

Money

Carry cash. Mali is a cash economy. Some big hotels in Bamako accept Visa cards, but most do not. *No one outside Bamako will even look at a credit card,* so if you are traveling to Ségou, *you will need to carry cash* for your stay.

The ATMs in Bamako or Ségou can be used with a Visa card (and only a Visa card; almost no one in Africa accepts American Express, which is little-used overseas, and Diners' Club is also unknown.). ATMs are always reliable, but they may run out of cash, and they may allow a maximum withdrawal of only $300. They are also expensive to use for getting cash.

When it comes to using cash, dollars and Euros are equally acceptable. Hundred-dollar bills are acceptable, but unfortunately, these bills are often counterfeited. Because of this, we advise you to ask your US bank to give you only *notes that have been printed within the past three years.* Older notes are often surcharged. Fifty-dollar bills will get you the best exchange rate. We recommend carrying your fifty US dollars or fifty-Euro bills with your passport in a pouch hidden under your clothes. A wad of one-dollar bills for tips can also be useful, in case you run out of small change in the local FCFA currency.

From experience, *we recommend <u>against</u> travelers' checks.* In a cash economy, you need to carry cash. You can transfer money through Western Union, but this is very expensive. We do not recommend trying to transfer money from your bank to a Malian account unless you do it two months ahead and are sure it has arrived.

Gifts

Americans are generous, and always want to bring gifts. Cheerful T-shirts are fine for Malian children, but not for adults, who will prefer useful gifts like unusual pens, jewelry, or tea towels, or flash drives or external hard drives for their computers. Children adore anything that helps their schoolwork, such as pens, calculators, and geometry sets. Schoolteachers love posters, atlases, wall maps, and wall calendars with pictures. Remember, Malians speak French, so US books are not very useful to young Malian students. Instead, they love footballs, basketballs, table tennis equipment, wooden picture puzzles (cardboard puzzles quickly get soiled and spoiled), packs of playing cards, and similar games. Ana gives art supplies, like colored pens. Robin always travels with colorful balloons, which are good for every age—but they do not last long!

Please do not hand out American flags or evangelical literature of any kind. Be sensitive to the way people in southern Mali perceive US and British foreign policy: in most parts of the world, NATO is seen not as a defensive alliance against communism, but as an imperial aggressor that likes to take out small countries using big weapons.

About the Authors

Ana Edwards, artist and educator, is a founder of Virginia Friends of Mali and of the sister city program between Richmond and Ségou, Mali's second city, which she has visited many times. She is chair of the Sacred Ground Historical Reclamation Project, which promotes the story of Gabriel's Rebellion and aims to reclaim Richmond's historic eighteenth-century African burial ground.

Dr. Robin Poulton raised his children in Mali. When his wife, Michelle, moved to Richmond as vice president of ChildFund, Robin taught university students about Africa, the Middle East, and terrorism. He also taught third-grade students and teachers about the medieval Empire of Mali, which was founded by the Lion King. His teaching led Mali's prime minister to visit Richmond with the invitation to become Ségou's sister city.

Glossary

Allah. Arabic name for God the Creator.

Amma. Dogon name for God the Creator.

ASA. African Studies Association (a 501.c.3 association), the premier association for African academic studies.

AUPAP. African Urban Poverty Alleviation Program, instituted by Sister Cities International to address urban poverty, and funded in part by the Bill & Melinda Gates Foundation.

Ba Djoli Ba. Bambara name for the Niger River meaning "great maternal artery" or "source of fertility."

BAFTA. British Academy of Film and Television Arts, based in London.

balafon. Mandé wooden keyboard, an ancestor of the xylophone, played by griots to praise kings.

bazin. Damask, a reversible luxury fabric of cotton and/or silk woven with patterns, invented two thousand years ago in Damascus. Mali is famous for the bright and beautiful designs of its dyed *bazin* cloth.

BHM. The Black History Museum, located in Richmond, Virginia.

Bogolan. Mudcloth, woven cotton dyed with leaves and painted with dark river mud.

CAFO. *Coordination des Associations Féminines,* a collective of Malian women's associations.

Chiwara. Mask or crest worn during dances to invoke agricultural fertility; symbol of community and cooperation.

CFI. ChildFund International, a 501.c.3. association for child development, based in Richmond.

CPEL. *Conseil pour la Promotion de L'Economie locale,* also known as the Ségou Region Economic Development Council.

CSO. Civil society organization.

daba. Bambara word meaning "hoe."

Dieu. French name for God the Creator.

djeli. Mandé word meaning "blood"; also used to refer to praise singers. See also **griot**.

dili bo. Fulani one-stringed guitarlike instrument from which the American musician Bo Diddly took his stage name.

ES. Elementary school.

FCMH. *Fondation Cheick Mansour Haidara,* based in Ségou.

FFF. French Film Festival, held annually in Richmond.

figh. Arabic term meaning "deep understanding" or "full comprehension"; the process of gaining knowledge of Islam through jurisprudence and the study of great scholars.

Guéno. Fulani name for God the Creator.

GMU. George Mason University, located in Fairfax, Virginia.

grand boubou. Three-piece embroidered Malian robes, used as formal dress.

griot. Praise singer, historian, and diplomat. See also **djeli**.

ICVA. Islamic Center of Virginia, located in Richmond.

Jingeraiber. Timbuktu mosque of mud brick built by Mansa Musa in 1326. Also spelled *Djingueraiber.*

JMU. James Madison University, located in Harrisonburg, Virginia.

kora. Multi-stringed West African classical harp.

MAN. MERLOT African Network. See also **MERLOT**.

mansa. Mandé word meaning "king of kings" or "emperor."

marabout. Charlatan; Muslim preacher; purveyor of charms.

MERLOT. Multimedia Educational Resource for Learning and Online Teaching.

MINUSMA. United National Multidimensional Integrated Stabilization Mission in Mali, a United Nations peacekeeping mission.

NAACP. National Association for the Advancement of Colored People, a civil rights organization founded in the US in 1909.

NCTA. National Council for the Traditional Arts, a folk arts organization founded in the US in 1933.

Nga, Ngai. Bambara name for God the Creator.

NGO. Nongovernment organization. These organizations promote development or a collective, nonpolitical interest.

ngoni. Three- to five-stringed African ancestor of the American banjo.

NOVA. Local term for Northern Virginia.

Opération Serval. French army operation to rid North Mali of jihadists, launched on January 11, 2013 and named after the serval, a fast and elusive desert cat.

Opération Barkhane. Six-nation military antiterrorist campaign based in Njamena, Chad, combining troops from the G5 Sahel states: France, Chad, Niger, Burkina Faso, Mali, and Mauritania. Named after a *barkhane,* a crescent-shaped sand dune sculpted by the Sahara winds, this operation replaced *Opération Serval* in 2014. See also **Opération Serval**.

pirogue. French word for a wooden canoe used for fishing and transport on the Niger River.

PVO. Private voluntary organization. See also **NGO**.

OXFAM. Oxford Committee for Famine Relief: a 501.c.3. association development agency

RPL. Richmond Public Library.

RPS. Richmond Public Schools.

RSCC. Richmond Sister Cities Commission.

RVA. Local term for Richmond, Virginia.

Sahel. Region of Africa located between the Sahara desert and the grasslands of the savanna in the south. A broad band of the Sahel runs directly through Mali.

Salafism. A political movement based on a literalist interpretation of the Koran, dedicated to imposing "original" seventh-century Islam by means of twenty-first-century technology like automatic weapons, satellite phones, and the internet.

SCF. Save the Children Federation, a 501.c.3 association that promotes child development.

SCI. Sister Cities International, a 501.c.3. association dedicated to building peace and friendship on an international scale through partnerships between individual cities.

SOL. Standard of Learning.

SWS. School of World Studies at VCU. See also *VCU.*

talib. A student of the Koran.

taliban. Arabic plural of **talib.**

ULSHB. *Université des Lettres et des Sciences Humaines de Bamako.*

UN. United Nations, an association of nations created in 1945 to promote peace and development around the world.

UDPM. *Union démocratique du people malien,* a political party formed in Mali in 1975 and dissolved following a coup in 1991. Beginning in 1979, it was Mali's single legal political party under the one-party state led by Moussa Traoré.

UNFM. *Union nationale des femmes du Mali,* an association for women created by the one-party state when it was in power in Mali.

UNICEF. United Nations Children's Fund.

UR. University of Richmond.

USAID. United States Agency for International Development.

USG. United States government.

UVA. University of Virginia, located in Charlottesville.

VCSSE. Virginia Conference of Social Studies Educators, the people who teach the Mali SOL.

VCU. Virginia Commonwealth University, located in Richmond.

VFoM. Virginia Friends of Mali, a 501.c.3 association supporting Richmond's sister city relationship with Ségou.

VMFA. Virginia Museum of Fine Arts, located in Richmond.

VSU. Virginia State University, located in Petersburg.

VUU. Virginia Union University, located in Richmond.

Wahabbism. Saudi version of Salafism; a nationalist and colonial political movement.

WARA. West African Research Association, a 501.c.3 association of academics based in Boston and Dakar.

WB. World Bank.

WHO. World Health Organization, a specialized agency of the United Nations.

List of Illustrations

Index of Proper Names

www.ingramcontent.com/pod-product-compliance
Lightning Source LLC
Chambersburg PA
CBHW060246100426
42742CB00011B/1660